BIGGER Isn't
Always *Better*

BIGGER Isn't
Always *Better*

The New Mindset for
Real Business Growth

ROBERT M. TOMASKO

ᴬMACOM

American Management Association

New York • Atlanta • Brussels • Chicago • Mexico City • San Francisco
Shanghai • Tokyo • Toronto • Washington, D.C.

This publication is designed to provide accurate and authoritative
information in regard to the subject matter covered. It is sold with the
understanding that the publisher is not engaged in rendering legal,
accounting, or other professional service. If legal advice or other expert
assistance is required, the services of a competent professional person
should be sought.

Library of Congress Cataloging-in-Publication Data

Tomasko, Robert M.
        Bigger isn't always better : the new mindset for real business growth /
Robert M. Tomasko.
        p.   cm.
        Includes bibliographical references and index.
        ISBN 0-8144-0866-4
        1. Corporations--Growth.   2. Sustainable development.   3. Creative ability
in business.   I. Title.

HD2746.T66   2005
658.4'06--dc22

                                                                    2005024600

Printing number

10   9   8   7   6   5   4   3   2   1

CONTENTS

Acknowledgments   vii

Introduction   1

PART 1
What Growth Is and Isn't   9

  1. Is Bigger Better?   11

  2. A Bigger Stock Price Is Not Always a Good Thing   28

  3. Growth Is About Moving Forward   48

  4. Are You a Fixer or a Grower?   75

PART 2
What Growers Do   97

  5. Know Where to Look   99

  6. Know What They Want   124

  7. Tell the Truth   139

  8. Create Tension to Generate Forward Movement   166

  9. Win Hearts and Minds   184

10. Master Momentum and Bounce   214

11. Know When to Let Go—and How to Share the Wealth   231

12. Epilogue   237

Notes   239

Index   253

ACKNOWLEDGMENTS

This book is a synthesis of ideas from many business observers, growers, and management scholars. Consider the notes at the end of the book as a partial accounting for some of my intellectual debts. These notes also make for good starting points if you would like to read further about any of the topics covered here.

I want to express appreciation for the time, thoughts, and general stimulation that a number of important individuals have provided over the many years I have been mulling over growth and what it really means: Bruce Aylward, Bill Bishop, Andrew Blank, Donald Calvin, Roger Conner, Matthew Davis, Jean Phillipe Deschamps, Joe Eldridge, JJ Finkelstein, Richard Goodale, Marvin Goodman, Kenichi Hattori, Don Heavy, Andre Hermann, Hisato Iguchi, G. K. Jayaram, Charlie Keifer, David Lange, Robert Lee, Robert Levering, Frank Louchheim, Michael Maccoby, Tim Mendham, Larry Miller, Alan Mottur, Maria Otero, Harrison Owen, Amram Shapiro, Bryan Smith, Herman Stein, Dena Stoner, Leon Sullivan, Shige Tabata, Toshiro Takeda, Greg Thielmann, Carl Tinstman, Martin Van der Mandele, Jan Wall, and Reid Weedon.

Several organizations also deserve special thanks for providing me with an opportunity to learn from them, as well as test out many of my ideas about growth: Air Products & Chemicals, Bain & Co., Center for Creative Leadership, Confederation of Indian Industry, Daimler-Benz, Econ Verlag, Grocery Manufacturers of America, Hartford Steam Boiler, Hy-Vee, IMD, Infosys, Innovation Associates, Institute for Management

Studies, Lipton International, Arthur D. Little, Inc., Mental Health Corporations of America, Mitsubishi, National Rural Electric Cooperative Association, Newspaper Association of America, NYK Lines, Österreich Volkspartei, Portugal Telecom, Rittal Werk, Sun Microsystems, Tetley, Toyota, and Yamaha.

I am blessed with a most supportive family; an encouraging agent, John Willig; and a great editor, Adrienne Hickey. Adrienne leads a superb editorial team at AMACOM, the best I've ever worked with. Any errors of fact or style herein are my own doing, of course, but there are far fewer of them than there might have been if not for the careful vigilance of Jim Bessent and proofreader Christina Orem.

This book is dedicated to my son, William. You can learn a lot about growth from business school classes and working in and for major corporations, but I am convinced you never really understand what it is about until you become a parent.

BIGGER Isn't
Always *Better*

INTRODUCTION

Life is occupied in both perpetuating itself and in surpassing itself . . .
If all it does is maintain itself, then living is only not dying.[1]

—*Simone de Beauvoir*

Some people seem to have a special mindset for the surpassing part of this equation—an ability to move things forward, generate effective action, and take a situation beyond what was there before. They are lighters of candles, not cursers of darkness. This ability is what growth is really about. Growth means progress, moving on to the next stage. It is not about getting bigger or having a record of unbroken success. Size and success are often growth's worst enemies. Real growth is about reaching full potential, not maximum size. It means progress, not excess; it is fueled by imagination, not expansion.

I like to call people who are especially good at employing this mindset *growers*. By looking closely at how they think and act, we all can become better at making new things happen and creating the kind of business we most want to see. If growers were better appreciated and understood, more recognized and cultivated, then the organizations where they work would accomplish more. This book is written for growers, prospective growers, and the people in organizations whose job it is to spot growers and nurture their talents.

Cultivating a growth mindset certainly beats the alternative: a life, or a career, spent being whipsawed by forces that we can only resist, respond to, or react against. If all we do is maintain ourselves, Beauvoir observed, then living is only "not dying." Resistance, response, and reaction are ways of coping, of getting by. They are escalating commitments to the status quo. Many situations call for these behaviors; short-term survival in the face of immediate danger, in fact, depends on them. But growth doesn't.

To paraphrase Martin Seligman, one of the growers profiled in several of the chapters that follow, business is not just about fixing what is broken. It is about taking what is best in an enterprise and nurturing its further development. Leading this kind of growth requires a very different mentality from that needed to manage ongoing activities. The best growth champions are often not the people who are in charge of today's successful organizations. What makes best sense for sustaining the status quo is often irrelevant or counterproductive for surpassing it.

Growers are people who want more than maintaining equilibrium. They are people who want to bring new things into being. Some start revolutions. Others nudge evolution along. These are people with a healthy measure of discomfort with the status quo, usually because they are able to foresee something better—something that they are able to move toward and encourage others to want. What they do, and how they do it, is what this book is about.

GROWTH IS ABOUT PROGRESS, NOT BIGNESS

Before these practicalities can be addressed, a myth about the nature of growth needs to be dispelled. The idea of "growth" does not have to be synonymous with "getting bigger." Growth is about forward movement, stretching beyond the limits that currently define and constrain the business. Growth is what Johnson & Johnson, Starbucks, and W. L. Gore still do in their sleep, what Wal-Mart used to do, and what Ford and Sony are trying to rediscover.

Solid growth has been a challenge for many enterprises. Too many have sought the appearance of growth through mergers, downsizings, stock price manipulations, and, occasionally, outright fraud. This book is about real growth, not the kind that accountants manufacture.

Part 1 of this book describes what growth is and isn't. In a world in which almost every business seems to be locked in a take-no-prisoners struggle to super size, we need a time-out to reconsider what viable growth really entails. Too often it has become confused with one of its by-products, expansion. Getting bigger may be a by-product of growth, but it is not growth's main feature. A business that takes the shortcut of pursuing an increase in size directly, instead of realizing it through the hard work of real growth, is like an athlete taking the steroid route to muscle building.

Bigness is a bit like self-esteem. It is a wonderful feeling when it is acquired as a by-product of doing well and achieving one's goals. When it is gotten this way, it can even serve as a flywheel to generate more success. But the kind of self-esteem that comes from blind optimism and putting a happy face on failure is brittle and unanchored. It tends to do more harm than good.

Bigger is not necessarily better. Bigness begets business bubbles and bullies. It bites back, too. A single-minded focus on getting bigger usually has a negative effect. Companies that successfully seek bigness soon find that their surroundings become less hospitable, resources less abundant, and organizations less functional. These are some of the ideas considered in the first chapter.

The second chapter zeroes in on why so many companies have sought bigness as an end in itself: a myopic focus on their stock price. Many of the flawed assumptions behind the "shareholder-value theory" are reviewed, including the assumption that it really helps long-term investors. Examples are also provided to show why a higher stock price does not always signify a better company.

WHAT GROWERS ACTUALLY DO

Chapters 3 and 4 offer a more useful definition of growth, one that is built around becoming better, not bigger. The purpose of Part 1 of this book is to change the way you think about growth. Part 2 then provides practical advice about how to make this kind of growth happen. Chapters 5 through 11 cover each one of the sequential steps taken by successful surpassers—from where to look for opportunities and how to rally support for pursuing them, to when to let go and how to share the wealth. Examples of growers in a wide variety of settings are used to illustrate these steps. Among the people you will meet here are:

- Bill Greenwood, who, from a sideline job in a backwater department of a railroad, created a multibillion-dollar business selling his company's services to its competitors
- Darcy Winslow, who helped testosterone-fueled Nike find growth opportunities by creating products for women that fit between the traditional jock-oriented market segments that had come to define, and also limit, Nike
- Michael Milken, who showed that growers can have successful second acts as he applied his management smarts to the task of revolutionizing the business model for medical research
- Al Bru of Pepsico, who found that being in the snack food business doesn't have to mean selling only junk foods
- Ko Nishimura of Solectron, who saw overcapacity in a factory as an excuse to sell more product, not a rationale for downsizing
- Three other seasoned growers who knew when to let go and how to give away the mindset for growth: Roger Enrico, a battle-scarred hero of the cola wars; Cate Muther, former chief marketing officer for Cisco; and Narayana Murthy, often called the "Bill Gates of India" for his ability to create a software business whose growth made several hundred of his colleagues millionaires

These are all growers from the world of business. But the enterprise ethic that they embody is not limited to the private sector. It can be just as alive in public institutions, in nonprofits, and even among some humanitarian and social-justice activists. So we'll also search for lessons from the efforts of people such as Bruce Aylward, a Canadian physician who set out to rid the world of polio; Leon Sullivan, an African American Baptist minister with a similar aim regarding apartheid; and a Bolivian immigrant to the United States, Maria Otero, who championed the idea of microlending and became a leading banker to the world's poor. Their stories, and those of growers trying to reform health care and broaden the discipline of psychology, are not added just for variety's sake. Growers need to know how to think differently about situations that they want to move forward. A good way to develop this skill is to look at the issues you face from the perspective of people dealing with them in other realms.

GROWTH IS A MINDSET GAME

What the people highlighted here all have in common is a stronger interest in building than in maintaining. They all share, to varying degrees, a common mindset, the mindset of a grower.

What is a mindset? It is how you think about what you are doing. It's your internal logic system, the model of the world that you carry around in your head. Your mindset gives birth to your beliefs and assumptions. It determines what facts you notice and what you make of them. And, even more important, it determines what you do as a result.

Simone de Beauvoir's perpetuators and surpassers both live in the same world, but they use divergent thought processes that lead them to very different conclusions about the nature of that world and what their role within it should be. This book distills some of the latest findings from cognitive psychology, brain science, and behavioral economics to help explain why some people, and the organizations they inhabit, channel their efforts in one direction rather than the other.

Growth is a subject that straddles both economics and psychology. *Bigger Isn't Always Better* synthesizes ideas from both disciplines—be prepared to think about both shareholder value and neuroscience, stock options and mental emotions. Organizational learning, as we will use the term here, is about building organizations that grow, not just learn. We will take some of its key ideas, such as mental models, personal mastery, and systems thinking, and link them to research results from the emerging field of positive psychology.

This book also borrows from Tim Gallwey's approach to learning tennis and other skill-related endeavors: Success requires mastery of both an "inner" and an "outer" game.[2] There is both an outer and an inner game of growth, also. The outer game is one of techniques—market research, product development, branding, sales force management, and customer service. It deals with core competencies, disruptive technologies, adjacencies, and synergies. Techniques, as important are they are, convey at best only a fleeting advantage. They are easily replicable, and they can be learned, and improved on, by opponents. There is a multi-billion-dollar worldwide industry, management consulting, dedicated to making this happen.

The inner game of growth is different. It's a mindset game. It's where the real leverage is. It's what this book describes. This is a game whose moves have to do with noticing opportunities where others see only obstacles, turning these openings into growth goals, and then rallying support around them. It's a game that feeds on brutal candor about the business's current situation and emotional ardor about its future prospects. It's a game of momentum and resilience, one whose best players also know when it's time to shift gears and share the wealth.

Growth is a narcissism-free zone. Being able to step back from yourself—from your ego, your self-image—is the best way to stay open to new opportunities and to change course as circumstances require. It's an ability that Herb Kelleher of Southwest Airlines had, GE's Jack Welch flirted with, and Enron's Ken Lay lacked.

GROWTH STARTS WITH PEOPLE, NOT STRATEGIES

Growth happens when new challenges are taken on and new capabilities are created or added to meet them. For this to take place in an organization, the same process must be going on in the people working within that organization. Businesses seldom experience sustainable growth unless the people within them do also.

The desire to acquire new skills and face tougher challenges motivates growth, just as greed and grandiosity are the twin drivers of bigness. People who want to grow a business have to have an urge to grow themselves as people first. Growers are people who need challenge the way we all need air. Without it, they are restless and bored; with it, they are gratified because they have an opportunity to show what they are made of by using or expanding their potential.

Before growth will happen in a business, it has to happen in the mindsets of the growers within it. These individuals need the ability to see possibilities that others may miss. Growth is an inherently liberal idea. I do not mean "blue state" liberal, but liberal as in "liberal arts": not limited to established or traditional attitudes, views, or dogmas; favoring proposals for reform; open to new ideas, broad-minded, and tolerant of the ideas and behaviors of others. These are hallmarks of people who are able to move an organization beyond its existing boundaries. They also must have the skills to bring along a critical mass of others to share a stake in that possibility, make things happen without being given a budget to do so, build momentum through a series of small wins, make midcourse corrections, and bounce back from setbacks.

Bigger Isn't Always Better draws from a 10-year effort. Its impetus came from one of my clients, who asked if there were characteristics common to the people responsible for driving the most successful and sustainable growth initiatives in his business. This inquiry was later extended to other industries; reviewed with several dozen executives in leading companies in the United States, Europe, and Asia; and used as a basis for in-company workshops and as part of a major information technology firm's leadership development program. As I talked with many of the growers profiled in this book, it was apparent that they were motivated more by progress than by expanding the size of their domains. Several also argued strongly that the popular definition of growth was overdue for rethinking, because bigger, in their experience, often got in the way of better.

In doing this research, I observed that growth is more frequently driven by people in the middle and on the sidelines of large organizations than by those at the top. This is a counterargument to the popular idea that real change always has to start with the chief executive. Many growers emerge from the margins of their organizations and industries, places where future opportunities are often more clearly visible and where people have less at stake in the status quo. These are people who are "in," but not "of," their organizations—a situation that can offer them a perspective many others lack.

On the other hand, CEOs, by the nature of their jobs, have divided loyalties. They are responsible for what currently is, as well as what might be. The only time they can play the role of pure grower is when they are starting up or turning around a company. Otherwise, they are often in a better position to stop things from happening than to spearhead new initiatives. Regardless, top leaders have a vital role to play in nurturing and supporting the organization's growers. How they do that is discussed in Chapter 11.

Read this book, as you would any business book, with your eyes wide open. What worked for another person or another company may not work for you. As Jennifer Reingold of *Fast Company* put it so well: "Business books are necessarily about generalizations; your company is necessarily all about specifics."[3] The examples offered here are given to help illustrate ideas, not to put anyone on a pedestal. A number of companies (including Apple, Ford, Kellog, Merck, and Samsung) and individuals are praised here for some of their actions and ideas, and criticized for others. No business, business leader, or business watcher (myself included) has a lock on wisdom that is good for all time. Figure out under what conditions an idea is a good one for you, and under what conditions it is best set aside. Address your issues on your terms, not someone else's. While growers cast wide nets for new information, they seldom get on bandwagons.

PART 1: WHAT GROWTH IS AND ISN'T

1

IS BIGGER BETTER?

The idea that growth is by itself a goal is altogether a delusion.
There is no virtue in a company getting bigger.[1]

—*Peter Drucker*

GROWTH HAS BECOME SYNONYMOUS WITH BIGNESS

What picture enters your mind when you hear the word *growth*?

Most of us associate growth with getting bigger. In business, growth is often depicted by a graph of some key indicator—sales, profits, assets, or stock price—rising from one time period to the next. The steeper the upward slope of the curve, the better, says the conventional wisdom. These images of growth as expansion or increase in magnitude are deeply entrenched in the way we think.

Growth, defined this way, is usually considered to be an unquestioned positive, something to be applauded and celebrated. Careers are made producing it. Bigness counts in the business world. The size of your paycheck is correlated with the size of the budget you are responsible for. A company making the *Fortune* 500 or its CEO appearing on the *Forbes* list of the world's wealthiest is seen as a hallmark of success. Consultants tell how important it is to be number one in your industry. Conference speakers warn of emerging competitive threats, and implore you to "grow or die."

The idea of growth as expansion is manifested in many ways: sell more products, hire more people, open more facilities, broaden geo-graphic scope, generate bigger profits, and increase the stock price. The last of these, increasing shareholder value, is often seen as the primary purpose of a business. Even in the less economically driven world of charitable philanthropy, the foundations that are most talked about are those with the most money to hand out, which may or may not be related to how much good their grants are actually doing.

Bubble Companies

Bubble companies are those that focus on size increases for their own sake. They put more effort into selling their stock than into selling their products. Sometimes led by charismatic narcissists, many of these com-panies achieve dramatic sales and earnings increases—for a time. Some manage sleight-of-hand pumping up of their stock price without really having added to shareholder value. But eventually, all of them discover that exponential rates of expansion are impossible to sustain. Success at expansion eventually limits, not enables, real growth.

When businesses fall short of ideas for real growth, they are tempted to make their numbers through gimmicks and fixes. They super size. They roll out unneeded upgrades. They pack their products with un-wanted features, and fill store shelves with mindless variations. Too few expansion-minded executives ask themselves the question the advertising guru Jay Chait raised about the firm he created: "How big can we get before we get bad?"[2]

Bully Companies

This is not to say that size doesn't have its advantages, and it may be a worthy goal for some businesses to pursue. But too many companies have pursued size for the wrong reasons. Some seek it for the bullying market power it can convey, others out of a fear of being left behind or devoured by larger corporate predators. "We're just not big enough to compete effectively,"[3] worried News Corp.'s Rupert Murdoch, leader of a $24 billion cable, movie, newspaper, publishing, and satellite TV busi-ness. It was thinking like this—buttressed by shaky broad-brush strategic concepts like "convergence"—that led to unwieldy media monsters such as AOL Time Warner and Vivendi. These bloated conglomerates are now busy unwinding their size-driven expansions, moves that, ironically, may reposition them to experience real growth for a change.

Other size seekers have sought to use their bulk as a weapon. *Fortune* called Enron "an awe-inspiring juggernaut"[4] with a visionary chief executive, Kenneth Lay, who valued the intellectual capital of his 18,000-strong workforce above anything else. *Fortune* also realized that there was more to Enron than a smart workforce,[5] and compared it to a high school bully using brute force to stimulate deregulation, breaking into new markets and boldly scooping up customers before its cowering competitors dared to react.

In business, the idea of growth has become badly confused with the idea of expansion. Growing businesses often experience expansion as a by-product, a correlate, or a symptom of growth. When expansion is substituted for growth, however, means have become confused with ends. Increases in size, scope, and profitability may be a result of forward movement, but they are not what drive it. Expansion is never a viable end in itself. In organisms, the single-minded pursuit of expansion is synonymous with bloat and cancer, and in the business world, it is synonymous with Enron, Tyco, and WorldCom.

The quest for bigness invariably comes with a lot of baggage. John Kay, a leading Oxford economist, asserts: "It is rare for the market power and scale economies associated with market dominance not ultimately to fall victim to the hubris, the insulation from the market, and the sheer bureaucratic inefficiency that goes with such size."[6] I would go further than Kay. What he describes is not just likely; it is inevitable.

BIGNESS IS NOT SUSTAINABLE

If growth is only about expansion, it's not going to go very far or last very long. Consider what happens when a small mutual fund gets hot. Its stock pickers, through shrewd insight and analysis (or pure dumb luck), manage to assemble a portfolio of stocks whose prices have soared far beyond those held by the fund's peers. The shareholders of the fund are happy. Their statements now show a healthy increase in their net worth. The stock analysts and the fund's management are happy because their compensation, which is based on the value of the assets they manage, rises. And the journalists who write the "What mutual fund should I invest in?" columns are happy, too. The problem of what to say in their next article has been solved. Thanks to their recommendations, word of the fund's stellar performance spreads, and investors withdraw money from its competitors and rush to buy shares of the new hotshot.

This makes the stock analysts even happier, at least for a while. As the new money starts to flow into their fund, its asset value (and their pay) rises, without them having to do any additional sleuthing for new stocks with undiscovered price appreciation potential. The increase in the size of the fund's assets doesn't have an immediate economic impact on the shareholders, though some may feel a psychic reward from having had the smarts to buy in before the masses discovered it. People like having their judgments affirmed.

The mutual fund's management is happy as well. It has learned a useful lesson: Assets can grow by attracting new investors as well as by hiring talented stock pickers. So the managers start to spend money on advertising the fund and its peer-beating track record. This attracts even more customers, increasing the fund's size even further. The management also offers incentives to brokers to steer new customers their way. All this promotion is costly, and has to be paid out of the fund's assets or taken from the budgets of the stock pickers, but it appears worthwhile if it produces a net increase in the fund's assets.

Success Does Not Always Scale

In the meantime, the stock pickers' job has gotten a lot harder now that the fund is on a real roll. To keep up with their reputation, they have to continually find new stocks whose potential is as least as great as those they discovered before, to buy with all the money that is now flooding into the fund. Of course, they could just buy more of the same stocks that propelled them to fame, but it can be risky to own too much of any one stock, and it can be difficult to do if the stocks are issued by smaller companies. And if they did buy these same stocks, they wouldn't necessarily be getting the great bargains they once did. It is a lot easier to buy and sell positions in a stock without negatively affecting its price when you are buying small quantities than when you are forced to invest vast inflows of new money. So pressures on the traders build, and some of them decide that life might be more fun if they cashed in on their past reputation and got a new job at another mutual fund, so they quit. The less-stellar analysts that remain tend to take the safe way out of these dilemmas, hedging their bets by buying a wide variety of stocks.

Where does this leave the mutual fund? Most likely with diminished investment performance because it has become so big that its portfolio reflects the range of stocks in the broader market more than it does a carefully selected subset of market beaters. This may not necessarily bother the managers, though. They have gotten good at bringing in new accounts through promotions and incentives, and they know that most customers are likely to stay put, hoping the fund will regain its past glory. But are the customers benefiting from the fund's rapid size expansion? Not really, as the returns have leveled off and future prospects are not as bright as when the fund was much smaller and focused.

This is a classic example of success in the form of size gain leading to mediocrity. Some mutual fund managers that want to compete on performance, not size, such as Dodge & Cox and Vanguard, have dealt with this situation by closing their funds to new customers and new investments when these threaten to kill the golden goose. Doing this is rare, though. It requires an understanding of the difference between real growth and size expansion. It also takes an ability to exercise self-control by leaving money on the table when necessary—qualities that too often are in short supply among today's size seekers.

Ironically, probably the best outcome for the early investors would be to hope that those who joined them after the fund became a superstar would become frustrated and bail out, reducing the total assets to just the right size for the magic of a skilled stock picker to work again.

BIGNESS BITES BACK

Bigness bites back in many ways. Jacques Nasser's brief tenure as chief executive of Ford seemed to be shaped by one basic objective: to over-take General Motors in sales. His quest to make Ford the world's biggest car company seemed ironic. Ford had already beaten GM on a more economically important measure: It was the world's most profitable auto builder. But Nasser sought the bragging rights that come with size. His path to expansion was based on the observation that only 10 percent of the total value of the car business was generated by actually making cars. The rest came from repairs, used-car sales, accessories, insurance, leasing, and finance. So in a quest to turn a metal-bending manufacturer into a diversified consumer products company, Nasser set up and bought many service-oriented businesses. As he and his executive group became caught up in what an industry observer dubbed "visions of grandeur,"[7] the performance of the core business they hoped to grow beyond seriously declined. The pace of new model introductions slipped. Quality rankings did the same. The Ford dealers, whom the company depended on to sell its cars, were up in arms, fearing that Nasser planned to compete with or dismantle the dealership system. After three years of Nasser's attempts at growth, Ford's board fired him, just before this one-time industry profit leader announced a $5.5 billion loss.

Ford was not the only automaker driven in the wrong direction by expansion. Consider the plight of Germany's big three. For Daimler-Benz, the vision of becoming a global car giant—rather than merely the aristocratic German builder—led it to merge with Chrysler, a company with a long history of roller-coaster economic performance. It also purchased a large stake in Mitsubishi, a profitless small car maker kept in business through zero-interest loans from Japanese banks. As happened at Ford, expansion distraction led to quality declines in Mercedes, the flagship product line, and a crimp in the company's overall finances.

Volkswagen's expansion ambitions took it in the direction that DaimlerChrysler was trying to move from, but the results were the same: Quality and cost problems with its mainstream cars, and financial losses with its others. A VW luxury vehicle, the Phaeton, was added to its more pedestrian car lineup, and the Bentley and Bugatti brands were acquired. VW may now be able to boast of competing in almost every segment of the auto market, but at the cost of a blurred image in the marketplace and diminished customer satisfaction, both precursors of difficult times ahead.

Even the creator of Germany's "ultimate driving machine," BMW, is showing early signs of the get-bigger-quickly syndrome. By adding a compact car, intended to compete with Volkswagen and Toyota, to its lineup, BMW runs the risk of this down-market, low-margin vehicle stealing sales from more expensive models and distracting management from the actions it needs to take to stay in tune with the company's more performance-oriented customer base.

Fast Growth Is Not Best Growth

Ryanair, Europe's pioneer discount airline, is frequently called that continent's Southwest Airlines. In some ways this is true, but Ryanair deviated from Southwest's slow and measured approach to expansion when the lure of being crowned Europe's biggest short-haul carrier led it to a financial near-meltdown. Ignoring Southwest's "don't bite off more than you can chew" example, Ryanair expanded its capacity by more than 50 percent for several consecutive years. As a result, borrowing requirements quickly soared, almost to the heights its planes fly, and its profitability took a nosedive. Southwest, Ryanair's role model, has many goals, but being the biggest has never been among them. It may now be a large airline, but it got there very slowly.

What's wrong with fast growth? A study by finance professor Cyrus Ramezani[8] shows that businesses that chase growth per se generate less wealth than those that follow a slower and steadier course. He reviewed the financial performance of several thousand companies over an 11-year period. The firms that were in the top quartile in sales and profit growth consistently made their shareholders less wealthy than those in the less glamorous second and third tiers. The triple-digit revenue growth (annual average 167 percent) of Ramezani's top-quartile firms was trumped by the slower, but still very respectable, 26 percent yearly sales increases of the next tier. When it comes to doing well over the long haul, the middle of the pack may be the place to be. What happened to the hotshot businesses? In many cases, their dizzying performance was impossible to sustain, a hint that attempting to "purchase growth" with the currency of sales and profits was the wrong approach.

What makes this so wrong? Why are rapid and unending expansions hard to sustain? At least three factors conspire to do in bigness: the company's surroundings lose their hospitality, resources become less abundant, and the organization becomes less functional.

Inhospitable Surroundings. A business's environment is always subject to change. Markets that were once eager and receptive become fickle and saturated. New predators emerge. Old competitors rebound. Technologies change, as do government policies and regulations. What worked well yesterday may have no relationship to what is required to keep a company growing tomorrow. Size attracts scrutiny, as Microsoft learned when its domination of the personal-computer operating systems market led regulators on two continents to constrain its ability to continue expanding by taking further advantage of its scale. Ubiquity, when you grow so big that you become your environment, also cuts your options. In many ways, Microsoft's biggest competitor is itself—its accumulated past successes. This kind of bigness is not a problem that a company can spend its way out of, either. Microsoft has invested over $30 billion in R&D since 1990, trying to create market-category-exploding products. This amount, more than the next five largest software makers combined have spent, has produced little in the way of breakthrough products during an era in which beleaguered Apple Computer and upstart Google stole most of the headlines. Blockbuster budgets seldom drive breakthroughs. Cash hoards are not the fuel of creativity; if anything, large financial reserves remove much of the impetus for doing things differently.

Wal-Mart is another example of a company that has felt the stings of a once-welcoming environment biting back. At one point it was what its former CEO, David Glass, described as an endearing underdog with a mission of allowing people of average means to buy more of the things that were once available only to the rich;[9] now Wal-Mart is the world's largest company in terms of sales and employees. Just keeping its current jobs filled requires Wal-Mart to hire over half a million new workers each year. New stores are opened daily. While praised for job creation and for its attention to selling goods cheaply, Wal-Mart's dominance has also spotlighted the connection between its deeply discounted prices and its efforts to keep labor costs low. Fewer than half of its low-wage store workers are covered by company health-care benefits,[10] and some local governments complain they are subsidizing Wal-Mart through the tax-supported public assistance programs these employees increasingly need to draw on. Wal-Mart has also become a target for sex discrimination and unpaid overtime lawsuits, including the largest civil rights class action ever brought against a company. Wal-Mart's bigness has even led

BusinessWeek to dub it America's most admired *and* most hated company.[11]

Resource Constraints. Resources are another constraint to unending expansion, for both Wal-Mart and its suppliers. Eventually Wal-Mart, if it stays on the path toward becoming the world's first trillion-dollar business, will absorb all the labor market surplus and find itself stymied by talent shortfalls. No one will be available to make the things Wal-Mart sells. Likewise, the red-hot growth of China's manufacturing sector (a key source of Wal-Mart's low-cost merchandise) will cool down as its factories require more raw materials and energy than the world has available. To the extent that China's expansion leads to environmental degradation and social unrest driven by increasing income disparities, the base upon which it rests is brittle. The rock-bottom "China price," so feared by U.S.-based manufacturers, is built on two unstable resources: low wages and an undervalued currency. Labor shortages are already occurring and pay rates are rising in some of China's manufacturing powerhouse provinces. The China price can only increase as the country's economic success propels increases in both its standard of living and the value of its currency.

Organizational Limitations. Expansion has a way of creating an inhospitable internal environment, also. All organizational structures have built-in limitations, constraints that become more troublesome as size and complexity increase. In this regard, organizations mimic biological organisms more than machines. Living creatures, unlike mechanical devices, just don't scale up very well.[12] Elephants are already fairly bulky animals. If they were to expand to much larger than they already are, they would require sturdier legs to support the added weight. But these legs would be so heavy that they would be impossible for the elephant to lift. Humans have a corresponding problem. We have reached the limits of development in terms of brain size. The amount of oxygen our brains would consume if they were to become larger, with a denser network of neural interconnections rivaling a supercomputer's processing speed, is considerable—so considerable that pumping that amount of oxygen from our lungs to our brains would require such high blood pressure that we would be likely to suffer a fatal stroke before getting much use from our expanded thinking capacity.

The same basic laws of geometry govern all organisms, and all corporate structures.[13] As the size of an object increases, the expansion of its surface area is measured by taking the *square* of the increase in its diameter. The *cube* of the change in diameter, however, determines its increase in mass. In other words, bulk happens. And most of it happens inside the expanding organism, not on its surface. So the bigger an organism (or organization) grows, the further away most of its mass will be from its outside environment. This is why big companies almost invariably focus inward. As a business grows in size, fewer and fewer of its employees have a direct line of sight to the company's customers and competitors. Market early warnings are missed, responsiveness slackens, more agile competitors prevail, and business expansion ultimately slows. The original Wal-Mart was not a Wal-Mart at all. It was a company that offered "everyday low prices" in the largest network of stores ever built. It was called the Great Atlantic and Pacific Tea Co. Now it is an almost-forgotten small division of a German retailer. A&P's leader in its glory years, John Hartford, presciently observed: "Sometimes the body gets so large that the pulsations fail to reach its extremities."[14] Ultimately, excess size tends to self-correct; market dominators like A&P are inherently poor adapters.

Some business observers have thought that the Internet and new forms of organization would change all this. They hoped that networks would replace hierarchy. Sadly, they didn't because they couldn't. Look at Microsoft, one of the world's leading users, as well as producers, of information technology. In 2002 Steve Ballmer, Microsoft's CEO, subdivided its megalithic organization into seven "sort of" stand-alone business units, each with profit-and-loss responsibility. "Sort of" because, while this decentralized structure was expected to stimulate entrepreneurial behavior and aggressive innovation, Ballmer also felt compelled to put a wall around permissible growth initiatives. He mandated that each business coordinate its activities with all the others, advancing only in directions supportive of Microsoft's overall strategy to defend and enhance the Windows operating system, its core product. Replacing autonomy with control and coordination is a good formula for preserving past success, but a strong brake on creating a future that is different from that past. Microsoft's leaders probably know this. Bill Gates is fond of saying that Microsoft's biggest competitor is its installed base. But a combination of fear of the unknown and the weight of responsibility for what already is keeps the company from seriously challenging this rival.

Gates himself is fairly mellow about this constraint, telling investors looking for companies with expansion possibilities to avoid the "big guys." In other words, don't expect Microsoft to become the next Microsoft. Perhaps he is mindful of how Citigroup fueled its ascendancy to the position of the world's largest bank by replacing an emphasis on controls and coordination with a hyperaggressive, push-the-ethical-envelope corporate culture. Known by some Wall Street analysts as the bankers with claws and fangs,[15] Citi's executives are now working over-time to repair the damage to its reputation caused by money-laundering scandals in Japan, questionable bond-market trading practices in London, and allegations of conflicts of interest during the tech-stock boom and bust. Now facing a regulatory environment less tolerant of the behaviors that once drove Citi when it was one of Enron's top banking partners, this mega-institution may have reached the limits of aggression-driven expansion.

This is a lesson that has not been lost on Wal-Mart, either. Its chief executive, Lee Scott, candidly admits: "Most of what size brings you is not positive." In his company of a million and a half employees, he guarantees that "at this very moment somewhere, somebody is doing something that we all wish they weren't doing."[16]

Bureaucracy Busting Can Backfire

Many other executives seem less sanguine than Gates about their size. Instead, they compulsively roll out program after program intended to teach corporate elephants "how to dance." When the consultants they hire wrestle with the problem of creating management systems that will enable big companies to innovate as well as small upstarts, the solutions they come up with tend to look a lot like those that Enron made famous. Royal Dutch Shell used one of these "bureaucracy-busting, innovation-inducing" programs to increase the size of its proven oil reserves. Called the LEAP program, it did not enhance the ability of Shell's oil explorers to find oil. It just creatively relaxed the accounting guidelines used to classify already-made discoveries as "proven," even though Shell was unsure these gas and oil fields could ever be tapped.

Calls to defeat the downside of bigness by becoming a "post-industrial organization," one that "conquers hierarchy" by "bringing the market inside the company," make for catchy slogans but dubious wisdom. Environment, resources, and organization all provide constraints that inevitably conspire to limit business expansion. Peter Drucker, a fan of the "don't get bigger than the minimum growth needed to keep abreast of the market" school of thought, maintains that there are few exceptions to the rule that "today's growth company is tomorrow's problem."[17] To the extent that growth means getting bigger, he's right.

BIGNESS IS COUNTERPRODUCTIVE

Where does the quest for bigness eventually take an industry? Almost invariably, the result is a competitive arena characterized by a small number of large players. Most markets evolve through a life cycle with a period of rapid expansion followed by a cooling down of new demand and a longish period of "mature" growth in phase with, not out ahead of, the overall economy. While adolescence seems the wild and dangerous phase of human development, businesses are more likely to be tempted toward self-destructive behaviors in maturity. This is when competitors consolidate and market power can become concentrated in a small number of large companies, as occurred in commercial insurance brokerage. In this global risk-management business, where brokers serve as intermediaries between corporations and the companies that provide them with insurance, two megabrokers (Marsh & McLennan and Aon) arranged coverage for 70 percent of America's companies. Environments like this stifle growth through innovation-based competition, instead tempting executives to drive future earnings by taking advantage of their market dominance. This apparently happened at Marsh & McLennan, where its chief executive was forced to resign after the firm was accused of obtaining half its profits through bid rigging, price-fixing, and receiving payments for steering underwriting business to favored insurers.

Situations like these are beacons for aggressive regulators, like New York State's Attorney General Eliot Spitzer, and are inherently unstable.

As happened at Citigroup, Marsh & McLennan's former CEO, Jeffrey Greenberg, set challenging profit-expansion goals, but failed to put in place a strong framework to guide how they were to be met.[18]

The Blockbuster Syndrome

Bigness also brings instability in the form of the category-killer or block-buster syndrome. It is easy to bask in the glory of the profits such high-volume products generate, and also ignore their inevitable downside. In the pharmaceutical industry, many of the top firms have developed an addiction to product portfolios of drugs that treat common diseases afflicting millions of patients. While these generate blockbuster sales, they also make the company susceptible to blockbuster-sized risks because so much of its revenue comes from a small handful of products. Almost every drug is accompanied by unwanted and harmful side effects. Drugs that are in mass use, however, are more likely to negatively affect great numbers of people in ways that clinical trials involving small numbers of patients cannot easily predict. This, in turn, generates product recalls, regulatory actions, and massive lawsuits, as Merck has found with Vioxx, Wyeth with Redux, and Bayer with its cholesterol reducer Baycol. Blockbuster drugs tend to have blockbuster direct-to-consumer advertising budgets. More money is spent in the United States to advertise drugs than to promote clothing or computers.[19] This approach to marketing expands sales, but it runs the risk of stimulating demand for the medicines by people outside the group of those who will most safely benefit from them.

The alternative is to develop and sell more targeted medicines aimed at a smaller number of users with more tightly defined ailments. Side effects are easier to spot and manage with such focused, personalized products. Uniqueness is also easier to claim. Almost 50 percent of the current blockbusters are me-too drugs, offering few benefits over their competitors, but requiring their makers to support them with many millions of marketing dollars—money that would otherwise be available to produce a profitable collection of treatments and cures for niche diseases. Had Merck freed itself from the blockbuster syndrome and applied this logic to its arthritis drug Vioxx, it would have sold fewer capsules, but to people at less risk of suffering heart attacks or strokes.

Merck also could have saved a good bit of the half billion dollars spent on mass-market commercials aimed at encouraging patients to ask their doctors to prescribe this painkiller.

Even the upside of blockbuster dependency is not all that rosy. It is hard for a company to meet Wall Street's unceasing expectations that it grow faster than the market when the company already accounts for a big share of the market. A blockbuster-dependent firm's biggest barrier to future growth is its bulging baseline. Innovations of the kind that propelled these businesses to the exalted places they now occupy are neglected because their promised return comes nowhere near the numbers needed to have an impact on today's enterprise. Blockbuster drugs produce revenues in the billions, targeted medicines merely in the tens and hundreds of millions. Like all addictions, blockbuster reliance is as detrimental to a company's ongoing health as it is hard to shake. Going cold turkey is never fun.

"Featuritis"

What do you do when you have a blockbuster on your hands, while awaiting the next one to emerge from R&D? The answer, for some market dominators, is to succumb to "featuritis." Add more and more bells and whistles to your product. Offer customers an unceasing stream of upgrades and variations. Stop offering support for earlier versions if customers balk at buying the latest release. A recent survey[20] of Microsoft users found that most of them used only 10 percent of the features built into Word, the ubiquitous word processor. The *Economist* interprets this as Microsoft offering a "90 percent clutter" product, with features layered on features that sometimes get in the way of what its customers really want the software to do. Attempts to prop up growth along these lines are not limited to the realm of high tech. McDonald's reaction to leveling demand (before it discovered that salads could be profitable, as well as healthy) was to supersize its menu of burgers and fries, in hope of increasing revenues by offering double portions for a less-than-double increase in price.

Blurred Focus

Bigness is at its most counterproductive, though, when it blurs a business's focus, when the business's size and success get between it and its customers. A good clue that this is happening is when the wrong numbers are most closely watched, managed, and rewarded. Charlie Bell, a McDonald's executive, who helped it recover from the ill effects of "supersize-ation," liked to warn of companies that "get fat, dumb and happy and take their eye off the ball."[21] This was an apt description of McDonald's by 2001, when customer satisfaction surveys showed that its once heralded philosophy of offering QSC&V (quality, service, cleanliness, and value) had fallen by the wayside. Rivals Burger King and Wendy's had much higher scores, and a University of Michigan consumer index[22] ranked happiness with McDonald's below that of every airline. The Internal Revenue Service's score on this index even trumped the Golden Arches'. Gimmicks and price cuts were not bringing in new customers, and its first-ever quarterly loss the next year led to the ouster of its CEO.

What happened? Look closely at what propelled McDonald's three decades of go-go growth in the years before these surveys, and you will find that much more of the profits and growth came from real estate operations and franchise fees than from selling hamburgers and French fries. The company's Golden Arches spanned these two completely different business models. Unlike most of its competitors, McDonald's owns or leases the land and the buildings that many of its franchisees operate. This gave McDonald's a great incentive to build more and more restaurants, even if some of them cannibalized the food sales of others. As fast-food saturation, labor shortages, and lower-priced competitors squeezed the franchisees' operations, McDonald's kept franchisees happy by slackening quality requirements without putting the brake on the real estate expansion.

The national program that graded the franchisees on QSC&V was eliminated in 1993. Service standards naturally declined, and minimal emphasis was given to inventing new menu items or staying abreast of changes in customer eating preferences. These were not priority concerns of what had become a property management company whose profits kept expanding as long as the number of stores also did. As service quality declined, the number of restaurants outside the United States more than doubled, generating enough earnings growth from being an international landlord to mask the problems back home. Ultimately this bubble, like all bubbles, collapsed. Unhappy customers led to fewer burgers sold and less franchisee revenue available to pay the rent. McDonald's was still the world's biggest fast-food company, but by few measures the best.

Measuring the Wrong Things

Kellogg, the maker of breakfast cereal icons such as Frosted Flakes and Special K, also offers a classic example of what happens when the wrong numbers are being watched. In the 1990s, all of Kellogg's management systems focused attention on the volume of cereal sold. When faced with competitive threats, like store-brand cereals and eat-on-the-go breakfast bars, Kellogg responded by cutting prices to keep shipments up. To maintain profit margins, new product development and marketing budgets were squeezed. Meanwhile, competitors such as General Mills and Post took quick advantage of Kellogg's hunkering down, introducing new products to steal its customers and dropping prices to force Kellogg to remain committed to its vicious downward cycle. When Carlos Gutierrez was appointed Kellogg CEO in 1999, the company's position in the market had deteriorated to such an extent that the board of directors gave him free rein to abandon the business's old ways. He took to heart Peter Drucker's warnings about volume fixation: "To use up more wood each year may be a rational objective for the Gypsy Moth. It is an inane objective for a paper company."[23]

Gutierrez began by gently interrupting any manager who talked about pounds of cereal sold instead of dollars made. He then reinforced his belief that volume is a means to an end, not the end itself, by retooling all the company's tracking systems to count cash, not pounds of product. Compensation plans that rewarded volume were tossed out and replaced with incentives for increased cash flow and profit. By eliminating the fixation on tonnage, Gutierrez was able to identify plants with excess capacity, shut them down, and invest the savings in R&D and promotion—the same areas that his size-obsessed predecessors had deemed worthy of cutting. Kellogg's financial results soon outperformed those of its peers, and President Bush tapped Gutierrez for a place in his cabinet.

Kellogg and McDonald's are food-for-the-stomach companies. Consulting firms, which are food-for-the-mind businesses, are just as susceptible to expansion distraction. I was a partner in one large international firm, and practice leader in another, during the era in which consulting morphed from small and medium-sized collegially managed professional firms into multibillion-dollar global behemoths. Once loosely organized like law firms or universities, their structures became taller and more hierarchical. Division of labor, profit/loss centers, and strategic business units abounded. Industrial-strength customer management systems were created, and in some firms top management's priority attention shifted from *practice* management ("What can we do to add more value *to* our clients?") to *account* management ("How much more revenue can we extract *from* them?").

Consultants are often conduits and gatekeepers for new business ideas. Could the increasing emphasis on their own expansion during these go-go years have led some to suspend critical judgment about one such big idea, "shareholder value"? This is a theory of what business is all about[24] that many advisers helped spread in the 1980s and 1990s. Its basic premise, that maximizing its stock price is a company's most important objective, has driven many of bigness's most dramatic failures. Stock price fixation may be the biggest management distraction of all. Managing the growth of the share price is not the same as managing the growth of the business, though in recent years this distinction has been frequently been blurred.

. . . .

A BIGGER STOCK PRICE IS
NOT ALWAYS A GOOD THING

. . . .

The stock prices of many firms have been too high.
That is to managers what heroin is to a drug addict.[1]

—Michael Jensen

BIGNESS IS BUILT ON DUBIOUS LOGIC

Michael Jensen undoubtedly meant well. As a young academic in the mid-1970s, this University of Chicago–trained economist, along with a colleague, William Meckling, set out to solve an important problem of that era: How do you keep business leaders focused on making money for their companies and their shareholders? What happened, though, was that his solution created an even bigger problem for companies 30 years later.

Shareholder-Value Theory

For much of the twentieth century, most chief executives' pay was based on how big a company they ran, and many appeared to be more attuned to building sprawling conglomerate empires than to growing profits and share prices. Both of those measures of economic well-being stagnated during the 1960s and 1970s. Jensen thought that the way to get businesses to better serve the interests of those who owned them was to put the company's stock price at center stage. Stockholders are the stars, the most important people in any company, according to his shareholder-value theory. Make them rich, and benefits will (eventually) also accrue to the supporting cast of managers, employees, customers, suppliers, communities in which the business operates, and the economy as a whole. The key to this all happening, said Jensen, was to reward the most powerful people in the business for acting in the best interests of the shareholders by tying executive pay to the stock price.

It took a while for this theory to get broad acceptance. For many years the Business Roundtable, made up of the CEOs of the 160 largest U.S. companies, emphasized that a key job of management was to balance shareholders' expectations of maximum return against the other priorities of the business and the demands of its other constituencies. In other words, businesses exist to serve customers and society, too. This is the sense of balance that disappeared during the hostile-takeover battles of the 1980s, when Jensen's theory was used to justify the tactics of aggressive investor-raiders like Carl Icahn and T. Boone Pickens. Wall Street soon joined the fray, as firms were created to do leveraged-buyout deals in which the acquirer would borrow money, buy out the public shareholders of a target company, install new management, and cut costs to cover the expense of all the new debt the company had just taken on. Eventually these target companies, or at least those that survived the deep cuts and high interest payments, would be taken public again, providing a large profit for the raiders when they sold out. During the 1980s almost half of the major corporations in the United States received such takeover offers. Those that did not succumb were often forced to prop up their stock price by downsizing their workforce and selling off their weaker business units.

Not wanting to be left out, executives of many public corporations wondered why they needed an outsider to do what they could do themselves, provided they were sufficiently well motivated. Jensen had some ideas about what it would take to encourage executives to behave like owners, and he soon became a leading advocate of mega-sized stock option grants to top management. At this point, his shareholder-value theory had caught on throughout American business. Lowell Bryan, a McKinsey director, asserted, "The size that really matters is market capitalization"[2] (the product of a company's share price times the number of shares outstanding). Jensen's course at Harvard was among the most popular in the MBA curriculum, and in 1997 the Business Roundtable reversed its earlier thinking about the proper role of business. It downsized the mission of the public corporation and its chief executive to a single objective: maximize shareholder value by keeping the stock price rising. A bigger stock price must be a better stock price, they assumed.

Only One Number Counts

The shareholder-value theory was popular because it seemed to codify common sense. Even though it was backed up with pages of mathematical models and equations, its basic conclusion was very simple: All it took to successfully manage a multibillion-dollar multinational business was to get one number (the stock price) right. *Most of us like things simple.*

The theory also received support from two other ideas that were commonly accepted in the business world. One of these, the efficient-market hypothesis, said that the stock market is all-knowing. At any point in time, it (somehow) manages to roll all the relevant information about a company's past, present, and future economic prospects into a single number. So, even if a stock price seems too high or too low, this appearance is wrong, not the number. *Many of us like to believe in magic.*

The existence of greed was another rationale for shareholder value. Economists often practice psychology without a license. They have to. Even though their expertise is usually quantitative, the issues they address are often more driven by the nature of human behavior than by the nature of money. To keep their equations manageable, they make simplifying assumptions about how people work. One commonly used set of these, called "Economic Man," assumes that we behave in ways that rationally, and sometimes even obsessively, advance our self-interests. We are never-satiated maximizers, always preferring more to less. To get people to do what you want (such as maximize a company's stock price), you should treat them as if they are Economic Man, and tap into their hard-wired greed by offering them stock options to make them very rich. *Even when our hearts tell us there's a lot of good in most people, our macho-tough instincts are more comfortable with explanations that acknowledge the dark side.*

A BIGGER STOCK PRICE DOES NOT SIGNIFY A BETTER COMPANY

Shareholder-value theory always had its skeptics. Union leaders, community activists, and corporate social responsibility advocates naturally never warmed to it. Many middle managers and workers, living in the world of 401(k) plans, not stock option grants, also wondered if they were bearing too much of the cost and not receiving enough of the reward. But it took an economist, unburdened by social pressures from business school colleagues and with a knack for asking probing questions, to look behind the veil of this immensely popular notion and explain why shareholder-value theory had a lot in common with the tale of the emperor with no clothes.

A Theory Built on Flawed Assumptions

Before becoming a Yale-trained economist, Margaret Blair's career was in journalism. Her experience as a *BusinessWeek* bureau chief taught her to start with questions, not assumptions, and to give emphasis to facts over theories. Blair's academic bases, at Georgetown and Vanderbilt law schools, distanced her from the conventional MBA wisdom of what a corporation is all about. Several years before the scandals surfaced at Enron, Tyco, and WorldCom, Blair's research raised many questions about the logic of shareholder primacy. Her examination found that it is "based on a series of elegant and facile, but deeply flawed assumptions about how financial markets work, how human beings work together in groups, and about what the law requires."[3]

When I was asked to join the board of a publicly traded company, I received a quick education about what the law requires. I talked with an expert in corporate governance in order to better understand just what I was getting into. What he said surprised me. My role was not to advise, nurture, and support the chief executive who had graciously invited me to sit on what he liked to call "his" board. Nor was I to think of myself as a representative of the people who owned stock in the company, even though they were the ones who actually elected me to the board. My legal responsibility was to serve the best interests of the corporation as an entity, not those of any one of its constituents. My marching orders were to serve as a fiduciary for the business, not as an agent for the shareholders. When I voted for a strategy proposed by management, I was to consider how it affected customers, employees, the company's reputation in general, government regulators, banks that lent us money, and our stockholders. All these groups had claims on the company and interests that had to be considered. As Blair points out, this is why U.S. law gives corporate directors very wide discretion to consider interests other than those of shareholders.

Stock Prices Do Not Always Reflect a Company's Real Worth

Blair goes on to argue that "shareholders are neither the 'owners' of corporations, nor the only claimants with investments at risk; stock prices do not always accurately reflect the true underlying value of equity securities; [and] managers will not necessarily do a better job of running corporations if they focus solely on share value."[4] Her assertion that a company's stock price does not necessarily reflect the business's real worth is in accord with the research that Robert Shiller,[5] another Yale economist, has done. He looked at stock prices throughout the last century and found that they were much more volatile than the actual economic performance of the companies they were supposed to mirror.

Blair also examined the efficient-market hypothesis and found that it does not do a good job of explaining how the stock market really works. It is simplistic as well as simple. While markets do respond quickly to good or bad news, they also take on a life of their own, going through periods of boom or bust that have nothing to do with the underlying fundamental value of the stocks. Look at the wild roller-coaster ride Amazon has given its investors. The stock peaked at almost $107 at the end of 1999, at the height of the Internet bubble. A few years later it bottomed at $6 a share. Amazon in early 2005 is trading at under $50 a share. Which of these numbers really reflected its "real" value? Through this entire period, Amazon CEO Jeff Bezos kept slogging along, building the world's most innovative cyber-retailer. Blair has found that markets respond very quickly to new information that is easy to interpret, but digest complex information sluggishly and imperfectly. Financial markets also overreact a lot. They are highly susceptible to bandwagon thinking, crowd psychology, and fads. This leads to share prices moving far out of line with reality, until enough investors wise up and sell an overpriced stock or buy one that is irrationally underpriced. Blair also warns that these tendencies to overreact and incorrectly absorb complex information give insiders opportunities to manipulate prices by giving out misleading information.

The bottom line is that there are many reasons for a stock price to inflate (or fall) that have nothing to do with the soundness of a company's strategy and how well it is being executed. Individual share prices tend to go up when the market as a whole is going up—something that it did fairly constantly for the 13 years after 1987. How do you separate the real increase in the economic value of a company brought about by wise management moves from the free ride the market gave many companies over those years?

Managing Earnings Instead of the Business

Individual stock prices also go up when the quarterly expectations of investment analysts are exceeded. This had led many companies to "manage" their earnings, constantly reporting numbers that are on target or just a little above what Wall Street was expecting. Enron, in its pre-bankruptcy days, was famous for always reporting rising quarterly profits. Few analysts were able to determine exactly where these earnings were coming from, but they took comfort (for a while) in knowing that Enron always seemed able to meet their optimistic expectations. Most companies have many buttons they can push to manipulate their profits. Accounting may appear to be a precise, quantifiable discipline, but its rules are full of allowable estimates, judgment calls, and loophole-filling gimmicks. I once asked an accounting firm partner how a common, but complex transaction ought be accounted for. His answer: "How would you like it to be accounted for?" Profit dollars can be generated from what is left over after covering expenses, or they can be created in the accounting department by hiding expenses, recognizing phantom revenue, treating pension gains as business profits, underestimating inventory losses, or overestimating inventory worth.

Lucent found itself caught in a no-win cycle of making special, expensive deals with its customers at the end of each quarter to pump up revenues for that period, only to find itself deeper in the hole the next quarter when it had to surpass the results of the previous one, as well as deliver on the uneconomic promises it made back then. Eventually Lucent ran out of rabbits to pull from its hat. The CEO who allowed the company to be driven by unmeetable Wall Street expectations was ousted, and his successor lamented that "the white-hot heat of driving for quarterly revenue growth"[6] had eventually destroyed Lucent's ability to execute any reasonable plan.

In the final analysis, a business's financial statement is a reflection of values and ethics as much as of economics. They are what determine how judgment calls about accounting practices are made. Very few businesses have operations that produce even and predictable quarterly results—there are just "too many moving parts,"[7] says one West Coast analyst. Companies that constantly report smooth and upward numbers are also reporting a top management fixation on the stock, not the business.

False Comfort from a Rising Stock Price

Is such intense attention to having a bigger stock price really all that bad? Yes, it is. An unwarranted rising stock price gives false comfort, another form of expansion fixation that distracts managers from closely evaluating how well the business is really doing. Actually, when all things are considered, too high a stock price is in itself a very, very bad thing to have. Just ask Scott Livengood, the chief executive of Krispy Kreme, who was fired less than two years after this famed donut maker was celebrated by *Fortune* as "the hottest brand in the land."[8] Livengood spent most of his tenure trying to grow the company fast enough to justify its once-soaring stock price, first by adding so many retail stores that the brand lost its novelty, then by trying to sell a product meant to be eaten right out of the oven in cellophane-wrapped boxes that sat for days on supermarket shelves. A stockholder lawsuit alleges that when both these moves failed to produce profit growth, the company applied its cooking prowess to its bookkeeping, sometimes shipping twice the number of donuts actually ordered to some grocers. Eventually the unwanted donuts would be returned, but not until Krispy Kreme had a chance to issue temporarily inflated revenue numbers.

Playing to Wall Street (instead of to whatever street your customers live on) does pay off, for a while. Investors are attracted, and the stock value initially soars. A study done at Wharton and the University of Michigan business school[9] looked at what happened to companies whose prospects were the most overexaggerated. When word of the overstatements gets out, as it always eventually does, share prices sink rapidly, with declines totaling over $100 billion in the companies studied.

Once a company's shares become overvalued, many managers, especially if a big part of their personal wealth is driven by the stock price continually rising, can be tempted to keep the stock that way and even encourage more overvaluation. This is the downside of Economic Man. Even if they know that the bubble is fated to burst, some people may hopefully assume that they can cash out first. What this leads to is limited candor coupled with creatively optimistic accounting. These managers may also launch initiatives—acquisitions and large investments in the technology trend of the moment—that look good to investment analysts, but make no strategic sense for the business. This is another big problem that accompanies myopic attention to share price—it lets others control your destiny.

Managerial Heroin

The misdeeds of companies such as Enron, Krispy Kreme, and Lucent have led Michael Jensen to an intellectual epiphany of sorts. Now an emeritus professor at Harvard Business School, he seems to have grown a bit skeptical of the shareholder-value revolution he helped unleash. In recent articles, he has acknowledged that stocks can be mispriced. "Companies do not grow in a constant fashion with each quarter's results better than the last," Jensen now also admits. "In the long run conforming to pressures to satisfy the market's desire for impossible predictability and unwise growth leads to the destruction of corporate value, shortened careers, humiliation and damaged companies."[10]

Overvalued stocks, Jensen observes, set in motion a set of organizational pressures that destroy, not create, shareholder value. Jensen has even gone so far as to call overvalued stocks the equivalent of "managerial heroin." Like a narcotic, Jensen says, they make you feel great. Your company is on TV; banks are throwing money at it; your stock options are going through the roof. The only problem is that all this requires a financial performance that is impossible to maintain. Managers keep struggling for ways to keep the earnings up. Some otherwise highly moral, honest managers, he says, are driven to lie, cheat, and steal. A Boston Consulting Group study found that nothing correlates as strongly with corporate illegalities as the value of the companies' outstanding stock options. The CEOs in firms found guilty of fraud received option grants in the years leading up to the crimes that were eight times larger than those received by chief executives of comparable companies never convicted of any bad deeds.[11]

BIGNESS LEADS TO RISKY BEHAVIORS

Addictions lead to risky behaviors. Many companies that have bought into maximizing shareholder value have followed Jensen's earlier advice of making executives think like owners by paying them with stock options. The problem with this is that they do not think like owners. They think like option holders. A shareholder has money invested in the stock. If the stock tanks, the shareholder loses real money. An option holder has a piece of paper giving him the right (but not the obligation) to buy the stock at a certain price. If the stock falls below that price, the option holder can just throw that paper away, losing nothing. An option is optional. Its owner does not have to exercise it.

Stock Options

Option holders make money when the stock rises above the price at which they have the right to buy it at. This gives the option holder the same reward as someone who has actually invested money in the stock, but none of the risk. It's nice work if you can get it—just don't confuse the perspective of the shareholder with that of the option awardee.

There is a valid place for stock options as a means of compensation: start-up companies. Most start-ups (and some turnarounds) are pure risk, offering either upside rewards or nothing. They are in sync with the logic of options in a way that larger, established businesses are not. Options are a useful, sometimes essential, tool that allows new, cash-short ventures to attract needed talent and to provide those people with incentives and rewards matched with the challenges that they are undertaking.

Granting senior executives of proven postembryonic businesses large grants of stock options gives the people in the company with the most power a lot more reason to focus on the upside of their strategies than on the downside. Their lack of personal risk can translate into greater risk for the business, though, if an "I've got nothing to lose (and a lot to gain)" mindset clouds their judgment. We have already discussed how this has led some managers to dishonest and unethical risky behaviors. But there are also perfectly legal risks that an option-loaded executive is susceptible to: short-time-itis, cash hoarding, and the urge to merge.

Living Quarter to Quarter

As already noted, the people whose judgments drive stock prices, the analysts, live in a quarter-to-quarter world. They like it that way. They are not forced to look very far into an uncertain future, so their credibility is at less risk. When the numbers of a company they once championed do not rise each quarter, anxiety sets in, which they quickly relieve by downgrading the stock. Executives, who are well aware of this proclivity, use two tactics to stay in the analysts' good graces. Some "smooth" the quarterly numbers, managing them through accounting discretion so that the results show a gentle, but constant upward rise. This makes for nice-looking PowerPoint charts, but it also takes away the likelihood that any short-term feedback that the market may be trying to provide through a dip in sales or an expense blip will be noticed, and midcourse corrections made while the correcting is still easy to do. Why go to all the trouble when the quarterly bottom line is fine and the stock price is rising? Another difficulty with final report cards coming out four times a year is that few, if any, real growth strategies are executed in three-month bites. Most, as we will discuss in Part 2, take years to bear fruit. Pulling a plant up too often to see how the roots are doing usually keeps them from doing very well.

Hoarding Cash

Shareholders make money in two ways: stock price appreciation and cash dividend payments. Executive with options are not eligible for dividends; they gain only through the stock price going up. So it is not surprising that since 1992, the heyday of big option awards, dividend payouts have fallen to their lowest levels ever.[12] Companies have a choice about what to do with their profits: pay them out to shareholders as a dividend, or try to get bigger by retaining and reinvesting them. While some companies develop wise plans for investing in themselves, the record shows that most don't.[13] Instead, they are more likely to use their surplus cash to expand their businesses beyond the point that makes the most economic sense.

As investment sage and author of *Against the Gods* Peter Bernstein observes, paying dividends is a great way to focus executives on what really matters. "Managements are more careful, " he says, "when they are not floating in cash."[14] Michael Jensen, now a convert to this way of rewarding shareholders, thinks that these payouts impose a needed discipline, encouraging managers to think twice about spending too much on iffy projects if that would endanger the company's ability to pay its expected dividend.[15]

The Urge to Merge

What is the biggest mistake made by people without this needed discipline? They go out and buy another company. Some, almost as if suffering from an addiction, become serial acquirers. Why not, if you are an adherent of shareholder-value theory? The fastest way to add earnings is to buy someone else's. When it becomes hard to find new customers, acquiring those of another company can be very appealing. Overvalued stock reinforces these tendencies to turn a strategic plan into a "buy another company" shopping list. Such stock is a tempting currency to use to get bigger because, being overpriced, it allows a company to purchase another at a discount. Discounts are hard to resist.

Making unwise acquisitions, though, is one of the riskiest moves a company can make—and most acquisitions turn out to be in the unwise category. Nobel Prize winner Daniel Kahneman is very direct about what happens: "Approximately three-quarters of mergers and acquisitions never pay off—the acquiring firm's shareholders lose more than the acquired firm's shareholders gain."[16] Why? According to the Boston Consulting Group,[17] it's simple: In the urge to get bigger, buyers tend to overpay to get the deal done. Whatever efficiency gains or strategic benefits the combination produces tend to go to the seller, not the buyer, by way of an inflated sale price. But the buyer is the one left with all the postmerger heavy lifting. Consultants at McKinsey & Co. call this "the winner's curse."

Addictive behavior is often characterized by excessive self-confidence. Businesspeople generally tend to be an optimistic lot (with at least 90 percent of them feeling that they are above average on whatever standard they are being measured by). This tendency is amplified in attempts to expand through acquisition. The main cause of the winner's curse is unwarranted optimism about the benefits that would come from greater scale, sales, and synergies. Most acquiring executives believe that with good planning and superior management skills, they will be able to avoid or easily overcome the problems that have kept others from realizing these benefits. Kahneman's research, and that of others, on postmerger performance says that they are usually mistaken.[18]

Scale. It once made sense to buy up related companies and become as integrated as possible. This was true in the days when Ford made the steel that went into its cars and railroads built their own locomotives. Grouping together interrelated functions added control and reduced transaction costs. That was then. Now, the age of global outsourcing has a different logic. Information technology and the Internet allow coordination to happen without a company's owning all the assets that need to work in harmony. The work done in the 1930s by Ronald Coase, another Nobel Prize winner in economics, is also now better appreciated. He studied what happened as companies expanded. For a while, transaction costs do drop. But at some point the expense of doing everything internally rises as the size and complexity of the organization grows. "Bigger is better—but only up to a point."[19] Economies of scale are still around, but the scale now has more to do with information than with bulk. This is a lesson that came too late for Royal Ahold, a once-successful Dutch grocer that in the wake of a billion-dollar accounting scandal had to dismantle significant parts of a decade-long global acquisition binge. Anders Moberg, the chief executive brought in to undo Ahold's past mistakes, admitted that moving into too many new markets and new businesses at the same time overwhelmed the company with complexity.[20]

Sales. Companies merge in hopes of increasing revenues. McKinsey and Southern Methodist University have extensively studied what happens to sales in the wake of mergers.[21] In 70 percent of the cases, the expected revenue boosts never came. Frequently, the two companies would have sold more if they had stayed apart and just expanded sales at the average pace of their industries. Both the acquirer and the acquired lose ground. The work involved in putting them together unsettles customers and distracts staff. Cross-selling opportunities are a frequent rationalization behind many business combinations, but very few of these bear fruit. Many customers just don't want to be cross-sold, and good salespeople are often reluctant to share their best customers. Companies like Charles Schwab and Hewlett-Packard have found that acquisitions intended to give them access to new customer segments actually just confused their old customers and blurred their image in the market. HP's merger with Compaq, for example, did add bulk, but it also essentially doubled the size of HP's worst-performing business. Not all sales are profitable sales.

Synergies. Synergy is a good thing. It doesn't scale well, though. Creative, boundary-spanning ideas occur in small, cohesive groups—200 people maximum, though teams of 20 work better. Synergy arises from trust among people who understand each other well and bring different perspectives to bear to achieve a common goal. It's a bottom-up process. It is seldom the result of cross-divisional negotiations or top-down mandates demanding coordination and cooperation. Sony has invested two decades of top management attention (with minimal success) in attempting to bring together its acquired music and movie "content" businesses and Sony's core of technical gadget "hardware" operations. But artistic creativity is not the same as technology innovation. Each may be "cutting edge," but in different realms with different corporate cultures and languages. The ability to design devices to play music and show movies is worlds away from what it takes to make the songs and films. Apple Computer, a company unburdened by this need to synergize, has been able to use its iPod product to capture the mobile-music market once held by Sony's Walkman. Continual references to high-level synergistic concepts, like "digital convergence," to justify combining disparate businesses are too often smokescreens that hide the fact that a practical plan to put together the parts of an acquired empire does not exist.

Eat or Be Eaten

The flip side of confidence is fear. Excessive self-confidence sometimes masks the real motivator for bulking up: the imperative to eat or be eaten. This urge often expresses itself when companies merge in hopes of obtaining a guaranteed market for their products: Viacom sells its shows to a captive CBS, Disney sells to ABC, and Time Warner distributes its content on America Online.

This quest for security usually backfires—sometimes tragically, as happened to Swissair, once one of the world's finest airlines, now out of business, with its successor only an appendage of Lufthansa. Afraid of being too small in an era of global airline giants and alliances, Swissair invested in a web of minority ownerships of many of Europe's weaker and smaller airlines. Its main objective was to lock these companies into being customers of Swissair's extensive aviation service businesses. To protect the viability of this expansion through diversification into maintenance, aircraft leasing, ground services, and catering, Swissair found itself forced to make huge capital injections into its struggling airline partners. The worldwide fall in air travel immediately after September 11, 2001, exacerbated the situation. Eventually something had to give in this "rob Peter to pay Paul" strategy—Swissair's solvency.

Mergers That Work

Not all acquisitions and mergers are bad. There is a lot to be learned from the minority of managers who know how to make them work or resist their temptation. Nestlé, a company that has grown by buying many other businesses, has preserved its gains by also knowing when not to buy, such as walking away from potentially owning Quaker's Gatorade business. Nestlé's chief executive, Peter Brabeck, candidly acknowledged that that sports drink could have more value for some of his competitors than for Nestlé. For Brabeck, being the best and strongest consumer company is much more important than being the biggest.

When used as a tool rather than as an end in themselves, business combinations can add economic value, not just bulk. Federal Express has a long history of making tightly targeted acquisitions that either round out existing product offerings or provide a focal point for new ones. FedEx anticipated that the market for its overnight delivery service in the United States would flatten, so it spent almost a billion dollars in 1989 to purchase Flying Tigers, a venerable freight-only airline with valuable rights to serve Asia's major cities. That acquisition gave FedEx a head start over its competition. It is now the number one express carrier to Asia, boasting an all-weather sorting hub in Anchorage and a network that includes over 200 Chinese cities. As the China market became red-hot and competing shippers scrambled to catch up, FedEx turned its sights back to the domestic market and identified a segment unserved by its main nemesis, United Parcel Service: less-than-truckload (LTL) freight hauling. This highly profitable business involved shipping items that were too big or too heavy for FedEx and UPS regular ground services, but too small to fill up an entire truck. FedEx purchased several well-established LTL regional haulers, combined their operations, melded them into its world-class information network, and is now the revenue and profit leader in this market niche.

Carlos Gutierrez made similar enabling use of acquisitions as part of his effort to restore Kellogg to a growth path. He purchased the cookie and cracker maker Keebler, not so much for its market position as because it had one of the largest direct-store delivery systems in the food business. By having the Keebler reps take along Kellogg's other products direct to store shelves, Gutierrez was able to streamline a lengthy supply chain by cutting out third-party distributors, using its own employees to ensure that Kellogg products received optimal placement on supermarket shelves.

In these instances, Nestlé, FedEx, and Kellogg all showed a degree of focus and judgment that has been missing in firms caught up in the urge to merge. Unfortunately, for every three examples of sound merger-and-acquisition judgment, it is possible to cite six or more where flawed reasoning was followed by poor subsequent performance.

BIGNESS IS DRIVEN BY THE WRONG PSYCHOLOGY

Business mergers are a lot like couples marrying. Both behaviors continue to be very popular, in spite of the not overly great odds that either will be successful. Second marriages have sometimes been called the triumph of hope over experience (with first marriages being driven by imagination over intelligence, according to Oscar Wilde). The same quips seem equally applicable to many organizational marriages and serial acquirers. When rational logic doesn't seem to be present in a situation, there is usually emotional logic at play. Love is the obvious powerful feeling behind human coupling. What plays the equivalent role in corporate combinations, and in the continuing quest for bigness in general? Why do otherwise smart, alert, and forward-thinking businesspeople repeatedly engage in activities that usually prove counterproductive?

This is a subject that has received a lot of recent attention. Robert Sternberg, a Yale psychologist, wrote a book to answer just that question. *Why Smart People Can Be So Stupid*[22] pulls together the research of several leading behavioral scientists to identify factors beyond avarice that have driven the kinds of dumb business decisions discussed in this chapter. A Dartmouth management professor, Sydney Finkelstein, also studied this phenomenon. His book, *Why Smart Executives Fail*, examines what was behind 197 instances of dramatic drops in market share and value. Nobel Prize in Economics winner Daniel Kahneman and behavioral economist Richard Thaler have also weighed in on these issues. The findings of all these scholars share a similar theme: Mistaken perceptions of reality can cause much more damage than willful misconduct. Self-serving behaviors have certainly played a part in many unwise business expansions, but they are far from the whole story.

Faulty Thinking

Mistaken perceptions come from faulty thinking processes. Sternberg identified five forms of flawed thinking[23] that can lead to counterproductive actions.

Unrealistic optimism. Optimism, as we will discuss in Chapter 9, is a powerful enabler of growth. Too much of it, applied in situations where it is unwarranted, can backfire by leaving people feeling so capable and on such a roll that they mistakenly think that they can achieve *anything* they set out to do. Samsung thought its great success with consumer electronics would carry over to a completely different business, automobile manufacturing. It invested $5 billion to enter a market that was already oversaturated and nearly profit-free. Exaggerating benefits and discounting costs is a great way to set a business up for failure, as Samsung soon learned after it was forced to turn over the direction of its ailing car business to a more experienced French company, Renault.

Egocentrism. Individuals who come to think that they are the only ones who matter are likely to make many perceptual errors. They will take personal credit for the good luck of having been in a buoyant economy or a market that has just taken off. Egocentrists act in ways that benefit themselves, often without a clue to what impact these behaviors are having on others. Their illusion of personal preeminence leads them to miss a lot that is going on around them. MIT systems researchers have spent several decades examining the dynamics behind growth. They have noticed that all growth initiatives involve two distinct processes—one that generates a self-reinforcing spiral of success, and another that attempts to balance this forward momentum with feedback from the rest of the world telling the grower to slow down a bit. The first process always runs up against, and sometimes causes, the second. Egocentrism (acting as if the world revolves around you) basks in the first of these, while ignoring the early warnings of obstacles ahead provided by the second process. Even as its sales declined, legendary Levi Strauss still thought of itself as *the* company that defined jeans and smart casual wear, and dismissed reports that young, fashion-oriented consumers saw its clothes as stodgy and outdated.

Omniscience. People who feel that they know all they need to know and do not need to seek or heed advice are the ones who are most likely to make decisions without considering all the ramifications of their actions. The chief executive of Rubbermaid in the mid-1990s, Wolfgang Schmitt, cultivated a reputation with his managers as a lightning-fast thinker who behaved as through he knew "everything about everything."[24] He ran one of the then most admired companies in the United States. Rubbermaid had a dominant position in many categories of household products and containers—at least, dominant until Schmitt missed that decade's shift of market power from makers of products to their sellers. Rubbermaid ignored Wal-Mart's demands for lower prices and deliveries at Wal-Mart's convenience, and found its place on this retailer's shelves quickly taken by cheaper items made by companies with retailer-friendly, just-in-time delivery systems. Rubbermaid's sales declined, and by the end of the decade the company was sold to a turn-around specialist.

Omnipotence. Feeling like an all-powerful master of the universe leads one to push harder in the same direction when obstacles arise, rather than heeding the potentially useful feedback the world is trying to provide. Assumptions about reality get confused with reality itself. After Nokia became the world's leading cell phone maker, it came to think that it could shape the industry because its market position was so strong. It resisted following its smaller competitors, forgetting how motivated these companies were to keep up with changes in customer needs that could offer a way to topple Nokia's dominance. As a result, when preferences shifted away from candy bar–style handsets and toward sleeker, clamshell phones, Nokia stayed with the older models too long and lost market share. Ironically, one of the companies it lost customers to was Motorola, the former wireless phone leader whose business had been devastated by Nokia's digital phones a few years earlier when Motorola clung too long to analog technology. Executives caught up in omnipotence overestimate how much control they have over events and completely discount the role that chance and one-time occurrences have played in their past successes. Their response to obstacles becomes stereotyped—they just push harder.

Invulnerability. Once thought to be only an affliction of teenage boys, the idea of being able to do whatever one wants to without fear of harm or exposure has crept into some boardrooms. Sometimes expressed by ignoring the law and social norms, and other times by failing to protect a strong position in the marketplace by adapting to evolving circumstances, this thinking fallacy leads to underestimating how aware and clever ones' opponents (and regulators) really are.

Grandiosity

These are all cognitive errors, not manifestations of greed. They drive bigness, and they are also reinforced by it. What causes people (especially *smart* people, as Sternberg and Finkelstein like to point out) to fall into these traps? We are all prone to distorted thinking from time to time, but when these become our modus operandi for dealing with the world, it is likely that we have become caught up in grandiosity. This is an occupational hazard to which many leaders are vulnerable. Psychiatrist Roy Lubit[25] notes that people in positions of power can become self-centered and grandiose when those around them treat them with excessive deference, fawn on them, feel reluctant to challenge their views, and fail to provide self-corrective feedback. Observes Lubit: "If you have power you are probably not as smart, funny, or good looking as people say you are."[26] Many leaders have risen to senior positions because of their expressed self-confidence, ability to generate enthusiasm in others, and willingness to make tough decisions quickly. As they advance in the hierarchy, they run the risk of having fewer people nearby who are willing to intelligently challenge or add balance to their views, further inflating their sense of self-importance and fueling any tendencies toward arrogance that they have brought with them. The tendency to provide rock-star-sized pay packages to senior executives reinforces all of this, putting additional distance between them and the others in their organization. Soon the stage is set for unrealistic optimism, egocentrism, omniscience, omnipotence, and invulnerability to take over, and the quest for bigness is primed to become the business's dominant driver.

SIZE IS A MEANS, NOT AN END

In this chapter and Chapter 1, I have tried to lay out the consequences of equating growth with size expansion. Success at expansion limits, not enables, real growth. It is more likely to stall a business than to move it forward. Bigness is not sustainable; it is counterproductive, and it often bites back. It is built on dubious logic, leads to risky behaviors, and drives otherwise smart people to think in dumb ways.

It doesn't have to be this way. What if we decouple the idea of "growth" from that of "getting bigger"? And what if we instead consider size expansion as a by-product of growth, but not growth itself? While it can be an enabler, it often becomes a disabler of ongoing growth. There are right and wrong sizes for every business. Some lack critical mass and must catch up. Others are imprisoned by too much bulk and need to seek other things. In an article explaining why size is not really a strategy, *Fast Company* editor Keith Hammonds hit the nail on the head: "Bigger, per se, isn't better. *Better* is better."[27] Peter Drucker agrees. He amplified the thought that began Chapter 1—growth by itself is a delusion; there's no virtue in a company getting bigger—by adding: "The right goal is to become better."[28] If growth is not the result of doing the right things, says Drucker, "It is vanity and little else."[29]

Smart Growth

Urban planners like to distinguish between smart and dumb growth. Dumb growth (extending a city with mile after mile of quarter-acre subdivisions built helter-skelter throughout the adjacent countryside) is usually a formula for sprawl and crawl, overstretched and uneconomic public services, and environmental degradation. Encouraging denser development along established transit corridors (smart growth) leads to shorter commutes, more affordable housing, and economically sustainable cities. More space is available for public parks, too. The key differentiator is sustainability—growth that meets the needs of the present without compromising the future. If we label "getting bigger" as dumb growth, what counts as smart growth in the business world? Or, to put it another way, where should all the energy, creativity, and resources that are now being spent pursuing bigness, shareholder value, unwise mergers, and faux synergies really go? That's what Chapter 3 is all about.

. . . .

GROWTH IS ABOUT
MOVING FORWARD

. . . .

> When paradigms change, the world itself changes with them.[1]
> —*Thomas Kuhn*

BEYOND THE LIMITS THAT DEFINE THE BUSINESS

Growth is about progress, not bigness. The point of growing is to achieve full potential, not maximum size. A business grows whenever it moves beyond the self-imposed limits that define and constrain it.

Examples

- When Howard Schultz focused on selling his customers an experience, not just a good cup of coffee, Starbucks grew.
- When Darcy Winslow championed a range of products for women who did not fit into the testosterone-defined market segments that had come to define her employer, Nike grew.
- When Bill Greenwood found a way to turn truckers, his railroad's most troublesome competitors, into its best customers, Burlington Northern grew.
- When Roger Enrico set his company on its own course, rather than defining it by its rivalry with Coca-Cola, PepsiCo grew.
- When Al Bru, one of Enrico's managers, spent $57 million to eliminate trans fats from Frito-Lay's snack foods, Frito-Lay's owner, PepsiCo, grew.

- When Deborah Henretta changed the mission of the troubled division she led from "producing the most technically perfect products" to giving customers a brand that "met the goals the customers themselves defined," Procter & Gamble grew.

- When Bill Ford turned his predecessor's (Jacques Nasser) expansion plans on their head and said that his goal was to give up market share and make more money by selling fewer automobiles, Ford Motor Company grew.

- When Arkadi Kuhlmann created a bank with no fees, minimum deposits, or branches; a narrow range of handpicked products; and a willingness to reject customers if they were looking for services he did not want to provide, his company, ING Direct, showed that it was possible to grow by challenging the central pillars of its industry's conventional wisdom.

- When publisher Jane Friedman developed plans to create in the minds of its readers a brand identity for her company as strong as that of its individual superstar authors, HarperCollins began to grow by reducing its economic dependence on blockbuster books.

- When Internet seller Jeff Bezos gave prominent placement on his web site to links that would take his customers directly to his competitors, Amazon.com grew.

- When Yvon Chouinard dropped 30 percent of his clothing line as runaway demand threatened to turn his outdoor sports apparel company into something he did not want it to be, a mass marketer, Patagonia simultaneously got smaller and grew.

- When Kenneth Chenault unwound his company's long-time strategy of becoming a giant financial services supermarket by spinning off its brokerage business, American Express grew.

This approach to growth is not limited to the business world. Martin Seligman grew psychology when he started a movement to broaden the field beyond its traditional fixation on rescuing people from mental illness and toward giving equivalent attention to discovering science-based ways for humans to thrive and flourish.

Roger Conner contributed to the growth of the "social activism industry" when he stopped being a passionate crusader for the human rights causes he believed in and became a broker who now helps dueling interest groups convert win-lose struggles into a search for common ground.

What Is Going On

Something similar happened in each of these instances of growth. The 14 individuals who drove progress all gave attention to:

1. Putting aside an old way of perceiving their situation
2. Assimilating, first within themselves and then in their organization, a new perspective
3. Building the capabilities needed to support that new perspective
4. Reorienting their organization, and its surroundings, around this new possibility[2]

HOW TO THINK ABOUT GROWTH

Real, lasting growth is hard to pull off, which may explain why a narrow focus on expansion so often substitutes for it. Not only does growth require moving beyond current boundaries, which themselves may be moving as well as hardened targets, but the business must also stay at the new destination long enough to reap rewards for having made the journey. And it has to do all this in a way that allows its newly found wealth to be shared with those who have contributed to its success.

For growth to be sustainable, it needs to offer some benefit to the environment in which the business operates as well as to the business itself, giving customers, shareholders, suppliers, and surrounding communities a stake in its ongoing success. This might sound like altruism, but the broader the base of people with an interest in a growing company's game, the greater the "home-field advantage" that company will enjoy. You can call it prosperity through reciprocation, the Jeff Bezos model for Amazon. Contrast the affection and support that is felt for Apple Computer and Google with the distrust and wariness that Yahoo engendered when, in reaction to a financial downturn, it changed its privacy policies to allow customers' personal information to be used to target them for unsolicited sales pitches. Yahoo endangered a great deal of accumulated goodwill when, according to industry observer John Ellis, it began to think narrowly of its user base as a revenue-extraction resource.[3] Yahoo made a common mistake: It attempted to expand blindly, without considering its actions in the context of its broader environment.

Seeing What Others See

Wise growers have the ability to see things as others see them, allowing them to anticipate the reactions that others will have to their moves. They are as sensitive to their context as they are to their intentions. They know that they are part of a broader marketplace that may not necessarily revolve around them and their immediate needs.

This is often where they get their growth ideas in the first place: by starting out with a different perspective on opportunities from the one that most of their rivals have. Deborah Henretta's way of doing this was very direct. She literally brought the consumers of her baby-care division to the floor on which she worked. By setting up a diaper-testing center a few doors down from her office at Procter & Gamble's headquarters, she made it impossible for her team of product designers and marketers (and herself) to avoid getting a firsthand earful of what was on their customers' minds. They learned that these mothers cared more about getting help with their baby's development than about having the world's driest diaper. This insight led to the creation of a broad range of new products, from training pants to baby wipes, that enabled Henretta's brand, Pampers, to gain share over rival Huggies for the first time in almost a decade.

Growth has a number of markers: increased sales, greater profits, and (sometimes) a rising stock price. But, as we have seen, these indicators can move upward for reasons that have nothing to do with real growth. When growth occurs, a company will always have a different view of its place in the market, and the market's perception of the business will also have changed. Each view will be re-formed based on new experiences and perceptions. Reorientation happens as new possibilities are envisioned, goals relating to them are set, and actions are taken to bring them to reality. If the grower is especially skillful and fast, there will be a time lag between a company's advance and its competitor's realization that something has happened (call it "perceptual arbitrage"), allowing room for midcourse correction, gain consolidation, and profit taking.

Growth Has a Direction

Growth is an ongoing process, not a state of being. It is movement, not a destination. The appellation "growth company" is a misleading categorization. It is a label that stock peddlers use to describe last year's flash in the pan. There is no such thing as a growth company; there are only companies that grow. Buddhists know that it is silly to talk about someone "being enlightened." Enlightenment is not a state of being. Being enlightened is always being enlightened about *something*, says Zen scholar Thich Nhat Hanh.[4] Growth always refers to growth *toward* something.

Progress in business, like evolution in biology, does have a direction. Natural selection affects organisms the way the market shapes organizations: Both tend to adapt to changing conditions by becoming more complex. Complexity implies that their component parts simultaneously become both more differentiated and more integrated; they are increasingly specialized while becoming increasingly better able to work together. Complexity allows new skills and capabilities to emerge; internal resources that were not previously available are manifested.

Complexity leads to greater awareness of an organization's surroundings. It is the opposite of inbreeding or hunkering down. Howard Schultz added music and wireless Internet access to further refine his idea of the Starbucks experience; Martin Seligman complicated psychology by calling on it to address happiness as well as illness. The payoff from all this is greater diversity—an enhanced adaptability to changing circumstances because a broader repertoire is available to draw from. The marketplace offers an incredible array of opportunities. The kind of complexity that accompanies growth allows more of this variety to be noticed, experienced, and exploited.

Complexity is not the same as clutter, which is diversity that cannot be digested. Both Kenneth Chenault and Bill Ford realized this when they refocused American Express and Ford, respectively, on the parts of the businesses with the greatest potential to move forward as integrated entities. Arkadi Kuhlmann's tightly edited version of a savings bank, ING Direct, avoided from its outset the clutter tendency that plagues most large banks, which frequently confuse their customers more than they serve them with ever-broadening ranges of products and packages.

ACCION International. Maria Otero, like Kuhlmann, has taken a segment of traditional banking and turned it inside out. But unlike Kuhlmann, who built a bank just for savers, the organization that Otero leads, ACCION International, has turned people with almost no money at all into good banking customers.[5] Otero is the leading banker to the world's poor. She is a champion of the idea of microlending—making small loans to poor people with no education, no collateral, and no credit history. The loans provide them with affordable working capital, allowing poor people to buy bananas that they might sell on a street corner, flour for tortillas that they would cook in a small marketplace stand, or leather that they might tool into belts. The loan recipients are members of the "informal" or underground economy, people who seldom show up on most bankers' radar screens. Before microlending began, the raw materials for these microbusinesses would be "financed" by local loan sharks, often at rates exceeding 10 percent a day. Most of the profits went for interest payments, locking the business operators into a daily struggle for survival, with no money left over to expand their businesses and work their way out of poverty.

Otero's organization changed all that. ACCION's lender network operates in 20 countries, and in the last decade it has made almost $6 billion in loans to over three million borrowers. First loans are typically small, about $100. Interest sufficient to cover the expense of making the loan is charged, but the rate is still much lower than the borrowers could otherwise obtain. ACCION's default rate is low—over 97 percent of its borrowers pay back their loans. Microcredit works so well because it is often extended to a group, not an individual borrower. This generates peer pressure on individuals to repay the loans or risk losing this source of funding for their community.

Since ACCION was founded, it has made significant advances beyond its previous limits four times, with each stage involving a sharpening of its focus and an increase in its complexity.

ACCION, an acronym for Americans for Community Cooperation

in Other Nations, began as a private-sector version of the Peace Corps. Its founder, Joseph Blatchford, was an amateur tennis player. In 1961, he completed a goodwill tennis tour of 30 cities in Latin America. While traveling, he was deeply affected by what he saw of urban poverty, hunger, open sewers, and overcrowded shantytowns encircling every major city. When he returned to the United States, he spread word of these conditions among his law school friends, raised almost a hundred thousand dollars from several corporations, and started a community development effort aimed at helping the poor help themselves. Blatchford began by flying himself and 30 volunteers to Venezuela. They built sewer lines, youth centers, and school buildings; installed electricity; and taught nutrition and job skills. Over the next 10 years, the program spread to Brazil, Colombia, and Peru and involved over a thousand volunteers. Blatchford received a good deal of recognition for his accomplishments, and he was selected to be the third head of the U.S. government–sponsored Peace Corps.

By the early 1970s, however, his successors at ACCION were becoming increasingly uncomfortable with the results of their work. While they were clearly improving some people's living conditions, it was less clear that their efforts were actually moving people out of poverty. They felt that they were reorganizing resources in a community more than increasing them. With these concerns in mind, they looked hard at an ACCION experimental program in Recife, Brazil. The staff there had wondered whether, if the small-scale entrepreneurs in Recife had access to capital at commercial loan rates, they would be able to lift themselves out of poverty. Over a three-year period, the program gave out 885 loans and found that over a thousand new jobs were created as a result, along with scores of self-sustaining businesses. Soon all of ACCION's programs were reoriented toward microlending.

Most of the money ACCION had available to lend out was raised through contributions and grants. As the scope of its operations grew, ACCION's capital needs outpaced its ability to obtain such gifts. While a half-million-dollar grant from the Inter-American Development Bank took 18 months to receive, ACCION lent this money out in two weeks. This led to a second major reorientation with the creation of BancoSol in La Paz, Bolivia. This was the world's first commercial bank dedicated solely to serving microenterprises, such as market vendors and seamstresses. BancoSol, the first of 15 for-profit financial institutions that ACCION started, raised its capital by selling certificates of deposit in the U.S. financial markets. By the mid-1990s, ACCION's role had changed again, from directly providing loans to poor people to organizing and supporting private-sector enterprises that would fill this need.

Otero's organization has an enviable ability to adapt itself to changes in its environment and avoid being a prisoner of its past formula for success. As the banking industry becomes dominated by large cross-border banks, many of the traditional national banks in Latin America are finding their middle-class and corporate customer base being eroded as megabanks from the United States and Europe set up branch networks in their home territories. ACCION is now having a big impact on these traditional bankers as they seek advice about how to find what is for them a new customer—profitably serving their country's poor with microloans. For Maria Otero, this evolution of ACCION's strategy has brought her career back full circle—she was born in La Paz, Bolivia, the daughter of a banker.

This development in Latin America has encouraged Otero to look to other regions of the world for growth. No longer focusing only on Latin America, she is now replicating ACCION's successes in Africa, Asia, and parts of the United States, hoping to triple the number of people receiving ACCION-supported loans by 2008. *Fast Company* magazine has called ACCION one of the top 20 groups that are changing the world.

The Growth Cycle

The smooth upward-moving curve on PowerPoint slides that has come to symbolize growth is not so much wrong as it is incomplete. Accelerated upward movement is only a portion of the complete growth life cycle. A growth trajectory, expressed visually, really begins with a long, almost flat horizontal line, usually beginning several years ahead of the upswing. This is when old ways of seeing the market are questioned and new perspectives are formulated and tested (and often reformulated). Capabilities are built, resources are acquired, and focused forays into the market are launched during growth's "quiet" period. At some point, assuming that the initiative resonates with its intended customers, the line moves upward. Sometimes the pace is slow and measured; other times, if the context is right and the growers sufficiently skillful, a tipping point is reached and demand soars as if it were propelled by an epidemic.[6] As the line's slope increases, the learning aspects of growth become less prominent, and market penetration and extension activities receive most attention. Eventually momentum wanes, the line's slope flattens, and hopefully a long period of stabilization and exploitation of the growth idea begins. During this period, growth consumes fewer resources and generates its biggest profits. Following this stage, there may be a time of diminishing demand, perhaps driven by the emergence of a competing growth initiative, and the growth curve slopes downward.

If examined closely, the line representing a growth trajectory is rough and jagged, influenced as much by seasonality, cyclicality, and random happenings as by management will. Business can be quirky; many opportunities (and threats) are surprises, not bullet points in the strategic plan. Profit windfalls are usually temporary, localized events, not ongoing trends. Internal complexity is built in fits and starts; organizational evolution is inherently discontinuous, involving lumps and bumps, not frictionless transformation.

Organizations are not like clothing that can be easily discarded and replaced when the old size no longer fits. No company grows with quarter-to-quarter consistency, though stretch goals and earnings smoothing can provide a short-term illusion that this is happening. The inherent uncertainties in every business cannot be willed away. Attempting to mask them, says Harvard's Michael Jensen, is like pushing on a balloon: "Smoothing out today's bumps means they will only pop up somewhere else tomorrow, often with catastrophic results."[7] The growth cycle encompasses much more than momentum-driven hot streaks, though these are what grandiose thinking and Wall Street expectations may fixate on. These fixations reflect a Peter Pan mentality more than real progress. They substitute getting big for growing up.[8]

Companies That Won't Grow Up

Peter Pan companies are those that let others set their course. They become locked into delivering quarterly earnings increases, an indicator that expansion has taken precedence over real growth. Their financial forecasts are not driven by where they are on their growth trajectory, but on what numbers they believe Wall Street analysts want to hear. This, in effect, turns strategic control of the business over to the outside analysts, as these companies' executives use Wall Street's often unrealistic expectations as the basis for the goals they set for their companies.

What do you tell Wall Street while you're awaiting the economic benefits of real growth? If you ask Jensen, whose thinking has gone through considerable growth itself since his years as the shareholder-value theory's greatest booster, he will say, "Just say no"[9] when Wall Street asks. Refuse to play the earnings projection game, Jensen now counsels, as companies such as Coca-Cola, Gillette, Mattel, PepsiCo, USA Interactive, and the Washington Post have found the courage to do. Donald Graham, Washington Post's CEO, goes so far as to say, "If you care about that sort of thing, you shouldn't own our stock. . . . Analysts won't live the consequences of good or bad decisions; shareholders will."[10] Graham wants his fellow shareholders to think like long-term owners, not short-term stock traders. This is the kind of environment that provides a fertile ground for real growth; these are the kind of shareholders that growing companies need.

Jensen has talked about the dangers inherent in the single-minded pursuit of the wrong measure of performance, stock price, and the narcotic-like temptations to escape from the reality of how a business actually operates that it offers. Is growth, as described here, also like a drug? Growth also offers escape, but it is an escape *forward* from current reality. It is movement that is grounded in reality. The end result of growth is that reality has been changed, not denied. The business, and the grower propelling it, becomes a conduit for the expression of new possibilities: Schultz's idea of Starbucks being a third place, between home and office, for its customers to congregate; Bru's effort to marry nutrition and snack foods; and Greenwood's plan to get trucks off overcrowded highways by transporting them, and the containers they haul, on top of flatcars.

WHERE OPPORTUNITIES FOR REAL GROWTH COME FROM

Historians like to talk about moments when the world changed. They add drama to their tales by focusing on critical events, great decisions, and major turning points. This can lead us to assume that in between these decisive moments, most things were congealed, constant, or fixed. But reality, especially marketplace reality, is in constant flux. Customers and competitors come and go. Their needs and behaviors change. Fashion preferences are displaced. New technologies slip into the mainstream, threatening to creatively destroy businesses built on older ones. Government policies change. Regulators awaken. All this cacophony creates a perceptual problem: How can we get on with things if much of what is going on around us refuses to settle down? The easiest way to deal with constant change is to ignore it, at least for a little while. When this becomes difficult, our common fallback is to categorize it.

Change Is Not Noticed in Real Time

The ideas and concepts we have about reality are often what stand between us and our direct experience of what is really going on. The psychologist Sidney Jourard sees concepts as "commitments to stop noticing . . . the disclosures of change incessantly being transmitted."[11] When we notice something new, we "rubricize" it, observing it only enough so that we can classify it. After we have put it into a category, we stop receiving new information about it (not that it has necessarily stopped sending data). We "freeze" situations, making a pledge to ourselves not to notice developments until they have reached a critical point beyond which they can no longer be ignored. Then we belatedly acknowledge change. Everyone does this to some extent; it is the price we pay for the ability to concentrate and focus. Multitasking is something that is successful only in computer processors, not in human minds. Change may be a constant, but it is experienced only momentarily. It is often said that the world changed after September 11, 2001, but what actually changed was many people's awareness of threats and issues that had been methodically building for almost a decade before that tragic day.

Awareness that things are different, and the sense of surprise that sometimes accompanies it, is not growth itself, but it is a necessary part of the process of growth. It always comes a little after the fact; as Jourard says, it is often a belated acknowledgment of "a change that has been inexorable and continuous."[12] What we make of the new information will determine whether it drives growth or not. Often the kind of information with the greatest potential to stimulate a new perspective is that which reports the failure of an old perspective. But it is not always easy for new awareness to get around old concepts.

Challenging the Ideas That Dominate

There are a lot of ways to look at a company. It is a collection of physical and financial assets. It is a portfolio of brands, products, patents, and other forms of intellectual property. It is an agglomeration of people organized in a certain way to tap into the knowledge and capabilities they represent. A company can also be thought of as a system of *dominating ideas*[13]–assumptions about how the business is defined, what it values, and how it deploys its resources. A firm can operate from within a set of such ideas, or it can, as in the examples at the beginning of this chapter, change the governing ideas.

Traditional business planning operates under the umbrella of the current dominating ideas. Goals are set, usually with reference to past performance, and alternative ways to achieve them are explored. A strategy is eventually settled on, and an effort is made to align budgets and what employees are doing with the strategy. Then, after a period of time passes, performance is measured against the plan. When results meet or exceed expectations, bonuses are passed out, and everyone is happy–at least, until the targets for the next period are ratcheted up.

Subpar performance presents a more challenging set of issues to resolve. Were the targets missed because an insufficient effort was made? If so, this is a problem of execution, and the common remedy is to try harder, work smarter, or assign blame and make whatever changes are appropriate. Anomalies are dealt with in this way when they are interpreted in terms of the existing dominating ideas. In most situations, they usually are. Dominating ideas are like the air we breathe–they are ubiquitous and taken for granted. They are also dominating, held and reinforced by the organization's most powerful people and part and parcel of its existing culture, image, and heritage.

It is usually much easier to take actions that support and defend the existing structure than to begin a process of questioning it. But that is what growth requires, *the ability to notice that assumptions that once made sense are no longer true, and then to offer an alternative perspective that is in better accord with today's reality.* Dominating ideas, like all concepts, have shorter half-lives with regard to their validity than to their robustness. An assumption failure is most easily noticed when a part of the business is failing—Ford Motor's loss of $5.5 billion was a wake-up call that was too loud to ignore. It cleared the way for a new chief executive, Bill Ford, and a new set of dominating ideas.

Thwarted plans do have the power to shatter outdated and misguided concepts, but failure is not the only way for assumptions to change and new opportunities to become evident. Al Bru's efforts to add nutrition to Frito-Lay's ingredient mix were not motivated by declining sales of snack foods. He did it because he sensed the way the wind was starting to blow in his marketplace. Likewise, Amazon.com was on a roll when Jeff Bezos decided to allow third parties to sell products on its web site, sometimes offering lower prices than Amazon's. This was a very controversial decision within the company, but one that gave customers more choice and more reason to keep coming back to Amazon.

Success, and the desire to keep it, can motivate movement beyond the limits that define it, as long as there is a willingness to stay attuned to the disclosures that the marketplace is constantly making. Bru was willing to go beyond the assumption that snack food has to equate with junk food; Bezos put aside the conventional business wisdom that says that anything that helps your competitors must hurt you. Chapter 5 explores in more detail how you can see opportunities the way Bru and Bezos did.

Being open to information that can overthrow deeply held convictions means being open to surprise. This is something that people who are caught up in the cognitive error of omniscience are not very good at. A "know-it-all" mentality is one that cannot afford to be surprised. A person with such a mentality has already decided that the marketplace offers nothing more than a playback of what has been expected or predicted. Success at growth is proportional to the extent to which concepts, interpretations, and assumptions can be held as tentative and provisional, subject to elaboration, modification, or even disconfirmation as new facts emerge. Growth feeds on dissonance between belief and expectations, on the one hand, and perceptions of how things really are, on the other. Growers work hard to see the market as it is, not as they imagine it to be.

IS GROWTH JUST ANOTHER WORD FOR CHANGE AND INNOVATION?

Growth sounds a lot like change because it *is* change, but it is change with a direction. Growth always implies positive movement. Growth is a vector—something with both a magnitude and a direction. Change has magnitude, but no implicit direction. You've changed as long as you are different from what you were before. Change can be from good to great or from bad to good. But it can also be from good to bad or from bad to worse. Growth is always in the direction of better. Which way is better? Growth results in a building up, not a spending down, of an organization's stock of capabilities and capital. These are new resources that are available to be drawn on in the future. Growth is movement in a direction that offers an enhanced ability to set a future course, a direction of greater independence and self-determination. Is change involved when growth happens? Always. Does change always produce growth? Not necessarily.

Change is something that happens to you, or that you make happen to others. You may dish it out or you may be on the receiving end of it, but you are always apart from it. Change makers focus on imposing their will on events. They resonate with the words President Bush spoke on September 20, 2001: "This country will define our times—not be defined by them." Inducers of change are shapers. They work hard to align reality, and those around them, with themselves.

Growers, however, align themselves, and those around them, with reality. Growers spot what's about to emerge, pick one of the many outcomes they see as possible, and put all their energy behind it. This doesn't mean that growers are passive, go-with-the-flow types. They instinctively believe that there is always more than one nascent reality, more than a single way in which things might work out. They grab on to the possibility they value most, and then bring it into being. For change agents, the focus is often on what they *don't* want: high costs, market-share loss, terrorism. These are seen as problems to react against. Growers, instead, obsess about the positive results they *do* want to see: game-changing products, high customer acceptance, a more peaceful world. Is this distinction a matter of semantics? Yes, but the semantics are a telling indicator of two very different thought processes at work, each leading to very different results.

Innovation

What about innovation? Apple Computer's Steve Jobs is a master inno-
vator. Is he also a grower? Innovation looks a lot like growth's front
end—discovery, invention, and introduction. It is growth's dramatic first
act. Innovation can provide the feedstock for growth. Apple, though, is
a business that has had a chronic inability to move beyond the first act,
to go from innovation to growth. Jobs's history is more one of serial
innovation than one of seasoned growth. Creativity, a word synonymous
with Apple, can be an important tool for growth. Creativity aims to
produce something original, something boldly new. Novelty can sometimes help, but it does not ensure a result that surpasses what was there
before.

People do change (and grow). Perhaps Jobs's foray into the music
business with the iTunes Internet music store and the iPod portable listening and storage device will be a vehicle for Apple's growth, reshaping
the industry as well as being expressions of striking, customer-friendly
design. If so, this will be a sign that Jobs has mastered growth's second
act—building a broad base of support, mastering momentum, and sharing
the wealth—with the same brilliance demonstrated by his creative innovations.

When Frito-Lay changed the shape of many of its snack foods by
adding a little curl to make them better scoopers of salsa and dip, it
innovated. Consumers were happy; more of what they were eating ended
up in their mouths, not on the floor. Sales of chips increased, too. Frito-
Lay grew, however, when it brought in an army of nutritionists to advise
it on how to rethink its product line and corporate mission. Soon after
holding a "nutrition summit" for its executives (probably a first in a
"junk food" company), Frito-Lay's leader, Al Bru, announced that trans
fats were persona non grata in all the salty snacks the company sold. Will
Fritos and Doritos eventually morph into health foods? Who knows? It
could happen. At least, that is the growth path that Bru has put his
company on.

BALANCE SUSTAINS GROWTH

It may take a strong push to start growth, but it is the ability to keep a
situation in balance that sustains it. If growth is going to have a lasting

positive impact, it needs to displace the stability that preceded it with a new and better equilibrium. Success at growth requires the ability to thrust forward and to build the next plateau, a blend of aggression and restraint. This pairing of opposite qualities is not common, but neither is real growth.

I was once trained in interviewing. My teacher, a seasoned consultant with the demeanor of a private investigator, told me that I needed to be a tough and tenacious questioner, totally focused on the facts I needed to find, and constantly on guard against attempts the subject might make to deflect my probes. Then I needed to know how to shut up and listen. I was warned that too many interviewers got so caught up in the chase for information that they were never ready to receive it when it was laid at their feet. Instead, they were too busy thinking about the next question, and they missed the significance of what they were being told.

The teacher went on to tell me that when one line of questioning was getting nowhere, I shouldn't dig in, raise my voice, and repeat the questions. Rather than mentally blaming the person I was interviewing for being unresponsive and resistant, I was to take the lack of progress as a signal to shift my approach and find another way to get the same result. While these suggestions might sound straightforward, this kind of mental agility does not come easily, the instructor warned.

Hardball

Switching gears is not easy in business, either—especially when it feels like caving in or admitting to having made a mistake. The fear of looking soft pervades business, perhaps a relic from when it was a male-only activity. The latest manifestation of this concern is "hardball," an approach to competition advocated by two Boston Consulting Group advisers, George Salk and Rob Lachenauer.[14] They say that the fundamental purpose of companies is to compete as hard as they can against one another, period. Winners in business, according to their worldview, play rough and never apologize for it. They enjoy watching their competitors squirm (though not publicly, lest the hardballer be seen as a bully). In this eat-or-be-eaten world, victory goes to those who want it the most. Those who do, according to hardball theory, follow strategies aimed at putting their competitors in situations where they inflict damage on themselves. Hardball players will use deception to drive up competitors' costs, unleash massive and overwhelming force, and plagiarize with pride. The consultants also note that since most legal standards are less than crystal clear, hardball players are aggressive pushers of the boundaries of existing regulations.

Hardball sounds tough, but it is a very superficial kind of tough. It is myopic, focusing most of a business's attention on its rivals, not its customers. It is unclear what customers get from all this. Some short-term savings might accrue while the hardball players fight one another to the death in a price war. But even that is likely to culminate in the winner's reaping monopolist pricing power in the market—not necessarily a favorable situation for its customers.

Accelerators and Restrainers

Two consultants in Boston put the idea of business-as-hardball together. In nearby Cambridge, on the more thoughtful side of the Charles River, a contrasting perspective on what happens to hard-charging forward movement was developed at Massachusetts Institute of Technology. The MIT Systems Dynamics Group has studied the process of growth for almost 50 years. As mentioned in Chapter 2, using the principles of systems thinking[15] (which they invented) and computer simulation modeling, they looked hard at the inner workings of growth. The MIT researchers were especially interested in companies that had been successful and rapid growers that suddenly stalled and failed. What they found seemed counterintuitive at first: The harder a business strives to grow, the more likely it is to undermine its chances of achieving growth. Hardball invariably melts into softball.

Growth is a form of movement, and like all motion, it follows some basic laws, including a variation on Isaac Newton's principle that every action produces an equal and opposite reaction. Unlike those of the physics law, however, the consequences of growth moves are not always proportionate and, initially at least, not in the opposite direction. Nor do they all happen at once. At growth's outset, momentum rules, and each success breeds more success. The MIT systems experts call this accelerating effect *positive feedback*: The introduction of a new product leads to new revenues, which provide funds for more marketing, which leads to more sales, and so on. This is the enjoyable side of the growth curve, the phase when it is pointed exponentially upward.

Unfortunately, acceleration never happens in a vacuum. It always happens *somewhere*, and for that somewhere itself to exist, it must have some degree of stability. Stability does not just happen; it takes a lot of hard work to keep something in place. The forces that do so (call them stabilizers) are usually invisible until something (like a growth initiative) disturbs them. We do not notice what keeps things at rest; we notice change. Just as it takes a while for forward movement to ramp up, there is a delay between when an accelerating force is far enough along to trigger a stabilizer and when the stabilizer starts having a visible impact. This delay adds to our confusion about what is going on. Humans seem hard-wired to deal with immediate feedback, but they have a hard time making the connections between cause and effect when there is a time lag between the two.

These restraining forces, also known as negative feedback, abound in every growth situation. For example, exponentially rising sales can (eventually) trigger:

- Shortages of vital raw materials or talent
- Increases in customer delivery times, resulting in diminished customer satisfaction
- Decreases in product quality as a result of pressure to meet surging demand
- New competitors noticing how attractive this business is and deciding to enter it
- Market saturation

These, and similar factors combine to slow down, and possibly at some point dominate, the growth process. They change the shape of the growth curve from an ever-increasing upward slope to a line that flattens and potentially curves downward. As product quality and buyer satisfaction drop, so do the number of customers; market saturation means fewer new purchasers; and more competition leads to less market share.

As soon as the effect of a restrainer is detected, two options for further action are available. Efforts to overcome the resistance can be redoubled (the hardball approach)—press forward with massive and overwhelming force. This is the tack that is most commonly taken, and the MIT researchers have found that it is the one that is most likely to fail. Managers like to crush targets; hitting the wall is akin to an admission of failure. These tendencies are counterproductive when confronting the stabilizers built into the business environment. All they do is feed the restrainers, making forward movement even more difficult.

Smartball

What is the smarter alternative? Let up a bit on the accelerator and pay attention to the source of the push-back. Find the factors that are limiting progress (capacity constraints, service or product quality slippages, and so on) and address them directly. Remove them, fix them, work around them—just don't ignore them. The even smarter alternative is to anticipate them before the initial growth thrust is made. It takes wisdom and maturity to realize that a wheel will squeak before the sound is audible. Ask what needs to be done now, so that as growth continues, the business's ability to handle its inevitable restrainers also grows. Hardball advocates might dismiss this as softball, but it is really smartball.

Accelerators and stabilizers are the two sides of the growth coin. You cannot have one without the other. Growth is not so much a matter of maximizing the gains possible only through forward thrusts; rather, it involves optimizing the big picture, including acceleration's side effects. What combination of forward thrusts and stabilizers will provide the most gain? When do additional sales become profitless ones? At what point will greater profits be obtained only by steep increases in risks to the business's future? Thinking about this best balance is the price of self-sustaining, rather than self-limiting, growth.

Coexisting Opposites

Balance is not achieved by averaging out opposites. Growers need the kind of perspective that allows them to appreciate the coexistence of opposing qualities in a situation, the ability to balance your interests with those of the people and entities around you. This is a perspective that Winston Churchill captured well when, as head of Britain's Conservative Party, he was asked for his views on business regulation. "We are for private enterprise, with all its ingenuity, thrift and contrivance," Churchill replied, then quickly added in the same breath: "and we believe it can flourish best within a strict and well-understood system of prevention and correction of abuses."[16] This is one reason why the vacuum of deregulation has led to so many growth failures. Lopsided victories in the marketplace can also have a similar result. When external checks and balances atrophy, internal restraint is necessary if gains are to last.

This idea of balance continually reemerges when growth's underlying processes are examined. Creativity is one of these. Mihaly Csikszentmihalyi, a Claremont Graduate University professor, has studied the characteristics of especially creative people. He has found that rather than possessing a single set of common traits, they have the common ability to shift back and forth on several dimensions, as their situation requires. They practice playful, out-of-the-box, divergent thinking when they need to come up with new ideas; they also use disciplined convergent thinking when it is time to put ideas back into the box and sell them. They balance a strong sense of direction, high energy, and vitality with an ability to calm down and be open to new stimulation. Creativity, Csikszentmihalyi has found, requires a strong reality orientation as well as an ability to engage in imaginative fantasy.

Optimizing growth requires striking a number of balances. Here are a few other key ones worth keeping in mind:

Short and long term. Growth is not only about a head-in-the-clouds concern for the future. Nor is it destroyed when concerns for immediate performance prevail. McKinsey & Company consultants studied the economic performance of half the S&P 500 companies over a 20-year period.[17] They examined both long- and short-term results, and they found that the top performers were the ones that did the best job of walking the tightrope between near-term operational results and investing in innovations that paid off in long-term growth. Companies that focused only on one time frame did less well. Long-term success is more than just the sum of a string of short-term tactical victories.

Affection and aggression. Hardball players do not know how to chill; growers do. Southwest Airlines is famous for touchy-feely attention to its employees, who, in turn, are expected to take loving care of its customers, but it also knows when to crush competitors by exploiting any apparent weaknesses. "We came, we saw, we kicked tail" was the headline of a Southwest newspaper advertisement as it moved into financially weakened US Airways' hubs in Philadelphia and Pittsburgh. Southwest shifts gears as the situation demands.

Capabilities and opportunities. Growth happens when challenges are well matched with capabilities. Companies with many perceived opportunities, but insufficiently developed skills to capitalize on them, tend to be anxiety-filled and burnout-prone. Likewise, businesses with a large stock of abilities, but a weak sense of growth possibilities, are sleepwalkers, with corporate cultures characterized by boredom and monotony.

Chaos and constraint. Growth is movement beyond the limits that define. Is it possible to move too far? Yes, says London Business School's Julian Birkinshaw.[18] He cites Enron as a company that had no real strategic focus, employees with too much freedom, organizational units with excessive autonomy and vague boundaries, and a free-market mentality unleavened by the system of checks and balances called for by Churchill. Just as bureaucracy can imprison growth, entrepreneurialism is a good idea that can be taken too far and put the business in danger. Free rein must always be granted within a set of defined constraints.

CONSTRAINTS GUIDE GROWTH

Limits actually play a big part in guiding growth. When they are self-imposed by a business's outdated dominating ideas, moving beyond them is a mark of progress. When constraints come from outside the business, they are not hurdles to overcome so much as guideposts to channel action. At times, they may serve to limit unwise actions, just as the discipline of paying dividends makes it more difficult to launch uneconomic business expansions. Few growers go out to seek constraints, but all successful ones learn how to live with them, and especially effective growers learn to extract some benefit from them.

When Sam Walton decided to expand his one-store business, his wife refused to live in any town that was not a small town. Walton, wanting both his company and his marriage to thrive, focused his expansion efforts in rural America, conveniently under the radar of the large, entrenched retailers like Kmart and Sears. This gave him time and a safe environment in which he could craft his personal approach to discount merchandising.

IKEA, another mass-market retailer, is well known for the cavernous, warehouselike structures adjacent to its showrooms, where customers use handcarts to pick out the items of furniture they want to purchase. These became part of IKEA's business model by chance when chronic shortages of stockroom employees led to long waits.[19] Frustrated customers in one store took matters into their own hands and rushed into the warehouse to serve themselves. The manager had the option of responding to this by putting locks on the warehouse doors, but he took a growth-driving move instead and redesigned the stock areas to make them customer-friendly. The cost of the improvements was soon returned through savings in labor costs and the increased revenue generated by IKEA's new reputation as a place that time-pressed customers could get out of quickly. Many of IKEA's other innovations, such as store-based child care and knockdown furniture in flat parcels, also arose as experimental reactions to pressing problems.

Likewise, Southwest Airlines' rapid turnaround of incoming aircraft was not part of its original master plan. It was improvised in Southwest's early, financially constrained days when one of its original aircraft had to be returned to its owners, and the airline's employees had to figure out a way to make the remaining three planes do the work of four.

Constraints Drive Creativity

Constraints, not freedom, drive creativity. They push us to think differently about our situation. We search for substitutes for resources that are in short supply. We invent alternatives that did not exist before the constraint emerged. Toyota, now the leader in making hybrid gas-electric vehicles, did not get to that point through a long-standing strategic intention to dominate the hybrid market. It gave attention to building these vehicles only because its conventional cars were not competing as well in Europe against fuel-efficient German diesels. Toyota was far behind the Germans in diesel technology. Rather than struggling to catch up, it moved in a new direction and developed the hot-selling Prius.

A different kind of constraint resulted in Central Park's looking the way it does today. In 1857, New York City officials held the first public landscape design competition.[20] Only one of the competing firms, Frederick Law Olmsted's, submitted a plan that met all the city's requirements. The troublesome constraint, that crosstown traffic be permitted to go through the park without destroying the park's pastoral feel, was deemed impossible to surmount by the other bidders. They resisted and resented it. Some refused to offer any roads through the park; others did so at the expense of vehicular traffic dominating the park's look and feel. Only Olmsted chose to think about Central Park as a three-dimensional space, which offered the possibility of sinking the four cross-cutting roads eight feet below the level on which pedestrians walked. The other designers, caught up in the mindset of the two-dimensional planning diagrams required for the competition, never considered what seems, today, like such a simple solution.

New England Lobstermen

Most constraints arise outside the business and are unwanted. But sometimes the most powerful driving forces for growth emerge when constraints are voluntarily imposed. Consider the contrasting situations of the lobster fishermen in New England and Australia.[21]

New England lobstermen work harder and harder each season, often getting less and less for their efforts. When many started catching lobsters several decades ago, they used small boats and sailed only a few miles into the ocean to submerge the traps they used to catch lobsters. Now they go 60 to 70 miles offshore and need large boats to hold the increased number of traps they need in order to bring home the same catch that they used to find much closer to home. As soon as one fisherman began putting out more lobster traps, the others from the same port would follow suit, creating a mini-arms race with no real gains for the fishermen. More lobsters would be caught with more traps, but the average size of each was getting smaller and smaller. Lobsters used to live for over 50 years. Catching one weighing 30 pounds was once not uncommon. Now overfishing has resulted in few lobsters over six years and most caught are just above the legal size limit.

Some New England fishing communities have tried to put limits on the amount of fishing taking place, resorting to social pressure and occasional (hardball-style) violence to implement them. These tend to be enforceable only close to the communities' shoreline, and most of the lobsters have migrated farther out into the open ocean, areas controlled by the state and federal governments. Government agencies, facing electoral pressure from the fishermen, have been reluctant to impose strict limits on the size of the catch. Instead, their policies—giving struggling fishermen subsidies, tax breaks, and financing for bigger boats—have served to accelerate the overfishing problem. One long-time lobsterman lamented that his only incentive is to go out and kill as many lobsters as he can. He has no motivation to conserve the fishery—any lobsters he leaves behind to grow bigger for next year's catch are likely to be taken immediately by his fellow lobstermen.

Australian Lobstermen

In Australia, things are different. These one-time New England–style hunter-gatherer fishermen have found good reasons to become homesteaders. Unlike the hardscrabble life of their Northern Hemisphere counterparts, many Australia lobster catchers live in large mansions and work from boats with outfittings that make them easy to confuse with luxury yachts. The Australians have plenty of time for recreation and hobbies also; their regulations prohibit them from working for more than 187 days out of their 211-day fishing season. New England lobstermen are often on the water 240 days each year.

Forty years ago, the Australians shared the plight of today's New Englanders. Their lives changed when government limits were set on the total number of traps that could be used by each port's fishing fleet. Each working lobsterman was assigned a license for his share of the traps, and from then on, anyone who wanted to fish for lobsters in the waters around that port had to acquire a license from someone who already held one. This is the same approach that governs seats on the New York Stock Exchange and the fixed number of taxi medallions (licenses) available in that city. Lobster-trap licenses that traded for $2,000 each 25 years ago now frequently sell for $35,000, making many of their holders millionaires. Why the sharp price appreciation? When given control over an asset that might appreciate in value, the lobstermen learned how to be conservationists.

The Australians started to take a long view when they saw the prices for their traps start to rise. Now they had two ways to make money: Sell their catch and take action to increase the value of their licenses. Realizing that the resale value of the licenses would determine how soon and how comfortably they could retire, they took steps above and beyond the government regulations to ensure that lobsters would be plentiful in the future. The Australian lobstermen hire scientists to monitor the size of the fishery; they put self-imposed strict limits on the size of lobsters that could be caught. In some ports the lobstermen limited themselves to 60 traps each—the New Englanders needed up to 800 to yield a similar harvest. Obviously, the Australians had a much easier workday and see a lot more of their families. Rick McGarvey,[22] a marine biologist, observed that the nature of fishing is such that more money can be made by doing less work. By fishing less intensively, more lobsters remain in the ocean to produce eggs for future catches, and those that remain get bigger, so that when they are eventually caught, they yield a better price.

What do the down-under lobstermen do with all their spare time? Some invest in thoroughbred racehorses or build bigger mansions. Others, though, have taken the growth lessons learned from lobsters and applied them to other types of fishing. In the 1980s, the tuna fisheries of the Australian coast were nearly depleted. The government took action again, assigning each fisherman a transferable share of each year's catch. This constrained their ability to kill as many tuna as they could catch, so they looked harder for ways they could make the most money from each tuna. Some came up with the idea of putting the tuna into large floating pens instead of killing them as soon as they were caught. The pens were then towed to their home harbor, where they became sashimi farms. The fish were fed special diets of herring and anchovies, cattle feedlot style, to add to their oil content and improve their color. Eventually, depending on the fish's weight and the number of upward price ticks in the Tokyo tuna market, they would be taken out of the pens and flown to sushi-crazy Japan, where they would command top dollar because of their appearance and farm-acquired high fat content.

Changing Outdated Ideas

The Australians showed a way to move beyond the self-imposed limits that defined and constrained their fishing industry. A few New Englanders, frustrated with working in a system that is bent on driving itself into decline, are studying the Australian model. Its benefits seem clear, but the path to turning what has traditionally been considered a natural freedom into a property right is very hazy. Unfortunately, it seems easier to kill off the New England lobster fishery than to change the outdated dominating ideas that are destroying it.

What would it take for this situation to move in a better direction? The New Englanders would have to do more than just ameliorate their immediate pain. That is what they have already done by using their political power to get government subsidizes to allow them to continue their old practices.

A critical mass of the fishers would have to be sufficiently stimulated by the Australian model to become conscious of their own potential. They would have to sell to their peers a vision of something that does not yet exist, an idea that is completely unproven in their part of the world. They would have to find surplus energy and resources to invest in transforming the way their fishery is managed. They would have to be willing to withhold part of their potential catch from immediate consumption in return for an expectation of much greater benefits in the future. They would have to prize self-determination—the ability to create their own future—sufficiently to let go of the mindset about fishing they have cultivated over many years. In short, they would have to grow.

LETTING GO

Growth and loss are intertwined. Letting go is easier to do if something is being offered in return for giving up old ways and ideas. The Australian lobstermen lost their freedom to fish as they wished, but they gained, after a time lag, a valuable appreciating property right. They "let come"— let something new come to them that then put them in a position to take best advantage of the changing dynamics of their fisheries. In like manner, the expansion of Wal-Mart has posed severe challenges to many retailers it competes with. Some, though, have thrived with Wal-Mart as a competitor. Costco, Target, Wegmans, Hy-Vee, Soriana in Mexico, and Aldi in Germany have all grown in Wal-Mart's wake. They have all let go of an understandably natural impulse to try to outplay Wal-Mart at its own game. They have given up whatever aspirations they had of being all things to every customer. Instead, they have defined, refined, and differentiated themselves from the world's largest retailer. They have let its entry into their markets serve as a grinding wheel to sharpen their identity and better align it with the needs of their particular segment of customers.

PepsiCo does not have an iconic product like Coca-Cola. This lack of sentimentality about its core brands has made it easier for PepsiCo to grow its business in directions led by changing consumer tastes. Coca-Cola, on the other hand, runs the risk of its values hardening into dogmas and its icon becoming a millstone, keeping it from pursuing the expanding markets for New Age teas, gourmet coffees, performance drinks, and health beverages. Sydney Finkelstein, a Dartmouth College management professor, warns his students of the danger of learning a lesson too well.[23] He says that many business leaders have a "defining moment," a key decision or choice they once made that has made them famous and thereafter has become what they are most known for. Unfortunately, many find themselves so defined by that moment that they keep trying to repeat it throughout their careers, regardless of how well it fits their current circumstances. It is not that they have not learned; the problem is that they have learned one thing too well. Letting go of proven past practices is a struggle, but it is a prerequisite for moving forward. As University of Michigan's C. K. Prahalad likes to say, the "forgetting curve" may be much more important than the "learning curve."

The opposite of letting go is "momentum thinking"—assuming that what prevailed in the past will continue to succeed. Sometimes it does. If the current formula is working well, and the world in which the business operates shows no sign of changing anytime soon, it is time to optimize the formula, not to set out in quest of a new direction in which to grow. But when dominating ideas are out of sync with reality, all the operational improvement in the world will not help things. And an escalating commitment to the status quo, in those circumstances, only puts the future at risk.

ARE YOU A FIXER OR A GROWER?

> Sometimes I get so busy fighting alligators,
> I forget I came here to drain the swamp.
>
> —*Common lament of many frustrated growers*

THE BURLINGTON NORTHERN STORY

I was excited. I was a rookie consultant, not long out of grad school, and I was getting my first chance to meet a CEO. I was part of a team of consultants that the Burlington Northern Railroad had hired to help it figure out how to get more productivity from its large fleet of locomotives. This was a big issue for Burlington Northern. Money was scarce. Each of these huge diesels cost hundreds of thousands of dollars, and minimizing the number of new ones that had to be purchased each year was vital.

The President

Early in the assignment, we were shepherded into the office of Thomas Lamphier, the railroad president. He wanted to give us his view of the big picture. At that time, the railroad industry was verging on the kind of massive upheaval that has since jolted the airline, electric power, and telecommunications industries. Congressionally mandated deregulation was about to change all the rules about how successful railroads were run. Competition would open up new options for railroad customers, and fixed prices for shipping freight would be eliminated. The president's response was to hunker down and prepare for a stormy time ahead. His main concern was running the railroad as efficiently as possible. The railroad's ability to survive in the future depended, he believed, on its ability to cut costs now.

Like many people in his industry, he was well immersed in railroad lore. Photos of large steam engines, long gone, lined his office walls. Models of sleek, efficient diesel locomotives painted in the company's new bright-green-and-white logo dominated the tops of his bookshelves. He was clearly a *railroader*. It seemed a part of his genetic makeup. When he found that I had planned to interview Burlington Northern employees along the rail route from Chicago to Seattle, he even offered me the use of his private railroad car and began to plot a schedule of what trains to attach it to and what routes to take.

As he unrolled a map of the western United States, I could not help noticing how closely the Burlington Northern tracks were paralleled by the interstate highways. It was an observation that I would have been better off keeping to myself. When I made mention of it, the muscles of his face tightened, his hands trembled, and the pitch of his voice rose several octaves. He lost all interest in planning what I had started a few minutes earlier to fantasize as a wonderful paid tour through the Rockies. Instead, all he wanted to discuss in the time that remained in our meeting was how the interstate highways were jammed full of merchandise-carrying trucks, and how angry that made him.

The Enemy

Like most railroaders of his time, Lamphier hated trucks and truckers—a natural reaction, I guessed, given the increasing competitive threat that they posed. He hated the fact that they rode on taxpayer-subsidized highways. He hated the fact that, unlike his capital-intensive railroad, trucking was a relatively easy business to enter. "Fly-by-nighters" was, I believe, the expression he used. And he especially hated the fact that they were stealing his customers.

What he, and many of the company's other executives, chose to ignore was that truckers were also customers of the railroad. At least, some were—those that took advantage of the service that Burlington Northern and other railroads offered in which their trailers or the containers they carried were hauled over long distances on top of specially designed flatcars, piggyback style. Top management's ambivalence about the trucking industry was reflected in the railroad's lack of aggressiveness in marketing this service. In 1981 Burlington Northern actually ranked at the bottom of the U.S. railroad industry in the performance of its "intermodal" business—which was not a big surprise, considering the depth of the president's negative feelings toward truckers, a hostility that had permeated throughout the ranks of this tightly managed organization.

It was heresy, in this company at least, to suggest that railroaders and truckers might cooperate to serve their common customers, so we kept these thoughts to ourselves. Our work had to do with trains, not trucks, so we thanked him for his time and went on to gather information about locomotive utilization and how the fleet was managed. The study went on for several months, and we were pleased to discover ways in which Burlington Northern could save between $100 and $200 million if it made some significant changes in its traditional operating practices.

While we conducted our productivity study, an internal team of mid-rank Burlington Northern managers was meeting regularly in a conference room far from the president's office. What this group was planning was to have a much more dramatic impact on the railroad than anything we outsiders would suggest.

The Greenwood Group

They were led by Bill Greenwood, a bright, aggressive, team-oriented middle manager who was based in Burlington Northern's backwater marketing department. As part of the "get ready for deregulation" planning, task forces were set up to examine the host of issues about to be facing the railroad. Most of these were perfunctory, going-through-the-motions efforts that produced pages of documents and little change. Greenwood's group was different. These people believed that they were going to make a big difference in their company's future.

Their charge was to map out the potential of the intermodal business. Considering top management's views of truckers, this was seen as a throwaway assignment, but Greenwood and his band of young Turks thought differently. In their meetings, they challenged every assumption the railroad's executives had made about truckers being, at best, a necessary evil. Looking outside the restricted traditional boundaries of the industry, it was clear to them that deregulation's new pricing freedom would encourage many Burlington Northern customers to move their goods out of railroad boxcars and into containers and trailer trucks. Greenwood, a natural optimist, saw this as a great opportunity for the railroad to grow its heretofore neglected intermodal business.

Greenwood assembled a team of six like-minded people from across the railroad's functional fiefdoms and from outside the industry. By using a series of carefully crafted carrot-and-stick scenarios, the team slowly, but surely, focused middle and senior management's attention on the opportunities for forming alliances with the truckers. They backed up these projections with detailed blueprints for constructing 22 intermodal hubs at points where the Burlington Northern freight tracks intersected the most heavily traveled interstate highways.

Hostile Reactions

As it became obvious that Greenwood's group planned to actually change the railroad, not just write another report, what had been indifference turned into active hostility. He and his team wore out their welcome as they lobbied for budgets to be shifted from boxcars to buy more trailer-ready flatcars. They advocated building a cross-functional organization that would topple the traditional boundaries between the people who ran the trains and those who dealt with customers. They even recommended developing joint marketing programs with the trucking industry.

Historians have considered the railroads to be the world's first modern industry. Their defining moment came in the 1860s, when they created organizational structures that allowed managers to supervise functional activities scattered over an extended geographical area. Railroads invented the first general management hierarchies. They emphasized standardization, top-down centralized control, and military-like discipline. These were significant management achievements, for the mid-nineteenth century. But as Greenwood and company found, more than a hundred years later, these practices still defined the ways things happened. Exploiting the intermodal opportunity required rethinking every one of them.

Greenwood's boss, seeing what a Pandora's box had been opened, came to regret having given him the assignment in the first place. Greenwood himself became convinced that his boss and other railroad executives were out to get him. The team's work was criticized, budgets were withheld, and one officer even kept the group from working with a preferred contractor to develop a new generation of piggyback flatcars by rigging a bid so that the vendor unfairly lost the opportunity to help Greenwood.

The hostility only served to steel the team's resolve. It fought back, creatively finding ways to obtain, through "back channels," the software pricing models, personal computers, and even voice mail that they were not officially supposed to have. Finally, after months of 16-hour days, the team members finished what they felt was a bulletproof, economically sound proposal for building a network of terminals where trucks could deliver their trailers to the railroad. These intermodal hubs were all outside congested urban areas, making them easily accessible to truckers. And to ensure that these competitors-turned-customers received a warm welcome, Greenwood's group proposed hiring ex-truck drivers to operate each terminal.

Pilot Project

After intense lobbying by Greenwood, the railroad president eventually agreed to give the plan a hearing. Most of the senior executives fought it tooth and nail. None of them believed that the business being projected would ever materialize. Probably afraid of the backlash they would get from Greenwood and his teammates, they decided not to reject the idea completely. They demanded, instead, that it be done on a pilot basis, and they selected for the pilot project the two geographic locations for hubs from among those the team proposed that were the most likely to fail.

Greenwood's group was discouraged, but the coiled energy that had been built up over the past months reinforced the determination to make this work. And in spite of one of the Northwest's coldest winters and a recession that slowed the overall freight business, the two new intermodal terminals exceeded all the revenue projections made for them.

Building Momentum

The team then scoured the railroad, looking for opportunities to cut costs so that they could raise funds to build more hubs. They advertised the intermodal service heavily; to the consternation of railroad traditionalists, they even excluded trains from the ads so that they would have more appeal to the target audience of truckers. Completing the network took additional years of political infighting and a healthy dose of what one team member termed "Jesuit management": It's always easier to ask for forgiveness than for permission. If the new idea works, nobody will ask if it was approved in advance; if it fails, you will be fired because it failed, not because you forgot to ask for permission.

In this instance, nothing failed, no one was fired, and the intermodal concept proved fantastically successful. Burlington Northern became the nation's number one intermodal carrier, and a new billion-dollar business was built in less than 10 years. By that time my client, the railroad president, had been retired for several years.

Who had his job? Bill Greenwood, of course.[1]

TWO WAYS OF LOOKING AT THE SAME SITUATION

Greenwood and the railroad president each faced the same situation, and each had dramatically different assumptions about it. One saw the cup as being half full; the other saw it as half empty. For the president, deregulation meant great danger. Truckers were sworn enemies. This was a time to hunker down, cut costs, and avoid risks (especially moving into a dubious business, like intermodal, that involved sleeping with the enemy). Greenwood was less troubled. From where he sat, deregulation offered great opportunities. Truckers were potential customers, not people with horns. This was the time to seize opportunities and grow.

Why did these two people see things so differently? Why did one see possibilities, and the other only problems? Why did one embrace the future and the other try to seek protection from it? These are the questions that this chapter will try to answer. They are important to consider because many growth situations involve the interactions of people with ideas similar to those held by these two individuals. To address these issues, we need to generalize beyond this specific situation.

Twin Missions of Every Organization

Every organization—business, government, or nonprofit—has two essential missions. It must maintain and preserve what it already does. It must also lay the groundwork for moving beyond the boundaries of its current activities. The first mission keeps the organization efficient and successful in today's world. The second ensures that it will survive and thrive in tomorrow's. One perfects the existing business formula; the other leads the charge to change it. Both missions are vital. Few companies can survive for long if they pay attention to only one and ignore the other, although in the short run the two missions are rivals for attention and resources. Both require people who are equally hard working, highly skilled, motivated, and committed.

A business model is a company's formula for success. It is built around the dominating ideas about how to best go about transacting business. These are often based on hard-won lessons from the past about what has worked best. They include assumptions about what customers want, what is the optimum way to meet these needs, and who the competition is. In a reasonably stable world, prosperity comes from finding a workable business model and sticking with it. In a less-than-static environment, the one most of us inhabit, life is more complicated. The business model, and all the day-to-day focus it provides, is still needed. But we also need a means for growing beyond it, for finding and shifting to whatever new formula best fits the future.

What makes the pursuit of these dual missions so difficult is that the mindsets—the basic assumptions required by each mission—are so different. Mindsets are shortcuts that we use to explain the world to ourselves. They are how we think about what we are doing, our internal logic system. Mindsets are the model of the world that we carry around in our head.

"Fixers" and "Growers"

To make it easier to contrast the mindsets required by the twin missions, let's give each a name. A "fixer" mindset is concerned exclusively with what needs to be done to maintain and preserve the business as it is, within the logic of its current dominating ideas. The "grower" perspective, in contrast, is focused solely on what is necessary to move beyond what currently exists. When the grower's mindset is employed, the business advances; when the fixer's is used, it stays afloat. Both are worthy objectives.

These are labels for mindsets, not people. It is possible to shift from one way of thinking to the other. But at any given point in time, you are most likely to be in a job or assignment primarily calling for (and rewarding) only one of these. So let's label the people in these roles as "fixers" or "growers," keeping in mind that they have the abilities and potential to use each way of thinking. The distinction is still helpful, because the beliefs and logic of each mentality vary considerably and can be strongly at odds with each other, just as people can be when they hold conflicting assumptions.

Fixers. Fixers know how to maintain and improve existing operations. They are the keepers of today's business model. Fixers keep the trains running on time. They are quick to spot any divergence from the plan. Fixers mount search-and-destroy missions to eliminate excess costs. They speed the flow of product to customers by streamlining critical business processes. They launch companywide quality improvement campaigns. They live in the worlds of Six Sigma and TQM, downsizing and reengineering. The fixer's idea of the future sometimes looks like the past, only without all the imperfections. Fixers are determinists; they like to control events, and they put a great deal of energy into eliminating deviations from expected performance. They are problem solvers par excellence.

Fixers like to see themselves as realists, as practical people. They like to quantify things, and they feel that there is an objective, measurable reality that may be different from how some people perceive (or misperceive) the world. They deal with events as they come. The status quo is something that they usually accept and try hard to work with, although at times they may feel skeptical or cynical about it. Sometimes they feel resigned to "muddling through" difficult situations, knowing that at best their efforts are likely to produce only incremental change. Fixers like to keep up with the latest management trends. They benchmark a lot, and they are diligent seminar goers, constantly looking for new techniques that show promise for improving the workings of the business.

Fixers think linearly—their world is one of proximate causes and immediate effects. Fixers often feel uncomfortable in times of chaotic change. They are more content when everything going on around them seems well under control. Future happenings, from their perspective, are largely determined by what has already occurred. They predict the future by looking at the past, always trying hard to stay keenly aware of the trends that are driving today's marketplace.

Growers. The grower's model of the future is quite different. For growers, the future is not fixed or predetermined. Marketplaces, they believe, are constantly in motion, fundamentally open to new influences, and full of possibilities. Yesterday's story does not have to be tomorrow's, they will argue. They are good at listening for what seems to want to happen next in the market. Growers believe that few trends keep going forever, and that small discontinuities in established patterns may be all that is needed to change entire industries. They relish discovering, or creating, these discontinuities. And then they make plans to take advantage of what is about to happen. For them, opportunities to create something new are abundant, and they are always alert for serendipitous events[2] that can provide leverage for their plans.

Growers have a similar perspective on the organizations in which they work. They value their ability to discover openings and leverage points in these structures. They believe that many internal rigidities and conflicts are rooted in misperceptions, which are correctable. Change, growers maintain, can arise from inside the organization. It does not always need to be imposed externally.

Different Goals; Contrasting Worldviews

Fixers and growers inhabit the same world, but they have contrasting assumptions about how to operate in it. Fixers are great problem solvers;

they are good at making something go away. Success happens for them when the problem has disappeared. Growers focus more on what they want than on what they do not want. They are opportunity seizers more than problem crushers. Success for a grower is the presence, not the absence, of a result. Growers are able to visualize an end result of their efforts—something that is hard to do with a fixer's goal, such as "zero defects." Taking action to bring something new into being—the process of creation—is the standard operating mode of a grower.[3] Growers want to go beyond what is now, rather than restore or perfect it. They are more concerned with "next practices" than with best practices.

Many of the activities of fixers are directed internally and deal with things that have already happened. Growers direct their attention outside the business and keep it more forward focused. While fixers are ready to give feedback about past mistakes, a grower will emphasize executive coach Marshall Goldsmith's technique of "feedforward": laying out exactly what to do in the future to have a positive impact.

Growers have a conviction that they can shape their own destiny, while fixers are more inclined to see themselves as being on the receiving end of circumstances outside of their control. One is proactive, the other reactive. The fixers' environment provides the stimuli for their actions, as they react against or respond to their circumstances. Growers are more internally energized by what they want to bring into reality, what they want to add to their circumstances rather than take away.

If you have a conversation with a fixer, you will soon notice that much of the discussion revolves around tactics, techniques, and technology. Mention the future and you will soon hear the fixer's thoughts about forecasts and predictions. Discuss the same issues with a grower, and you will find that less is said about what is likely to be and the mechanics needed to bring it about, and more about alternative ways in which things might work out and what would be required for each to occur. Growers like being on the initiating, the shaping, end of change. They believe that the best way to predict the future is to invent it.

The idea of commitment has a different meaning for fixers and for growers. A fixer exhibits commitment by sticking with a task and pouring on whatever discipline is needed to succeed, come hell or high water. Growers are also determined and hard workers, but their commitment

FIXER MINDSET	GROWER MINDSET
Fear and anger	Hope and optimism
Determinist worldview: sees problems	Future is open: sees opportunities
Incremental, piecemeal change	Small discontinuities lead to big opportunities
React and respond	Create something new
Carrots and sticks	Want something because you want it
Hide and deny mistakes	Uncover mistakes and learn from them
Keep up with best practices	Leap ahead with next practices
Predict the future	Create the future

is more tied to the end result they foresee than to the particular path they are taking to get there. Place an obstacle in front of a fixer and he is likely to redouble his efforts to push it away; do the same to a grower and she will more likely find a way to go around it.

The fixer usually directs strategies against what he sees as wrong. A grower might agree completely with a fixer's assessment of a situation, but would more likely try to replace what is wrong with something better. Growers have internalized a perspective on change first articulated by Swiss psychologist Carl Jung,[4] who felt that many important problems are fundamentally insoluble. Solutions may be attempted, but they do not last. Fixes often fail because problem solvers are driven by the intensity of the problem they are dealing with. Once the intensity abates, new squeaky wheels replace the old ones. As a result, the motivation to act on the underlying causes of the initial difficulty is reduced, and the old problem eventually reemerges. This reinforces the fixer's view that fate, more than effort, determines the future.

For Jung, the only way out of this cycle was growth, a broadening of perspective or outlook so that the insoluble problem loses its urgency. It is not solved logically on its own terms, but fades into the shadows as new priorities emerge. A fixer might call this "sweeping problems under the carpet;" to a grower, it is more like moving to a new house.

THE PIVOTAL ROLE OF EMOTIONS

Looking at the same situation, people with the grower's mindset notice the opportunities; those with the fixer's, the difficulties. Why? Mindsets give birth to beliefs and assumptions. They determine what facts are noticed, what meaning is made of them, and—most importantly—what is done as a result of this interpretation. Emotions are the mechanism that makes all this happen, the link between thoughts and actions. Different emotions are triggered by each mindset, and these feelings, in turn, are what guide perceptions and behaviors.

What we do, and how much energy we put into what we do, is driven by how we feel about it. Emotions energize effort, but what fuels emotions? Some early psychologists believed that feelings were the product of a bubbly cauldron of primal desires and drives buried somewhere deep in our psyches. Recently, more science-oriented researchers armed themselves with brain-scanning MRIs and computerized EEGs and went searching for this hot pot of our minds. They didn't find it, but they discovered instead that several discrete clusters of brain cells produced emotions, not independently, but when we entertained certain thoughts.

Negative Emotions

Human sentiments come in two varieties, positive and negative, and each has a different point of origin in our brains[5] and a unique neurochemistry. Each also appeared at a different stage in our evolutionary development.[6] Negative emotions came first—anger, anxiety, and fear. These emotions served solo cave dwellers well, alerting them immediately to threatening predators. They served as a sensory alarm to mobilize and find out what was wrong, and they provided the energy needed to eliminate it—the stock-in-trade of the skillful fixer. Anger drives an urge to attack; fear, an urge to flee. Negative emotions adapted our ancestors to survive in a short-term world of win-lose, eat-or-be-eaten struggles. The best fighters-and-fleers were the best heeders of their negative emotions. They were the ones who survived and passed on their hard-won emotional intelligence.

How do negative emotions work? The brain seems wired to produce these momentary sensations when an event occurs that we interpret as a sign of danger. The emotion itself does three things. It provides a wake-up call by making us feel uncomfortable. It sets off specific physiological changes that get our body in gear to respond to the danger. If fear is manifested, additional blood flows to our large muscle groups to make it easier for us to run away from the pending danger.

Negative emotions also change the way we perceive reality. Since their job is to gear us up to take immediate action, fight or flight, our attention is narrowed so that we see nothing but the problem at hand. Our peripheral vision is switched off. No multitasking is allowed. We are in an "if I do this, that will happen" mode of thinking. Our thinking is as narrow as our vision; we are less concerned with why something has happened and more with what to do about it. This is not a time to entertain new ideas or to practice toleration; we feel compelled to act right away.

The part of our brain that produces emotions such as fear, the amygdala, is located adjacent to an area associated with memory, the hippocampus. This is convenient. It allows for quick reaction to new events that are judged to be threatening. We compare what is happening with stored memories of similar occurrences in the past, and we repeat what worked for us then. This is how, in part, defining moments come to define us. In a crisis, perceived or real, our brain is set up to make it as easy as possible to respond instinctively.

The president of Burlington Northern did a number of things to arouse negative emotions in the railroad's employees. He constantly *warned* of the risks and dangers that deregulation would pose. He *feared* that the trucking industry would take unfair advantage of the situation, and he *scapegoated* truckers, *blaming* them for whatever economic losses the railroad might suffer. He encouraged others to share his *anger* at competitors who used government-subsidized highways. He mobilized his employees to *attack* costs by being more productive because the company's very *survival* was at stake.

Are negative emotions like these only vestigial artifacts of human development, impulses that humans should have grown out of by now? This seems unlikely; evolution certainly has not removed them from our repertoire. But over time, people have developed a supplementary set of emotions that serve to broaden our range of abilities and undo some of the effects of fear and anger.

Positive Emotions

Positive emotions came later, according to evolutionary psychologists, as humans banded together in cooperative hunting parties and communal agriculture. Group cohesion was highly valued, and it was fostered by expansive, joyful, and tolerant thinking. Inspiring others about future possibilities from which all might benefit became very functional. The win-win, grower thinking needed to direct efforts toward building on what is good about a situation eventually began to coexist with the reactive fixer vigilance necessary to cope with the darker side of existence.

While negative emotions have been studied ever since the field of psychology began, it has only been in the past 10 years that significant attention has been given to their positive counterparts. The leading figure in advancing the scientific understanding of positive emotions is Barbara Fredrickson, a Stanford-trained psychologist. Now based at the University of Michigan, she directs a laboratory whose sole purpose is to answer the question: "What good is it to feel good?"

Fredrickson's research has identified a number of benefits that go beyond the ability of positive feelings to strengthen existing social bonds and create new ones.[7] Positive emotions do much more than signal the absence of a threat, she found. By priming the volunteers in her laboratory with stimuli from movie clips, stories, or pictures designed to elicit either positive or negative feelings, then giving them tests that measured their cognitive abilities, she found that positive emotions enhanced the ability to:

- See the big picture
- Stay receptive to new ideas
- Integrate diverse sources of information
- Discover novel and creative approaches to adapt to changing situations

These are all important attributes of growers. The experimental subjects who were exposed to stimuli for negative emotions performed poorly on each of these dimensions. They tended to focus on the trees, not the forest. They rejected new ideas, and they were unable to creatively combine concepts or invent new strategies.

Her studies found that people experiencing positive emotions are also less likely to engage in many common habits of faulty thinking, including succumbing to premature closure and becoming so wedded to their first impression that they are unwilling to change their mind when they are presented with new information. However, after a person experienced the perceptual distortions brought about by negative feelings, Fredrickson found, exposure to positive emotions actually undid most of the harm, restoring expansive and tolerant thinking and reactivating peripheral vision.

Positive emotions, such as confidence, hope, persistence, and zest, do not arise as instinctively as negative ones. They often need to be primed, as Fredrickson did in her lab. Their cranial home base also serves as a center for certain types of reasoning and understanding. This zone of the brain is sometimes short-circuited in times of immediate danger, but when it is activated, it makes possible the cognitive benefits that undergird the grower mindset.

Bill Greenwood took on the task of activating positive emotions, first with his teammates and then throughout the railroad. He offered a *hopeful* alternative, growing the intermodal business, to address the challenges of deregulation. He appealed to people's *sense of rationality* by offering a clear vision of *what could be* and a set of steps for getting there. He focused attention on *future opportunities*, not past problems. He redefined truckers as potential *allies*, not enemies, and he *forgave* them for stealing business from the railroad in the past. He even found a *creative* role for ex-truckers in his plan, to be the operators of the new intermodal terminals.

Pros and Cons

Our Ice Age hunter ancestors had only negative emotions to help them survive. As agriculture and industry offered alternatives to what had once been primarily a win-lose existence, evolution supplemented them with positive feelings, but did not replace them. This suggests that positive emotions alone—and the grower mindset that can activate them—are not sufficient for all the challenges that we face.

When we have positive feelings about a person or a situation, we are encouraged to approach. They are markers for a win-win encounter ahead. Negative emotions signal the opposite. They are the flashing red lights that warn us to avoid something.[8] Both signals are useful. Each offers both benefits and unwanted side effects. Skillful growers take advantage of both positive and negative emotions to advance their cause.

On the plus side, positive emotions make us open to new ideas and expansive thinking. We are happier, more tolerant, and even more altruistic when they drive us. We are more likely to attract a band of followers when we offer hope rather than doom and gloom. The price we pay for this is occasional wishful thinking, unaddressed problems, and excessive optimism. At their worst, positive emotions will sugarcoat reality, and so excite us about our lofty visions that we prefer thinking about the future to taking action in the present.

These positive emotion–induced contortions of reality might be the cost of creating an environment that nurtures dreams and embryonic ideas. A University of Michigan management professor, Kathleen Sutcliffe, has studied the behaviors of business leaders who are especially good at playing the role of grower.[9] She finds that the most effective leaders are not usually those with the most accurate reading of their competitive environment (a core fixer skill). In fact, growers consistently overestimate market volatility, growth trends, and general business prospects.

This overoptimism serves an important purpose. It contributes to a sense of enthusiasm and persistence in their organization and fosters a willingness to experiment and improvise. Sutcliffe also found that while the best growers feel very positive about the opportunities available, at the same time, they are modest and humble about their expected ability to control the future course of events. A leader who admits to not having all the answers about how to proceed (while remaining highly confident about the benefits of moving forward) creates an environment that encourages others to take the initiative and act creatively.

Negative emotions also come with a downside. They can induce paranoia and all the reality distorting that accompanies it. They limit our ability to invent creative and flexible options to deal with the challenges we face. They also focus us only on the extremes: fight or flight, all or nothing, us versus them thinking. But in return, negative emotions offer useful assistance. They promote vigilance and speed, as well as provide an energy burst and intense focus. The perils they signal help us to attract the attention of others. We will be more likely to cut our losses when we are in their sway. Our short-term accuracy in solving problems is also likely to be enhanced by a manageable dose of negativity.

A Mix of Two Vital Ingredients

Emotions are the raw materials that mindsets organize. What varies by mindset is the proportion of each emotion brought into play. Positive emotions dominate the grower's mindset, negative emotions the fixer's. Both types of feelings are inherent parts of the human fabric. It is difficult, and dysfunctional, to operate from only one of them. If either mindset were to evoke all positive or all negative emotions, the actions it stimulated would be crippled by the downside associated with that type of emotion. But when both are drawn on, each type of emotion has the potential to continually correct the other's weakness.

The extent to which one family of emotions can dominate the other is still a matter for psychologists to sort out, although some tentative conclusions are emerging from their research:

• If positive and negative emotions are called up in equal amounts, negative will always trump positive,[10] probably because the brain is wired for the negative emotions to trigger first. This suggests that fixers can get the benefits they need from negative emotions and still employ up to an equal amount of positive emotions, as fits their situation.

• If positive emotions are to work their expansive-thinking magic for growers, they need to be *three to five times* as prevalent as their negative cousins.[11] Therefore, effective growers need to be masters at drawing on and eliciting positive emotions, and infrequent users of anger, fear, blame, resentment, and the like.

Marcial Losada, a University of Michigan management researcher, examined how 60 strategic planning teams went about their grower-oriented work by listening to and analyzing the content of their discussions. The teams were then rated on how much of an impact their work had on the performance of their companies. Losada discovered that the teams that benefited their businesses the most had a positivity-to-negativity ratio of three to one. This meant that, in the verbal interactions among

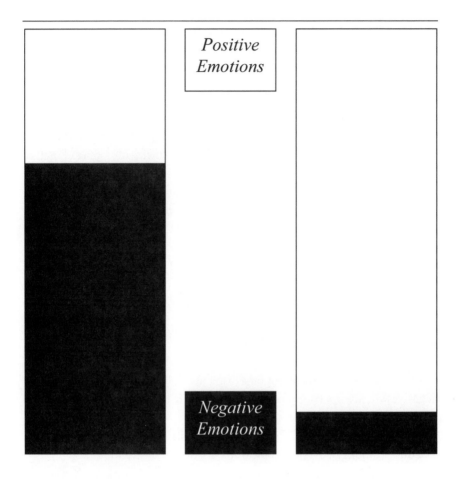

Fixer   **Grower**

the members of the strategy team, teammates were encouraged *three times as frequently* as they were reproached for their ideas. The lowest-performing teams were so mired in critical, negative comments that their team members became too self-absorbed to focus well on external opportunities for their firms.[12]

Mindsets and Emotions Reinforce Each Other

Fast-forward a few millennia from the era of cave dwellers and early hunter-gatherers, and we find mindsets that drive, and are in turn being driven by, each type of emotion coexisting in most people, societies, and corporations. Freud maintained that emotions are what drive thoughts. More recently, cognitive psychologists have argued that it is the other way around: Thoughts drive emotions. Actually, both of these are true.

The prevailing mindset (fixer or grower) will determine which type of emotion (negative or positive) is stimulated the most. It does this through the interpretation of events (threats or opportunities) that its logic system makes. That emotion, in turn, affects how reality is perceived and what kind of thought processes are employed to deal with it. Perceptions and thought patterns also tend to reinforce the mindsets from which they originated, turning them from a one-time set of tentative beliefs and assumptions into an abiding disposition.

It is when we allow a mindset to become an abiding disposition, though, that we open ourselves to trouble, because we then tend to deal with every new situation in the same way. It is better to think about a mindset as if it were an item of clothing, something to be put on and taken off to fit the occasion, rather than as an always-worn straitjacket.

ARE GROWERS BETTER THAN FIXERS?

Keep in mind what we have been talking about are mindsets, sets of assumptions, ways of thinking—not people or the roles they play. The title of this chapter asked: Are you a fixer or a grower? Or, in other words, which mindset should you operate from? The right answer, of course, is that it depends on what you want to accomplish. Ferreting out what is wrong and eliminating it is enabled by the negative mood of the fixer. The grower's more positive and spirited approach helps to identify what is right in a situation and determine how to build on it.

One mindset isn't better or worse than the other; it's just more or less appropriate to specific situations. The ability to shift mindsets means that we must discern which one is governing our actions, stand back from it, and critically assess its appropriateness for our aims. Though it is popular to call the business world a dog-eat-dog (fixer's) jungle, it is not really that bad, at least most of the time. Threats to our survival seldom leap, unexpected, from the underbrush. Most markets are large and diverse enough to allow for more win-wins than sudden deaths. There is often room for both you and your competitor to grow, provided that you do not both try to behave like the mirror images of each other.

The fixer also has an important role to play in growth. Moving forward usually requires making an investment. The savings generated through the cost-cutting efficiencies of a thrifty fixer can fund a grower's initiatives. That is what happened at Burlington Northern. The terminals and railroad cars that Greenwood's group of growers required for their plans would never have been bought without the surplus cash generated by the cost cuts and locomotive efficiencies championed by the railroad's fixer president, Thomas Lamphier. Greenwood never saw himself as being on the same team with his internal adversaries, but in a sense he actually was.

Carlos Ghosn, the chief executive of both Nissan and Renault, is an object of national adoration in Japan, where he is credited with reviving a car company that many had given up for dead. Ghosn closed Nissan factories (a "thinking-out-of-the-box" move in Japan) and ruthlessly cut costs, then he shifted his fixer's zeal for efficiency to a grower's antipathy to boring-looking cars. He gave his designers free rein to create a lineup of curvaceous, muscular-looking vehicles intended to define new market segments, not just fit into the existing ones. Nissan now leads its industry in operating margins and is worth more than every other automaker except Toyota.

Ghosn shifts mindsets the way drivers shift gears, a talent perhaps enabled by a polyglot upbringing (he also speaks five languages). He was born in Brazil, but his family returned to its native Lebanon before he was a teenager. He was educated at an elite French engineering school and learned turnaround artistry in the United States, where he overhauled troubled tire maker B. F. Goodrich.

Goshen embodies Simone de Beauvoir's perspective on the need to surpass as well as perpetuate (or else "living is only not dying," as quoted in the Introduction). We need to do both: to conserve what is essential to our existence and to try to move beyond these essentials. Beauvoir has also written that the effort to perpetuate, if it is going to make any sense at all, must be integrated into its surpassing.[13] These are not two separable, stand-alone activities.

FROM MINDSET TO ACTION

Few of us are all fixer or all grower, but if we are in a situation calling for one mindset too long, our abilities to perform in the other may be weakened and eventually even be lost. This is a real problem in companies where past success has been driven by belt tightening, mergers and acquisitions, and attention to internal improvement. Outward-looking growers have been lying low. Some of them, attuned to the way the winds have been blowing, have acquired the fixer's tool kit. Others may just have gone elsewhere, either voluntarily or as the result of downsizings. Many positions of power and influence have been awarded to those who best accomplished the business's old fixer-related priorities. Growers may be in short supply—or to be found hiding in the woodwork, in relatively marginal jobs.

In many businesses today, being a grower is hard. While most companies devote tremendous efforts to keeping everyone on the same page, growers excel at putting things out of alignment. Organizations naturally compartmentalize people and knowledge; growers work across hierarchical levels and bridge the boundary between the organization and what's outside it.

Many guides exist for fixers. The shelves of bookstore business sections are heavy with volumes on change management, control and measurement, financial analysis and balanced scorekeeping, forecasting the future, information technology, quality and productivity improvement, reengineering, and outsourcing. These are all vital concerns for those involved in managing today's business.

But there are fewer ideas in circulation about the central concerns of the builders of tomorrow's enterprise: where to look for opportunities; how to build support for seizing them, create momentum, and bounce back from missteps; and how to know when it's time to change course. Issues such as these define what was called in the Introduction "growth's inner game." Growers are a very diverse bunch, but when you look closely at how they do what they do, common themes emerge. The second part of this book highlights their hallmarks. Chapters 5 through 11 describe what growers actually do, and the sequence in which they do it. This is the raw material that you can use to sharpen your own mindset for growth.

PART 2: WHAT GROWERS DO

KNOW WHERE TO LOOK

Products that one way or another redefine how people think of things tend to be something that a couple kids put together in three months. They just look at the world in a slightly different way, and then in retrospect everybody goes, 'Oh, of course.'[1]

—*Marc Andreessen, Web browser inventor*

THINKING DIFFERENTLY

"Think different" is more than just the clever marketing slogan that Steve Jobs used to propel Apple Computer's recent rebound. It is the idea behind many types of growth, not only the industry-shaking, block-buster product–driven triumphs that we usually associate with knowing where to find new opportunities. The key to spotting openings for growth is to cultivate an ability to see the world in a slightly different way. Fortunately, this is not a gift that is limited to youth, though it is worth considering what Andreessen's "kids" have that the rest of us may lack.

Thinking differently is also what happened when:

• *Ko Nishimura visited an NCR factory near Atlanta.*[2] NCR, once the world's biggest builder of cash registers, had decided to get out of the manufacturing business and focus on software and service. It would still sell retail payment systems hardware, but the machines themselves would be made by others. NCR wanted to sell the factory and agree to buy back its production. Several outsourcing vendors had checked out the factory, but they all insisted on making significant layoffs as soon as they took possession of the facility—it was the only way they knew of making the deal economically feasible.

Nishimura, the chief executive of Solectron, looked around, realized what an underappreciated operation it actually was, and quickly offered to buy the factory and keep its workforce and management intact. He planned to use the plant's excess capacity to serve Solectron's other outsourcing customers. The revenue from them plus what NCR promised would turn a money-loser into a profit machine. Nishimura saw a great growth opportunity where others, who looked at the factory as something that had to stand alone economically, perceived only a fixer's downsizing challenge.

• *German automaker Porsche decided to get into the rental business.*[3] Porsche does not rent its speedy sports cars, but it does let other carmakers borrow its bright and talented engineers and designers. Porsche's people, used to working on hundred-thousand-dollar vehicles like the 911, also designed Opel's first compact van, the Zafira. They have also contributed to Harley-Davidson's motorcycle engines and have found a way to keep DaimlerChrysler's once-troubled A-Class compact cars from tilting at autobahn speeds. Porsche initially started renting its engineers as a tactic to avoid layoffs when economic downturns cut demand for its expensive product line, but the rent-an-engineer business soon proved to provide returns as good as those the company got building cars. At any one time, a third of Porsche's technical staff may be busy on projects for others, all the while picking up new ideas to bring back to Porsche. This allows Porsche to thrive as a low-volume car company while most others in the industry are attempting to survive by pursuing bigness strategies.

• *Billy Beane played by the numbers so that he could do more with less.*[4] There are probably more statistics kept about baseball players' performance than about performance in any other sport. Almost every move every player makes in every game he plays is carefully tracked and recorded. But the teams that can afford to do so often make recruiting decisions based on a player's celebrity status, or on a few popular indicators like home runs and batting averages, rather than by taking a hard, cold look at all the numbers. Billy's Beane's Oakland Athletics is a team that cannot afford that luxury. So Beane has found a way to be very successful by completely rethinking how baseball talent should be valued. He revisited the truisms that have made certain players worth so much and others worth much less. Beane found that what really mattered were things like a player's ability to get on base, even if all he did was tire out the pitcher and get walked. This does not make for very exciting games; it does help win them, though. Using insights such as these, he identified players fitting his statistical profile who were undervalued in the talent market. He hired these players and used them until their compensation caught up with their value, then he traded them to richer teams and started the process over. Using this form of arbitrage, he turned one of the poorest teams in baseball into one of the most successful, frequently competing head to head with the powerhouse New York Yankees, whose payroll dwarfed that of the A's. As Beane found, resource constraints can encourage you to notice facts that others miss.

• *Alan Willner avoided the overwhelming temptation to do what marketers usually do when a product seems to be catching on.*[5] A few years ago, Pabst Blue Ribbon Beer was a near-dead brand. It had hardly been advertised in decades. Pabst had shut down its brewery and hired one-time competitor Miller Brewing Company to make enough for its remaining fans. Its owner's plan was to slash costs and let the company profitably decline. Then in 2002, sales mysteriously rose by 5 percent. The next year, the rate of sales increase doubled. What happened was that the brand's obscurity fanned its popularity, especially among people 30 to 40 years younger than those who still loyally drank it regularly. It became a favorite of bike messengers, punk rockers, and skateboard fanatics—as well as people who were fans of these sorts of people. It was cheap. It had cachet because it was not marketed and was sometimes hard to find. It was also seen as an underdog brand, looked down on by most beer drinkers. Pabst's brand identity was being created (or reinvented) by its drinkers, not its owners.

When products reach a tipping point like this, the temptation to ratchet up the marketing effort to build more momentum is strong. But ideas like taking out ads on alt-rock stations and seeking endorsements from underground musicians or extreme athletes were all rejected by Alan Willner, Pabst's vice president of marketing. He feared getting too trendy and creating a backlash among the people who had adopted "his" brand more than he did losing a few incremental sales. In a measured and very limited way, Willner quietly sponsors local music events and an occasional bike polo tournament—but nothing that could be seen as boorish and corporate-like. Some kinds of growth happen best when they are allowed to happen with a very light touch. Sometimes a grower's best move is to sit still.

• *Lillian Stroebe looked out her window while riding a train through the Champlain Valley.*[6] Stroebe, a Vassar College German teacher, had a problem. It was 1915. German had become a "strategic language," as Russian was to become and Arabic is now. She knew that the best way to meet the increasing interest in learning fluent German, since the war in Europe made it impossible to send students to Germany, was to create a setting in which students could be completely immersed in the language and culture. This was not possible on her campus, but in a chance glance out the train window, she spotted an isolated and self-contained cluster of college buildings on a pretty foothill of Vermont's Green Mountains. Stroebe quickly appreciated how ideal the school would be for her vision of a distraction-free intense summer language program.

Fortunately, Middlebury College's facilities were unused in the summer, and the school's president quickly saw the wisdom of the idea. The first session began the next summer, and soon "No English spoken" signs began to appear across the campus classroom buildings, dormitories, and dining halls each summer as programs were added in French, Spanish, Russian, and Italian. Middlebury has become world-renowned for these immersion programs, and several additional languages have been added since.

While it took an outsider to help the college initially discover its distinctive advantage, soon after Stroebe's initiative was launched, several of Middlebury's English professors decided to learn from her success. They created another summer program to take advantage of a nearby mountain inn that had recently been donated to the college. The support of a local poet, Robert Frost, was enlisted, and they began what has become one of America's most famous literary institutions, the Bread Loaf Writers' Conference.

Chance can play a significant role in growth. Had Stroebe been distracted and not looked out her train window when she did, Middlebury College might never have become a global magnet for people wanting to learn writing and languages through intense interaction in an inspiring setting.

*   *   *

These are all examples of seeing openings that might otherwise be missed or misinterpreted, and then using them as a basis for actions that shape the future. Management author Michael Maccoby distinguishes this kind of foresight from the more common activity of extrapolation, in which we simply transfer the rules of one day to the next.[7] Foresight is something that happens in a person's head, not in a strategic planning process. It is sometimes associated with "gut feel," the instinct that comes from a deep and detailed knowledge of a subject, but it really has more to do with the mind than with the stomach. Our gut feelings are stimulated by how we think.

For many people, the ability to spot opportunities is an acquired taste; many of us get along just fine by extrapolating. But it is a taste that is not impossible to acquire as long as we are willing to remove some of the blinders we may have acquired from experience and our normal course of development. This may make us a little more like the kids that Marc Andreessen mentioned at the start of this chapter. Then, after we have removed some of the limitations on our vision, we may also find it useful to move ourselves to a point, at least temporarily, from which it is easier to see the future.

TAKE OFF YOUR BLINDERS

Growers cultivate clarity. They know that markets are dynamic and alive, while the concepts that most of us hold about them are static and always out of date. We all tend to see the future through the lens of the present.

It is this gap between reality and common perception that provides the openings that growers seize. Their trick is to directly experience what's out there, not to approach it through intellectual abstractions that may or may not reflect actuality. For a grower, a market is something with a life of its own, independent of whatever is thought about it or what the company's strategic plan says. To see like a grower, you must turn off some of the noise in your head: your past experiences and your repertoire of analytic tools. Pay attention, instead, to changes in your surroundings. What voices are you hearing, those of customers in the market or the ones in the back of your head? Distinguish factual observations from judgments and inferences you make about them. Put your assumptions on the table and mull carefully over what you actually observe. And don't do this alone—multiple perspectives on a situation are a better way to combat myopia. These are all among the "special accommodations" that growers need to make. They are necessary because our brains, unfortunately, are not wired appropriately to help us see things differently.

Is Our Brain a Supercomputer or Just a Big Database?

Jeff Hawkins has made over $100 million by thinking differently. He created the handheld computer industry when he invented the Palm Pilot in 1994. He also invented its handwriting recognition system, the first such software that actually worked. Hawkins's real interests, though, have always had more to do with how people think than with how machines work. To further them, he has invested a lot of his accumulated wealth in a different kind of start-up organization, the Silicon Valley–based Redwood Neuroscience Institute.

This group of researchers is helping Hawkins flesh out a new understanding of how our brains actually function.[8] For many years, the prevailing view was that the mind acts along the lines of a powerful supercomputer, taking in data, processing it in some way akin to computing an answer to a problem, and then letting us know what the result is. This view suggests that intelligence is related to our data processing ability. Hawkins's work suggests a different perspective: Intelligence is rooted in our brain's ability to access memories rather than its ability to process new information. Rather than computing an answer, we retrieve the answer from our memory. We are intelligent, he maintains, to the extent that we remember things, and then use these memories to make predictions by comparing what is new with what we remember. We access our previous experiences, see how they match up with whatever new information we receive, and then use the comparison to make predictions about what will happen next.

Seeing What We Believe We See

This hypothesis (that thinking is more about memory than about computational skill) has been applauded by several top scientists, including Nobel Prize winners Eric Kandel, investigator of the physical changes occurring in the brain due to memory and learning, and James Watson, co-discoverer of DNA's structure. It is also supported by recent investigations of how our neocortex, the cauliflower-looking gray matter that is the brain's home base for perceptions and thoughts, works. When we look at something, our neocortex immediately starts downloading predictions (from our memory) about what is being seen to the parts of the brain that are crunching detailed data from our eyes about the shape and color and size of what we are looking at. This memory accessing and downloading happens faster than the data processing, often short-circuiting or overriding the information from the eye. This is not all bad. It explains why we do not have to learn how to drive all over again each time we get into a new rental car. If our brain were merely a giant supercomputer, we would need specific instructions about every discrepancy between the rental car and whatever vehicles we were already familiar with. Fortunately, it is not, and we can get through a lot of life by just knowing generally how things work. We adapt to new circumstances more by comparing than by starting to figure things out from scratch.

Social psychologist Karl Weick sums this up by saying that it is not so much that we believe what we see, but that we *see what we believe* (based on what our stored memories are telling us).[9] We often notice only what we have been previously prepared to notice. At times, what we think we are seeing can be more a product of our imaginations than of our pure perceptions. Don't think of this as a flaw in our brains. It's a feature, and one that probably made a lot of sense when humans dwelled in caves, survived by eating before they were eaten, and had little time to spend on strategic planning or new product development. But the world is more complicated now. Growers thrive on the complexities; that is where they find opportunities that others miss. This is especially important when they operate in a well-defined industry that others may have written off as mature or in decline. Labels like "mature" are invitations to simplify, to disregard facts in favor of preset ideas or memories.

The Psychology of Noticing Things

Neuroscientists, like those Hawkins has pulled together, actually look into the inner workings of the brain with expensive computer-supported imaging technologies. Psychologists often lack the fancy equipment, but just by studying people and their reactions to different stimuli, they have also made important discoveries about how things get noticed (or not).

• When people are overloaded with information (sound familiar?), their ability to pay attention to more than one thing is severely limited.[10] To see complexity in the marketplace accurately, it is essential to limit diverting stimulation. Do not attempt to make any long-term plans in an office with the phone constantly ringing, e-mail messages piling up, and colleagues constantly dropping by.

• When something becomes the focus of attention for a long time or has had a special significance attributed to it—a competitor, a trend, a key person in the company, an old customer preference—it becomes very easy to overattribute everything that happens in the market to that thing. Called "illusory causation," this tendency makes it hard to spot emerging driving forces in time to take best advantage of them.[11] Things that were seen as powerful in the past turn into today's superstitions—they still have power in people's minds to explain why things are the way they are, but their ongoing validity is seldom tested. Growers test ideas and pay attention to distinguishing superstition from fact.

• We are most likely to notice things when we have been "primed" in advance to look for them.[12] What we read and whom we talk to now to will have a great effect on what we are likely to notice, or miss, in the future. So watch out for "selective exposure"— limiting yourself to only a narrow bandwidth of information. If we tend to maintain our beliefs by selectively exposing ourselves to information that we know is likely to support these beliefs, our abilities to spot new opportunities will be severely crippled. Good growers read widely. They seek out opinions and perspectives that they are not especially comfortable with. Growers also take advantage of priming. They immerse themselves in all that is known about a market, region, issue, or technology that they want to explore. This gives them a framework on which to organize new information as it comes in. Attention always serves as a filter between the outside world and how we experience it. We cannot eliminate the filter, but we can use priming to control and direct it.

SEEING OPPORTUNITIES

The more we know about how our minds operate, the better position we will be in to enlist them as allies in the growth process. Many of our natural mental processes can help, as well as hinder, a search for growth opportunities. Hawkins sees creativity as basically a way of predicting something by analogy. You do not so much look "out there" for a new idea; instead, you reflect on the patterns that are already stored in your cortex and see which ones might be analogous to the issue you are trying to deal with. Jean Nidetch, the grower behind Weight Watchers, did not make the company successful through the composition of its diet. She made the diet effective because she combined it with mutual-support techniques that she borrowed from Alcoholics Anonymous.

Picasso liked to talk about good artists borrowing and great ones stealing. This might be true, but a lot of the theft is from what is in their memories. This is where age and experience come in handy, as they provide a large supply of patterns to draw from. Trying to look at your situation in different ways may make it easier to jog loose some of these memories. Frank Louchheim did this when he started what has become the world's largest outplacement firm, Right Management Consultants.

Rethinking Outplacement

Right, a human resources services firm hired by employers to help their ex-employees find new work in the wake of layoffs and downsizing, grew from one office in Philadelphia to a large international network operating in 300 locations in 35 countries. When Louchheim put his plan for Right together in 1980, he made an important decision about division of labor that was responsible for driving much of the business's growth. The traditional pattern in most professional services firms is for those who sell the work to also do it. Partners in accounting, law, and management consulting firms tend to wear both hats, and this is something that their clients have come to expect. Louchheim was new to this type of business and was more familiar with the way industrial firms were organized: Those who made the product were usually in a separate unit from those who marketed and sold it.

His inclination to set up a sales organization that was separate from the group of career counselors he would hire to teach job search skills was further reinforced when he looked at the kinds of advice his counselors would be offering. They started their counseling with a battery of diagnostic tests to help a person seeking a new job better understand what kind of work he or she was best suited for. These tests invariably showed that good counselors had a very different profile from did star salespeople. This was enough for Louchheim to confirm his hunch. He hired different types of people for each role and put them in separate organizations, with different titles, career progressions, and compensation systems. Clients did not mind, because the nature of outplacement is that the people delivering the service are dealing with ex-employees, not with the people who bought and paid for the service. Right's competition almost invariably followed the unified organization pattern, hoping that good counselors would also make good sellers. They generally did not, and Right's business expanded to the point where it became the dominant career-transition firm.

Rethinking Executive Search

Outplacement is a bit like headhunting in reverse. When Egon Zehnder founded the executive search firm in Zurich that bears his name, he also flouted the expected business model for his industry.[13] He had worked for a large American recruiter for five years before starting his own firm, so he had a lot of exposure to the traditional ways this business was run. Search firms typically charge their clients a percentage of the first year's pay for anyone they help recruit. This bothered Zehnder. He felt that it created a clear conflict of interest, giving the search firm an incentive to find candidates who could command the highest salaries rather than those who might be the best fit for the job. It is also a practice that, over decades, has helped fuel the mega-pay packages that have created immense gaps between the pay of executives and that of others in their companies.

Zehnder, whose firm is now among the world's largest, insisted on charging flat fees based on the level of the job and the estimated difficulty of the search. Executive recruiting had until then been dominated by American firms. Zehnder's firm was the first to expand rapidly in Europe because his approach to fee setting was more in accord with that continent's conservative approach to compensation. It also fit better with European expectations of professionalism.

Zehnder also broke from traditional professional-service-firm internal-pay practices when he decided to pay all his associates based on their seniority, rather than on their background or their individual or office performance. This radical rethinking reinforced Zehnder's idea of professionalism. He wanted colleagues who would want to stay for a long time; would cooperate, not compete with one another; and would build a strong, unified firm, not islands of rival fiefdoms. It also forced him to do as Louchheim did: Practice what he preached. Zehnder's pay system puts tremendous pressure on the firm's ability to recruit carefully and choose people who will thrive in its unique culture. Selection errors will quickly lead to deadwood and disruption. But relatively few mistakes have been made; this is a firm that is very good at doing what it does best: matching the right people with the right jobs.

Turning Off Our Autopilot

If we cannot find ways to take advantage of our mind's natural ways, then it may be more useful to try to short-circuit them or slow them down. Our brains seem very willing to automatically, from our memory, create meanings and interpretations for things we experience. These may be helpful, but they are limited by what is already in our "database." Left to its own devices, the process is fast and unconscious. What if, instead, we turned off our mental autopilot by slowing down our thinking process and making it a more conscious one? Doing this requires us to distinguish between the *direct observations* we make and the *spin* with which we almost automatically surround them. This is something that is most productively done with a colleague, preferably a friendly and trusted one. When discussing trends in your marketplace, for example, slow down the pace of the conversation. For every assertion you make about where things seem to be heading, lay out:

- The observable facts upon which you have based your conclusion
- All the assumptions you are making related to your conclusion

See if your colleague has additional facts to add, or notices assumptions that are missing. Test your assumptions. How valid is your basis for them? Ask each other what could happen that would make them untrue.

What making the effort to have these "conscious conversations" provides is a way to become very clear about why we see the world as we do. It is a better alternative than jumping to unconscious conclusions based on the way our brain automatically uses its memories. Comparing our perspective with others' can then serve as a way to spot growth opportunities and openings for change.

The idea here is not to hide what you are thinking, but to bring both it and the thought process that has led you to it to the surface. For this "bringing to the surface" to work, growers need to be as open to being challenged as they are to arguing for what they believe. This is a variant on a standard part of the scientist's tool kit. Scientists call their beliefs "hypotheses." The norm in science is that you do not prove a hypothesis so much as you offer others ways to show how it might be faulty. If it is not found to be faulty, the hypothesis stands. A hypothesis that remains standing after a couple of rounds of this is elevated to the status of a "theory." Theories are considered valid as long as they seem to provide an explanation for facts that are observed. When they cease to do so, it is time to begin the process again.

Reality Is Often Whatever We Think It Is

We may find ourselves behaving like a large elephant if we do not keep testing and retesting our assumptions. Vivek Paul was formerly vice chairman of one of India's largest technology companies, Wipro.[14] He likes to explain his firm's success at growth and transformation by referring to a discussion he had with an elephant trainer in the jungle outside Bangalore. Paul noticed that several large elephants were kept in place by being tied to small stakes planted in the ground. He asked the trainer how such an enormous beast could be restrained by being tethered to such a small stake. The trainer replied that when the elephants were small and restless, they tried to pull out the stake. Since they were weaker then, they failed; and now, even though they are much stronger, they seem to remember the lesson of their youth and never bother to try.

Paul's company may be based near elephant-inhabited jungles, but it has none of the elephants' mentality. Wipro has gone through several cycles of evolution: It started as a maker of toilet soaps, lightbulbs, and cooking oil, and is now a leading provider of information technology outsourcing and consulting services. Its plans call for eventually pulling away from the software tether as it adds capabilities in hardware and product design.

John Child is one of the relatively few academics concerned about business who has actually spent a significant amount of time working full-time in a global corporation. As a result, many of his observations are often closer to reality than to lecture-hall theory. One of my favorites is his view that a company's environment is not an objective factor in business decision making. Instead, it is something that is constantly being disputed and reinterpreted by top management and others throughout the organization.[15] Growers thrive on this kind of debate. A group of them has formed within Nike and has been working hard to change how the company perceives its surroundings.

Nike Goddess. In Greek mythology, Nike was the goddess of victory, daughter of Pallas and Styx, and a resident of Mount Olympus. In business history, Nike is an athletic-shoe company, founded by a jock and his track coach in Beaverton, Oregon. The shoe company may have been named after a woman, but for most of its existence, it has been a male-focused company, either treating female customers like men or completely ignoring them. It takes a special kind of grower to nudge an established company away from its fixed ways and broaden its business model to something that reflects more of the future than the past. Darcy Winslow is one of these. She and a group of her colleagues, including Mindy Grossman, Martin Lotti, Jackie Thomas, and Cindy Trames, created a grassroots movement within Nike.[16] Dubbed Nike Goddess, its goal is to help this testosterone-fueled company grow by creating a range of products for women that didn't fit into the jock-oriented market segments that had previously come to define (and limit) Nike.

Nike has been a company built on brash ads and male athletic fantasies, according to Jackie Thomas. The black space on its organization chart is all about sports—running, basketball, or soccer. Darcy Winslow, now general manager of women's fitness, has been at work in the white space of the chart. This is the large, and mostly unoccupied, turf in every company where "the rules are vague, authority is fuzzy, budgets are nonexistent, and strategy is unclear."[17] In other words, this is where all the entrepreneurial action happens. This is where businesses get reinvented and renewed.

What Nike Goddess got the company to pay attention to was where opportunity could be found in these in-between places on the organization chart. The group knew what it wanted to do at a time of upheaval and change within Nike (often a very good time for well-prepared growers to advance their ideas). Business had fallen off. Phil Knight, one of the company's founders, had returned to an active management role. He led a business rebound, shifting Nike from a shoe company to a fashion-oriented sport and apparel business, and then brought in an outsider as his replacement.

In the midst of all this turmoil and rethinking, Nike Goddess spread the word that there were certain things that Nike needed to do if it wanted to reach the vast women's market, and that these would not be the same things that were successful with male jocks. They got the idea across that women do not dwell on superstars the way men do, nor do they think they'll run as fast as so-and-so just because so-and-so's name is on their shoes. Women define high performance differently, too. For many of them, it is about fitness, not competitive sports.

The results to date have been impressive. Nike Goddess is now also the name of a newly rolled-out chain of retail stores intended to have more the feel of a comfortable residence than the loud locker-room ambiance of Nike's existing stores. Smaller versions of these will appear in leading department stores. The stores will be filled with fashionable fitness-oriented shoes and apparel, including Air Kyoto, a black slip-on that is Nike's first yoga shoe. Winslow has just unveiled a women's fitness dance collection, part of her effort to show that Nike now defines sport as activity beyond traditional courts and playing fields. Her message is one with two targets—the female consumers in the marketplace and the male Nike executives in Beaverton. She is reaching both.

The Business Case for a Positive Mood

As Nike moves beyond the limits that used to define it, one key aspect of its culture is very unlikely to change. It is a very "up" place. It has an optimistic and positive tone to its work environment. Determination, perseverance, and hope are coded into Nike's corporate DNA as well as its advertising copy. This is fertile growth for growers and growth initiatives.

The grower's mindset cues us to notice the hopeful features in our surroundings—things that might be missed or dismissed if we approached things less optimistically. "A positive mood jolts us into an entirely different way of thinking from a negative mood,"[18] says University of Pennsylvania's Martin Seligman. The different way is one of big-picture thinking, according to the results of a National Science Foundation study, just the opposite of the hunker-down-and-focus mode of the fixer mentality. Happier moods promote a greater focus on the forest; sadder feelings encourage people to dwell on the trees.[19] Brain researchers have also found that a rush of positive feelings does more than just make us happy. It provides cognitive glue—new information connects more firmly to old knowledge.[20] This happens because the chemicals that are produced by the brain's pleasure centers are also energizers of the neural pathways involved in making these connections.

So feeling happy is actually good for business, especially if the goal is growth. Positive interpretations of the competitive environment add to people's general sense of enthusiasm and their willingness to persist in the face of adversity. Leaders with a positive orientation create a better context for learning and creativity, thanks to the mechanism of cognitive glue. Is the world an open place, full of potential and possibilities? Or is it a predetermined realm, closed and bounded, one that, at best, allows movement only back toward what is remembered as having once been good? The mindset of a grower sees things the former way, and this is why opportunities emerge for them that are often missed by those who are caught up in the fixer's world.

Desperation works in the opposite way. Amgen, a California biotechnology company, had a 10-year stretch with no successful new product introductions. It had been growing rapidly on the strength of two older products, but now its chief executive feared that the expansion would be unsustainable. So he went into what he calls "submarine mode" and stopped listening to the marketplace and objective outsiders about the potential of a new drug to help people with rheumatoid arthritis. He needed it to be a big success, so he dramatically overestimated the revenue potential of the drug and spent money on its development and marketing based on these estimates. When the real sales were nothing like he had hoped, Amgen lost millions. Kevin Sharer, the CEO, has fortunately found one way to recoup some of his ill-fated investment: He has had the situation written up as a case and teaches it in Amgen's executive leadership development course. He uses it to show his top 400 managers how negative feelings can actually drive overoptimism, with disastrous business results.[21]

APPRECIATIVE INQUIRY

David Cooperrider of Case Western Reserve University has spent almost 20 years pioneering a new branch of organization-development consulting that is a good complement to Seligman's positive psychology. It is called appreciative inquiry (AI), and its purpose is to shift attention from what does not work to what does.[22] As we have discussed earlier, our minds tend to work in ways that lead us to generally find what we are looking for. If we search for problems, we invariably will develop a long list of them. And along with the list will come a generous amount of negative emotions that are likely to bog people down and get in the way of finding good solutions.

But what if we started off by identifying what is good in a situation? Then we would have a catalog of an organization's best successes, its strongest capabilities, and its best moments. Another by-product is likely to be generated: a surge of positive feelings, enthusiasm, and forward momentum. Cooperrider teaches consultants to use interviews throughout an organization to collect stories about these positive episodes. People are asked to talk about the best team they were on or the best meeting they ever attended. What is this place like when it is most productive and vibrant? Interviewees say why they are proud of their organization and describe how they would like to see it in the future.

Consulting has tended to be about what is wrong and how to fix it. AI can also lead to things getting fixed, but by a less direct route. Information might be gathered about a problem-prone department, but it would be data about how that department and the departments it interacts with see its positive features. These, in turn, would be used as the basis for improving or redesigning it, with the key objective being: How do we do more of what is right? The same result is achieved, but using a different starting point and mindset. Actually, the result is often better. When questions focus on problems, the list tends to grow longer and longer; clients internalize the negative feelings and become depressed and anxious, and often nothing happens. Focusing on what is effective, the AI approach, is much more likely to lead to action.

Thinking Differently About Health Care

Let's see how a grower might apply some of the principles of positive psychology and appreciative inquiry to a pressing national problem: health care. This is an issue that has been resistant to past attempts to resolve it. It is one that is of serious concern to many millions of under- and uninsured people, and its costs rank among the largest line items in many corporate budgets. Some automakers and other manufacturers are finding that they are spending more on health care for employees and retirees than on basic materials such as steel.

Most analyses of "the crisis in America's health-care system" focus on cost escalation, and the remedies that are most commonly proposed involve limiting the consumption of health care through some kind of rationing coupled with new cost-cutting arrangements such as managed care, health savings accounts, or a single payer (the government or some national insurance program) of all health bills. For a variety of reasons, these solutions have found little political or popular acceptance in the United States. They also typify a fixer's approach to this issue.

David Cutler is an economist and a battle-scarred veteran of the ill-fated Clinton-era health-care reform attempt.[23] Now a Harvard dean, he has had a chance to reflect on both the failure of that attempt and the way the broader issue has been defined. Cutler now applies the grower mindset to health care, and he has come up with a new diagnosis and prescription. He feels that a direct assault on high costs, in addition to attracting tremendous opposition, will not really address the underlying problem of the system. Too much attention has gone to the expense side of health care, and not enough to figuring out how to maximize its benefits.

Cutler's rethinking began, along the lines of appreciative inquiry, by looking at what is *right* with the current system. He found that spending on health care has certainly increased, but not because of price increases as much as because of a demand surge. People are consuming more health care, which, in itself, is not necessarily a bad thing. When Cutler traced these extra inputs as they moved through the system, he found that they were not necessarily being converted into the desired output—a healthier population. The real issue, as he probed more deeply, was a management one, but not one of lax cost management.

The underlying problem with American health care, says Cutler, concerns effectiveness more than efficiency. Pills are prescribed, but they are not taken. People with chronic conditions are expected to monitor their conditions, but they do not. Doctors are frequently inconsistent in the treatments they recommend, and they overly rely on oral means of communication with their patients. Communications between specialists and primary-care physicians are seldom timely or detailed. Patient survival rates are seldom tracked. Neither hospitals nor doctors make a regular practice of comparing themselves to others, nor do they make good use of quality improvement techniques that have been used for decades in manufacturing industries.

Cutler has also found a way out of these difficulties. Doctors and hospitals, according to his research, are very responsive to incentives. The problem is that the present system gives them the wrong incentives if the ultimate goal is to increase the level of health of those they treat. Most are paid on a fee-for-services basis. They are rewarded for each unit of "care" they deliver, but not necessarily for achieving an end result, such as "better health." A try, even a not especially good one, will count financially as much as a spectacular success. This, Cutler finds, is especially an issue for people with chronic diseases, such as asthma, diabetes, high blood pressure, and obesity. Their well-being requires a consistent approach to long-term care, lest their conditions worsen and complications ensue. What happens, though, as Cutler's research found, is that few doctors do a good job of following up to ensure that medicines are properly taken and their advice heeded. Doctors admit to this failing, often noting that they are not paid to do follow-up work.

Cutler has a simple reform recommendation: pay them. Set performance goals for blood sugar and cholesterol reduction, daily consumption of correct medicine dosages, weight loss, and smoking cessation. Provide bonuses for meeting the targets. A large health plan in Minneapolis tried this, and it found that the incentives tripled the number of patients who were doing everything that they were supposed to. A Florida hospital that improved the consistency and speed of the care it provided cut in half its record of deaths from heart attacks and strokes.

Paying physicians for producing better results in the treatment of chronic conditions can have a big economic impact. Half of the health-care spending increases now go to treat these conditions. Measures that would better control them would make significant cuts in the number of these patients eventually requiring expensive hospitalization and chronic-care facilities. Investing in quality care the moment a chronic condition is diagnosed can have a significant cost-reduction payback.

General Electric, a company that pays over $2 billion annually for health care, is beginning to put these ideas in place. It has a system that splits the resulting savings with doctors who provide better care for diabetics and heart patients. Information technology is also being used, not so much to cut costs as to provide physicians with ongoing rapid feedback about their own performance. GE is applying a proven principle from the factory floor: What gets measured gets managed. By focusing on patient results, not on controlling the costs of the inputs that produce those results, health goes up and total health-care costs actually decline over a patient's life span.

GO WHERE THE VIEW IS BETTER

We are often a prisoner of our immediate environment. Eric Bonabeau, chief scientist of decision-support tool maker Icosystem, warns that we often live in a vast echo chamber. We also miss opportunities because of where we are. That is easy to remedy: We just have to move to where the view is a little better. To make the trip worthwhile, we may also have to change how we notice and think about things.

Get Out More

Growers have an uncanny knack for spotting what's about to happen next. They internalize William Gibson's sage wisdom: The future is already here, just unevenly distributed. They look for the automobile of tomorrow in Southern California, see the shape of the upcoming mobile Internet in Tokyo, note the next generation of interactive computer games in South Korea, learn the secrets of micromerchandising in the rural villages of India, go to Germany to discover the state of the art in recycling, and go to Holland to find an economy that has moved far along the path to replace checks and cash with bits and bytes.

Samsung was once a back-of-the-store brand, a company that barely survived the last major Asian currency crisis. Now it is a direct rival of Sony, with twice Sony's market capitalization. Samsung's electronics business is also larger than Sony's. Samsung dates the start of its turn-around to a trip its chief executive, Lee Kun Hee, organized in 1993. He flew all his senior managers to Los Angeles, where they spent days just touring the retail stores to see how the company's products were not being taken seriously. The trip made a much stronger impression than all the statistics in all the market research reports they had seen back in Seoul. Samsung's products looked blah in comparison to others on the store shelves and were lost in the crowd in the U.S. shops. The group immediately vowed to change that, giving top priority to product design. Now Samsung has the reputation of making some of the coolest-looking gadgets on earth.

Make a Stale Situation Fresh

This idea of getting out and shifting perspective to make a stale situation fresher is starting to catch on.

• Procter & Gamble chief executive A. G. Lafley took all 40 of his business-unit direct reports to San Francisco for a one-day shopping immersion. The idea was for them to understand firsthand what consumers experience when they shop, in hopes of stimulating some future product innovations. One group went out to buy music, starting at a funky local music shop, then going to a large retail chain store, and then going online. Another paired up with poor people to understand the kind of trade-offs that people with almost no extra resources make each day.

• Ford did something similar to help its executives understand how consumers without a six-figure salary make the trade-offs involved in purchasing a car. Early one evening at a product planning immersion session, the Ford executives were told to put their wallets and credit cards on the conference table. Then they were each given $50 cash and told to take a bus to an Old Navy store. There they were given 20 minutes to buy the clothes they were to wear to the next day's session.

• Ford also sells luxury cars. To help the team of designers, engineers, marketers, and senior executives involved in updating and refining the Lincoln brand, Ford required the group to spend time in settings that represented the idea of "American luxury" that the company wanted this car to convey. Stops in New York City included a Four Seasons Hotel, an expensive Upper East Side restaurant, Christie's auction house, and several fancy Soho boutiques.

Leave Your Baggage Behind

Growers are more than jet-lagged time travelers, though. They know that what you see depends on where you stand—preconceptions drive perceptions. There is no point in traveling to Southern California, Tokyo, South Korea, India, Germany, or Holland if you carry with you the same mindset that you had at home. Direct experience always trumps reading postcards and trip reports, but for direct experience to actually be direct, we need to make sure that we are actually observing what is in front of us. Take the time to describe in detail what you are seeing. Otherwise your mind is likely to start judging it or evaluating it. Observe what you are seeing; do not try to figure it out. That can wait until you get back to your office.

Blinders from existing business models or getting caught up in the hot concept du jour (convergence, deregulation, Internet-means-everything-is-different, and so on) will also limit our ability to see the market clearly. When we see something new, we seldom stop to appreciate it for what it is. Instead, evolution seems to have trained us—hard-wired our brains—to slot things into categories or explanations that are derived from our past experiences. In pigeonholing things this way, we run the risk of filtering out what it is that makes the novel new. When Konosuke Matsushita was building his electronics business from the rubble of war-devastated Osaka, he constantly implored his colleagues to approach things with a "mind that does not stick."[24] He wanted them to rethink the business from the ground up, with fresh eyes focused on the future, not the past. This is good advice for any grower.

Pick the Right Place; Set the Right Rules

Microsoft has a not-too-elegant phrase to describe how it does product development. The company expects its software developers to "eat their own dog food." By that Microsoft means that as your ideas (or software) are being developed, they should be used as quickly as possible to develop more. This is a great way to test the validity of new ideas. It is also an approach that Martin Seligman has taken to heart as he has grown the field of psychology by guiding the development of positive psychology. As discussed in chapters 3 and 9, positive psychology is about how people can thrive and flourish. It deals with such things as positive emotions, pleasures, gratifications, optimism, and people's strengths and virtues.

When Seligman annually gathered groups of leading psychologists to work with him to ponder the directions this new discipline should take, he shunned the usual cheerless urban university or hotel conference rooms in favor of a setting that was more likely to buoy people's moods. He invited the psychologists to spend a week in Akumal, a modestly priced vacation town in Mexico's Yucatan. Ground rules included no neckties, families were welcome, the preset agenda was minimal, and the week was deliberately underscheduled. The psychologists would meet as a group of 30 for a few hours each morning and again in the evening, focusing on the key topics and new research findings that were important to shaping the emerging field. In the afternoons, small triad groups (Seligman calls them pods) were to meet or just chat about the specific aspects of positive psychology that they were committed to working on together after they left Akumal. These sessions were commonly rated by the participants as one of the best intellectual experiences they ever had.[25] How does this compare with the typical off-sites you have attended?

Look From the Outside In

The key point of sessions like these is to broaden people's perspective. To the extent that such sessions can help people let go of their narrow, company-centric view of the world, they are more likely to pay off in identification of new opportunities. Jack Welch created a growth trap for General Electric when, early in his tenure as chief executive, he mandated that all businesses be number one or number two in their markets; otherwise they would be sold off or closed down. This was a classic fixer ploy—use fear and intimidation to get people to change. Welch's managers, a smart and survival-oriented lot, quickly figured out how to "game" his requirement. They cleverly defined their markets so narrowly that the segments their businesses occupied were, by definition, ones that their businesses owned.

Welch, to his credit, quickly caught on to what was happening. He borrowed an idea from Coca-Cola's then-CEO, Roberto Goizueta, and changed his rule. Now, all businesses leaders were required to redefine their industry in such a way that their market shares were only in single digits to mid-teens, then submit plans for doubling their share. Moving from the perspective of a big fish in a small pond to a small player in a big ocean can do wonders to illuminate new possibilities. Managers who once saw their job as product makers soon discovered growth opportunities in selling services like finance and maintenance to those who once bought only their hardware.

The best place for a grower to stand is on the outside of her existing business and market, looking in. Otherwise, opportunities are easily missed because you'll see only what you thought you'd see before you looked. When you see things from the outside in, you notice surprising things, such as that people often buy products for what they're not, not just for what they are. Nonfeatures can be more important than features. Whole Foods, one of the fastest-growing U.S. supermarket chains, built a business on selling groceries for what they are not: full of fat, additives, and pesticides. So did Wal-Mart and Costco with their unrelenting focus on "expensive-free" goods.

Company-Centric vs. Customer-Centric Information

To help an organization move beyond its limits, the growers within it must move beyond theirs, cultivating an ability to see their operation as an outsider might. This is much easier said than done. Ask most chief revenue officers about last year's sales results. You will be likely to hear something along these lines:

Companywide revenues were such and such, up 10 percent over last year. Here's how the sales break down by product, geography, and organization unit. Here's how each number compares to last year's results and this year's forecast. Here's a list of salespeople arranged by who exceeded, met, and missed their quotas. Here is our win-loss record for major contracts we competed for.

A response like this is common, and it provides some comfort that the business is under control. Contrast it, though, with what you might hear from a chief revenue officer who was more attuned to growth:

We sold x dollars last year. Seventy percent of this revenue was from goods sold to people who bought from us in past years. Of these people, 10 percent were happy campers, 60 percent were too lazy or dumb to look elsewhere, and 30 percent were smart enough to look elsewhere, but didn't have the time.

Thirty percent of our annual revenue came from new customers. Half of this amount is from first-time-ever buyers of this category of product; the rest we weaned away from our competitors.

Minus y dollars was the amount we didn't sell to people who bought from us two years ago. Of these lost sales, 25 percent were due to no need for our products on the part of our former customers, 45 percent were due to their finding a lower price elsewhere, and 30 percent were due to our having messed up on quality and delivery of past orders.

What's the difference? The first perspective is company-centric; the other is customer-centric, rooted outside looking in. One has a clear view of sales dollars, the other of customers. One is well prepared to ask: What can my customer base do for me? The other is more focused on laying the groundwork necessary for finding what the company can do for its market. Relatively few companies try hard to see themselves as others see them, which provides great opportunities for those that take the trouble to do so.

Thinking in a customercentric way does not come easy—even to some of the business world superstars like Jack Welch, former General Electric chief executive. Welch's book *Winning*[26] describes his core business principles, and he lays out five questions to guide the creation of a winning strategy:

1. What does the playing field look like now?
2. What has the competition been up to?
3. What have you been up to?
4. What is around the corner?
5. What is your winning move?

These are all good commonsense concerns. They are also very ego-centered ones. They are all about what I am doing to my competition, or what my competition is doing to me. Minimal consideration is given to customers, how they see themselves being served by me, and what their future needs might be. Welch lives and writes about the fixer's world of technique. Growth, for Welch, is something a "player" imposes on his environment—which might explain why more than twice as many pages in *Winning* are devoted to mergers and acquisitions as are given to organic growth.

* * *

Knowing where to look for openings and opportunities often requires changes in how we think and where we sit. Going to all that trouble has a nice payoff: It provides a holistic idea of where your business might be headed. Actually getting it moving in that direction then requires setting a specific target, making an honest assessment of how far you are from it, and using creative tension to overcome inertia. Let's start by looking at how growers figure out what they want to happen.

KNOW WHAT THEY WANT

I have only one purpose, the destruction of Hitler,
and my life is very much simplified thereby.[1]

—*Winston Churchill*

ERADICATE POLIO BY 2008

Like Churchill, Bruce Aylward knows two things when he wakes up every morning: what he is trying to accomplish, and how far from that target he is. Aylward's job is to bring about a polio-free world. He is a Canadian physician and the coordinator of the World Health Organization's efforts to eradicate polio by 2008. Aylward is project manager of an endeavor of staggering size. His organization has raised $3 billion and recruited 20 million volunteers to immunize over 2 billion young children. His activities have literally touched every country in the world. This is the largest public health initiative ever attempted, and it is only the second time an effort has been launched to free the earth from a disease. Its success can pave the way for similar global-scale campaigns to address malaria, measles, tobacco use, and eventually AIDS.

Fixers control and treat disease. Growers set out to eliminate it—in this case, to wipe out forever one of the leading causes of permanent disability. Fifty years ago, Dr. Jonas Salk created a vaccine that ended the annual polio epidemics that had crippled and killed hundreds of thousands of Americans since 1900. Children were most vulnerable, but

Franklin Roosevelt was 39 years old when the virus infected him. Salk's and another researcher's (Albert Sabin) vaccines were quickly adopted by most developed countries' health systems, but polio was still rampant in many third-world nations. Since the disease spreads easily by contact with an infected person, as long as one case exists anywhere in the world, the rest of the world remains vulnerable, and even polio-free countries must continually immunize all their children. Aylward sees the goal of eradication as the ultimate in health equity and justice, as it offers an identical and universal benefit to every person in the world.[2] Meeting this goal also makes good economic sense. It means that all current polio control measures can be stopped, freeing up over a billion dollars a year to spend on more pressing health needs.

Aylward lives this goal, but he did not create it. Credit for that vision goes to Rotary International, a 100-year-old international voluntary service organization. Rotary undertook a five-year project in 1979 to deliver polio vaccine to six million children in the Philippines. The success of this and other Rotary service projects in developing countries convinced Rotary that polio was a conquerable disease, but that the conquest had to be a worldwide one if it was to be lasting. Rotary has backed up this vision with over half a billion dollars to help organize and then support the international effort that WHO coordinates. Over a million Rotary members have also volunteered to be part of the immunization teams, traveling from remote village to remote village in the world's poorest countries to administer the vaccine.

WHAT GOALS CAN DO

Seeing opportunities clearly is vital, but it is not sufficient. Oracles seldom move things along. A good possibility remains just that—a possibility—until someone with the mindset of a grower is able to convert it to a clear, achievable, not-too-distant goal. Going from opportunity to objective requires giving a vision a practical shape. This is the point when you move from hesitancy to commitment, from possibility to action.

This is also the point where you put yourself on the line. Even if no one else knows of your plans, you still risk the anxiety and depression that can come from not meeting the expectations you hold for yourself.

If you go public with your plans, other people's expectations are raised, and your reputation is at stake. What do you get in return?

Goals Change What We Notice and How We Interpret It

William Hutchinson Murray, leader of several Himalayan mountain climbing expeditions at the time Mount Everest was first scaled, maintains,

> The moment one definitely commits oneself, then providence moves too. All sorts of things occur to help one that would never otherwise have occurred. A whole stream of events issues from the decision, raising in one's favor all manner of unforeseen incidents and meetings and material assistance, which no man could have dreamed would have come his way.[3]

While it is unclear that commitment always elicits divine intervention, Murray is right in saying that knowing what we want can change us. What changes is our awareness of what is around us, and what meaning we make of what we now encounter. When Aylward took on the polio eradication campaign, Bill Gates was no longer just the maker of the software running on Aylward's desktop computer; he was a potential funding source. Rotary International was no longer just a large fraternal organization; it was a willing partner and a reliable source of grants and volunteers. Aylward's friend Carl Tinstman was not just another United Nations buddy to commiserate with about the rigors of travel in the third world; he was a trusted ally at a sister organization, UNICEF, who could help dovetail that group's work with WHO's.

When a commitment is articulated, it changes how others see us as well as how we perceive the world. Most of us find that just muddling along through life is a sufficient challenge in itself. So when we meet a person who is radiant with excitement about an important task he has taken on, we notice. If we feel empathy for what he is doing, some of his energy may rub off on us, and we are likely to be attracted to him and want to support his cause. Charisma is not an artifact of a select few's unique personality; it is a result of the kinds of commitments that people have made and how we respond to them.

Goals and Purpose

Knowing where to look is an outside-in process. Knowing what is wanted from an opportunity is more of an inside-out matter. It is driven by values, a sense of purpose, and knowing what you're willing to trade off to accomplish something. Goals do not emerge out of thin air; you do not just make them up or formulate them in a vacuum. They arise in a particular context: either your own values and purpose or those of the organization in which you operate.

Goals can be powerful when they resonate with the purpose of your organization. Companies like Amgen, Johnson & Johnson, Nike, and Starbucks have found ways to cultivate a strong sense of what they stand for—a sense of mission that has given birth to many growth initiatives at each of these companies. Many organizations, though, fail to make use of purpose as a tool to unify or organize people's efforts. They may have the paraphernalia often associated with a sense of purpose—mission statements, lists of values, annual reports organized around the customary themes of serving the customer and valuing the employee—but they lack its substance. Other companies have a mission that has served them well in the past, but is no longer relevant to their current situation. For decades Coca-Cola's growth was well served by a simple purpose: to put a bottle or can of Coke within arm's reach of everyone in the world. This objective has been largely achieved and does not serve to generate growth ideas the way it once did.

How do you know if people in an organization share a common overriding purpose? The two best clues are:

1. Most people's attention is not fixated on the usual annoyances and internal irritations that plague every business.
2. All parts of the organization adjust rapidly to outside events that either threaten the business or offer a way to accelerate its progress.

Goals Are Beacons, Not Blinders

Make sure that the goal you choose takes you somewhere you are excited about being—somewhere you intrinsically want to be, not a place that fear drives you to. Picking a goal means picking a motivator. You can't excite others about something that doesn't excite you. Make the payoff inspiring. Fixer goals seldom are—they are too rear-view-mirror oriented: how to keep what you have, or how to get back to a point where things were thought to have been better. A good grower goal, in contrast, should evoke images and create expectations of new things to come. It is something that a grower can see. It is something personal, wanted so much that it can almost be tasted.

Choosing a goal also means picking a new master. Bryan Smith of Innovation Associates likes to describe the "custodial" sense that commitment to a goal can evoke: You become a servant to the goal you have chosen.[4] If you find yourself in servitude to your goal, just be sure it is voluntary servitude.

Being committed to a goal is not the same as being blinded by it. If you become too attached to the result you are seeking, you are likely to miss the point when, as a result of changed circumstances, the goal is no longer serving the purpose of growth. That is when it becomes a millstone, not a beacon. A goal is a tool to keep you on track to achieve your purpose. Its "why" is as important as its "what."

Goals are the wedge that can break the inertia of the present. They give you a way to identify with what could be the future. They enable you to do battle with entropy, the tendency for the status quo to get worse unless energy is added to it. A good growth goal generates energy when it is articulated.

FIXER GOALS AND GROWER GOALS

Fixer goals arise from necessities, grower goals from desires. A fixer may carefully design a product that is in accord with existing customer tastes and preferences. A grower, when deciding what to do, will also keep in mind that these preferences and tastes are not static and can be influenced by the grower's actions. Growers shape new ideas, fixers respond to old ones. Growers are active, fixers reactive.

Fixer goals are reductionist in nature. They beget schedules, budgets, and PERT charts. These are useful aids to getting things done, but they are not necessarily the best tools to use when the objective is to move beyond the existing limits of your situation. Grower goals are intended to offer a direction that makes the choice of the next step to take clearer and easier. Sequence and priority are their by-products.

Roger Conner and the Search for Common Ground

Fixer goals are rooted in negative emotions, grower goals in positive ones. Sometimes the distinction is clearest in the arena of social activism. Roger Conner was described in Chapter 3 as a person who is working hard to move activism beyond the limits that have defined it. Conner once described himself as a passionate advocate for causes he believes in: "I fight evil and do good." And he has a résumé to prove it. A public-interest lawyer since graduating from University of Michigan Law School, he has fought oil drilling in environmentally sensitive areas. He has started and led activist groups that dealt with issues ranging from shutting down street drug markets to immigration reform.

Then he changed. He realized that, in a country increasingly polarized by Red/Blue gridlock, being a passionate crusader often serves only to strengthen the resolve of those on the other side. You may win a few, but the gains are seldom sustainable and always in jeopardy. So he joined Search for Common Ground, an organization that operates in 14 countries to transform the way the world deals with conflict: away from adversarial approaches and toward cooperative solutions. As the head of the organization's programs in the United States, Conner traded in his "fighter of evil" job description, but he kept his zeal and intensity.

Conner's goal changed from winning to transforming. Now he assists community groups in shifting win-lose struggles into game-changing goals shared by both sides. He has brought together groups as divergent as the Southern Baptist Convention and the American Civil Liberties Union to find points of common interest regarding ways in which religious organizations could assist in solving social problems. He found roles for both district attorneys and public defenders in cooperating to ease the reentry of released convicts into their communities. He wants a search for win-win outcomes to be the first reaction when a dispute arises, not the last resort considered only after each side has bloodied and exhausted the other.

What Conner has done, both in his career shift and in his current work, is to use educational techniques that draw on the positive emotions of the grower mindset. They help conflicting parties to better understand each other, rather than assume the worst, and to use this as a basis for finding a direction in which they can move forward together. His new role as a mediator and trusted intermediary has changed (grown) his perspective about what happens in situations of conflict. Conner observes that people often choose their strategy based on what they think is the strategy of the other side. But, most of the time, they are wrong in how they perceive their opponent. They tend to see the other side as more of an enemy and more eager to use force than it really is. Negative emotions of fear, anger, and distrust predominate. These cause overreactions, escalating the conflict and making it harder to resolve differences. By shifting both parties' attention to the positive outcomes that each wants, Conner also shifts their mindsets toward those of the grower. The positive emotions of aspiration, hope, and optimism that he helps bring into play defuse some of the conflict and create an atmosphere that is more open to compromise and alliance building.

Robert Levering and the 100 Best Places to Work

Robert Levering, the man behind the annual *Fortune* lists of the 100 Best Companies to Work For, is another good illustration of the power to be gained by shifting from negative (fixer) to positive (grower) goals. Levering, an active Quaker and a graduate of Swarthmore College and Martin Luther King School of Social Change, has always been concerned with social inequities. Early in his career, he worked as a journalist in San Francisco, writing about labor and business issues. The orientation of the newspaper writer, especially the investigative reporter, is often that of the fixer. Bad news sells newspapers; exposing inequities arouses anger and disgust, and sometimes may force change. Levering decided to take a different tack. Even though his personal experience and research told him that most workplaces were bad places to work, full of alienation and humiliation, and were reservoirs of wasted talent and energy, he realized that there might be limits to how much good would come from writing muckraking stories about these obvious realities.

Instead, Levering took the stance of the grower and set out to try to drive away the bad with the good. He invented an incentive, and a reward, to encourage companies to behave the way he felt they should.

Levering began by seeking out American companies that had gone against what seemed to be the grain and created positive working environments where people thrived and felt genuinely happy about their employment. His objective was to celebrate the right-doers, not to catch the laggards. This has led Levering to write several books about the best places to work as well as preparing the annual *Fortune* workplace scorecard.

Getting on Levering's list has become the goal of many corporate human resource departments, and most companies that do make the 100 Best list feature that recognition prominently in their recruiting efforts. His definition of a great place to work is one in which employees trust the people they work for, have pride in what they do, and enjoy the people they work with.[5] His contribution was inventing ways to measure these "soft" dimensions of a workplace. All of these, not surprisingly, are the kinds of attributes that a grower would aim for and are rooted in evoking positive emotions.

THE WRONG KINDS OF GOALS

Grower goals differ in many ways from the kinds of goals that serve other purposes. To illustrate some of the key differences, here are some characteristics that grower goals avoid:

Too many. Growers do best when they are facing one overriding goal at a time. Multiple targets, triple bottom lines, and balanced scorecards can be great tools for fixers, but growers need a sharper focus.

Too vague. Before her ouster from Hewlett-Packard, CEO Carly Fiorina would continually speak about her ambition for HP: to become the "world's leading technology company."[6] She never specified what company currently had that mantle, the company that HP was supposed to surpass. Nor did she define any attributes of such a company, or any milestones that would need to be passed on the way to achieving that title. However, for all her failings as a growth leader, at least Fiorina did not succumb to the most common growth platitude: "taking this company to the next level."

Too specific. Committing to making so much money by such-and-such date is fine for an annual budget, but it provides none of the wiggle room needed for a growth initiative that is taking the company into uncharted waters. Too many specifics in a goal can also provide opponents with details to latch on to and use to disparage the entire objective.

Too soon. Goals that are to be achieved in the next year or two do not allow enough time for multiple ways of achieving the goals to be tried, or missteps to be rebounded from.

Too distant. Objectives beyond five or six years from today may be made irrelevant well before their hoped-for achievement.

Too sterile. While every automaker has a comprehensive set of quantified performance targets, very few of these leap off the pages on which they are printed. Output goals like productivity, profits, or return on assets lack charisma. They do not offer easy ways for people to identify with them. A Japanese car company avoided this problem by supplementing its numbers with a two-word statement of intention. This goal focused everyone's attention on exactly what most needed to be done: "Beat Benz."

Too negative. "Beat Benz" may have worked for that automaker, but "Be the next Benz" or "Be better than Benz" might have done even more for it. For growers, goals that emphasize widely held common values usually trump more negative ones.

Too defensive. Growth is about advancement, moving forward. Fixer goals are often about survival—how to keep from losing what you have. "Not losing" is a hard goal to accomplish; when is it really finished? Survival is important, but it is not growth.

Too tactical. Implementing a new process, system, or technique may be a worthy task, but it is not a growth goal. The goal is the "what" that the tactic is to deliver, not the "how." Measure the effectiveness of philanthropy by the results achieved, not the amount of money donated. This is something that is often lost when considerable effort and ingenuity need to go into the "how." NASA learned this when its once-routine space shuttle missions seemed to be undertaken just because they could be, rather than to advance any plan for space exploration. Some observers have said that the shuttle's goal has become keeping Americans in orbit, making the effort more of a *place* program than a space program.[7]

Too rigid. Growers believe that the world is fundamentally open and subject to unexpected change. For them, goals are tools to use to enhance their ability to adapt to new circumstances, not walls that box them in.

Too cute. The purpose of a goal is to stimulate thought and action, not to serve as a motto for memo pads, coffee mugs, wall plaques, or desktop mementos. Companies that use these goal gimmicks in hopes that they will reinforce behaviors usually mean well, but usually find them poor substitutes for real growth goals that people have internalized and made a personal commitment to.

Too personal. Even growers who are the first to initiate a goal know that it may have a greater chance of happening if it is not seen as exclusively "their" objective. So they orchestrate ways in which others may be seen as having proposed it or can become identified with it.

Too public. Some goals, initially at least, are best left unarticulated, as the experiences of the Green Bay Packers, Lufthansa, and Canon that follow illustrate.

HOW GROWERS USE GOALS

Growers will often evolve their goals to fit the stage of development of their initiative, along the lines that Vince Lombardi used when he became head coach of the underperforming Green Bay Packers.[8] Rather than starting off with a bold "stretch" objective, he announced only that the job of the team was to be a "winner." This was a broad, positive-sounding aspiration. It appealed to the players, fans, and owners, but it did not raise any false hopes. Since the team's record until then had characterized it as a "loser," Lombardi was offering change in the direction of getting better. He then worked intensively with the players on the basics of football (running, blocking, and tackling) and set a series of increasingly rigorous step-by-step improvement goals for each skill. Achievement of these heightened the players' confidence.

Then Lombardi focused them on achieving their first preseason victory, then their next. He waited until the team had achieved a string of victories in regular-season play before announcing the next objective—winning an NFL championship, which in due course they did. Had Lombardi started off announcing his aspiration to be league champions, the aim would have been dismissed as unreal, and this lofty goal would have cast a shadow on what was otherwise a good plan for methodical re-building.

Lufthansa's Business School

Football is an American sport, but using goals progressively is an inter-national pastime. When Thomas Sattelberger left Daimler-Benz in 1994 to head the human resources function at Lufthansa, he brought with him a dream: to create the Lufthansa School of Business, Germany's first corporate university.[9] He could not have picked a bleaker time for such a lofty plan. Lufthansa was still in transition from a state-run airline to a private-sector business. Many of its basic human resources processes were outdated, inefficient, and error-ridden. A companywide cost cutting program was in place that required every department to reduce expendi-tures by 4 percent each year for the next five years.

Sattelberger quickly sized up the situation, realized that he had best keep his dream to himself, and began the work of work of reorganizing the broken HR processes. He never abandoned his overall plan; instead, he positioned, in his mind at least, the necessary fixer tasks in front of him as creating the foundation on which the Lufthansa university would be built. This motivated him to tackle them, not as ends unto themselves, but as steps toward his ultimate goal. He then used the credibility gained from his improvement projects to start a series of individual projects and programs, each aimed at creating what he thought of as the pillars of his university. He presented these learning initiatives as stand-alone efforts, not as part of a grand design, and sought approval for them one by one.

One project involved systematically emulating best practices from leading companies like General Electric and Deutsche Bank. Another was a popular program that provided a forum for managers from across Lufthansa's ranks to learn from one another, and a third was a more traditional training program for newly appointed managers. Like Bill Greenwood and his intermodal team within the Burlington Northern Railroad (Chapter 4), Sattelberger had to be creative in how he found funding for these projects. At one point he persuaded his boss to allow him to rent out some of the training rooms he built to other companies as a way to cover Lufthansa's costs.

By 1998 many of the elements of his plan were in place. Sattelberger then learned that his former employer, Daimler-Benz, had decided to start its own university. Taking this news to Lufthansa's top management and taking advantage of its desire to be seen as Germany's best-managed corporation, he obtained quick approval to announce the immediate establishment of the Lufthansa School of Business, Germany's (and Europe's) first corporate university.

Since then, the Lufthansa School has gone on to offer master's-level and nondegree management courses, and has partnered with leading academic institutions worldwide. It has also proved to be a key driver of culture change in the airline's privatization campaign. Throughout the four years, Sattelberger coped with many setbacks and delays, but he never lost sight of his objective. He patiently bided his time, incrementally crafting the university's key elements and letting each small success serve as the platform for what was to come next. And, most important, he avoided giving others the opportunity to veto his dream as something that was impossible at a time of financial retrenchment by not presenting it in its entirety until it was a fait accompli.

Canon vs. Xerox

At Canon, in Tokyo, secrecy also played a key role in a major growth initiative, but in this case the object was to keep Canon's intentions from its competitor, not its executives.[10] Canon's top management aspired to move beyond the company's traditional role as a camera company. Office equipment was an attractive market segment, but both IBM and Kodak had tried to challenge Xerox's dominance of the copying business in the 1970s and had failed. A decade later, Canon succeeded by quietly reinventing, piece by piece, the rules of the game.

Canon started by challenging its engineers to design a small, inexpensive copier suitable for the home market, an area that was of minimal interest to Xerox. The engineers quickly found that it was impossible to just make a cheaper version of the traditional machine, so they reinvented the copier by developing a disposable cartridge to do the work of the complex image-transfer hardware in traditional copiers. Canon then introduced the first models in Japan and Europe, markets that were off Xerox's radar screen.

When Canon felt ready to take its product line to North America, it deliberately avoided the moves IBM and Kodak had made to match Xerox's large sales force, nationwide service force, and large leasing company. Instead Canon sold (not rented) small (not big) machines directly to the people who used them (not the heads of corporate duplicating fiefdoms). Its redesigned machines were so reliable that minimal maintenance was required, and the machines were distributed through independent office products dealers, not an army of Canon salespeople. Canon's stealth approach surprised and, for a time, paralyzed Xerox in a market it had once owned. By the time its competitor responded, Canon had won a reasonable share of the lucrative U.S. copying machine business and had clearly established itself as more than a photography company.

Timing Really Matters

Growers can do well by imitating Canon's search for back doors, Sattelberger's willingness to play the role of fixer as a way toward his grower goal, and Lombardi's use of progressively expanding objectives. While it is always important to know what you ultimately want to have happen, signaling all your intentions at the outset of your efforts can be counterproductive. Depending on the grower's situation, some goals are best announced, not in advance, but in the wake of their accomplishment. And there are some goals, like Bruce Aylward's interim target for the polio campaign ("have things far enough along by the end of 2000 that it will be impossible for the sponsors to turn back and curtail the effort"), that it may make sense never to make public.

Within a short period of time in the 1960s, Boeing lost both a major competition to build the giant C-5A cargo plane for the Air Force and the opportunity to develop the first American supersonic transport. Within weeks, the Boeing management announced that it would, using its own financial resources, go ahead with a plan to build the jumbo jet itself and sell it to commercial airlines to haul passengers and freight. From that day forward, the devastated morale of Boeing's plane designers and engineers soared, and in a decade the plane they created, the 747, became one of the industry's greatest commercial successes.

Goals Bring Unintended Consequences

Growers use goals carefully and sparingly. They know that announcing objectives can instantly centralize an organization.[11] Once the destination is made public, colleagues and subordinates know that certain issues are closed for discussion and that whatever thoughts they might have about alternative courses of action have become irrelevant. Ironically, some growers find that they have to resist requests to set goals because they know that if these requests are granted, it will reduce the freedom and initiative of the requesters, people the grower needs to depend on to be aware and adaptable.

Goals attract supporters. They also crystallize opposition. Sometimes they provide the focal point for otherwise fragmented opponents to organize around. Many growth initiatives have failed because the grower-in-charge became so identified with the nobility of his cause that he failed to take into account the reactions that others around him might have to it. Building step-by-step consensus around aspects of a plan may seem tedious, but successful growers have learned to move in a tortoise-like manner when the situation calls for it.

Polio was far from WHO's top priority when Aylward joined the eradication initiative in 1996. At that time, the project was buried in the bureaucracy concerned with all infectious diseases. Rather than expending energy fighting these other focal points within his organization, and possibly turning them into an unintended countercoalition, Aylward spent time cultivating the support of influential outsiders such as Bill Gates, UNICEF, and Ted Turner. Their enthusiasm and financial backing eventually made it possible to move Aylward's group out from the other operating units and have it report directly to Lee Jong-Wook, the WHO director-general.

James Brian Quinn, a professor emeritus at Dartmouth College, has studied how effective managers really use goals. He finds that very few follow the conventional textbook wisdom about clearly announcing specific targets in advance. Instead, the few goals that they, and most growers, will announce tend:

- To be either reflective of or contributing to building an evolving consensus about where the organization should be going

- To be sufficiently broad in concept to allow a lot of flexibility and opportunism
- To be sufficiently far away in time that several alternatives are available to ensure their achievement[12]

FINDING YOUR GOAL

Sometimes knowing what you want is not as easy as it sounds. Most fixer goals are imposed on us, either by circumstances or by the hierarchy in which we live. Growth goals are different. They are things we want. We have to make them up ourselves.

The best way to find a goal is to look backward from the future. Otherwise you fall into the trap of just making incremental improvements on whatever is today's baseline.

Many growers have discovered a useful technique to help them tease out what they most want from the openings and opportunities that they sense are available. Imagine that it is three or four years from now. Your growth initiative has begun to bear fruit, and you are starting to receive plaudits for all your hard work. A writer from *Fortune* (or *BusinessWeek*, the *Economist*, or whatever makes the most sense for what you hope to accomplish) has just interviewed you and your team. A three-page cover story about the initiative soon appears.

What will it say?

For what accomplishment will you receive acclaim?

What kind of a difference did what you accomplished make?

How will the article describe the steps, and the missteps, that were taken?

This is a good exercise to do with your teammates, first individually, and then as something to circulate and discuss among yourselves. Look for the common "what I want to happen" themes that emerge. They are the raw material from which a good goal can be crafted.

Without a growth goal, it is hard to focus and easy to be distracted. Having a goal means always having a source of immediate feedback—as long as you are willing to tell the truth about your current situation.

TELL THE TRUTH

> Most companies don't face reality very well.[1]
>
> —*Larry Bossidy*

TRUTH PROVIDES TRACTION

Growers are positive and upbeat about where they are going, and equally confident in their ability to get there, but they never allow this to blind them to the realities of their current situation. They know that it is hard to see how far they are from where they want to be if they do not have an accurate reading on where they stand. It is difficult to break out beyond the limits that define and constrain them if they do not know where those limits are, what they are made of, and why they are in the way.

Larry Bossidy, former chief executive of Honeywell, observed that most companies do a poor job of executing because they do not do a good job of facing reality. They put too a great premium on giving every event a positive interpretation. They believe their own PR. They live in fear of demotivating their sales force or spooking the stock market. Living in the world-as-you-wish-it-were can have some appeal, but the problem with life in the clouds is that it doesn't provide a good source of traction. That's why turnarounds are often very successful. For once, everyone is free to admit what the current state of the business is. Everyone has a common foundation of truth from which to move forward.

Without this reference point, growth goals are ephemeral aspirations, dangling somewhere out there, just beyond our reach.

Creating such a reference point was clothing retailer Gap Inc.'s objective when its annual report for 2000 began with these words to shareholders:

> Our performance in 2000 was disappointing. We failed to execute well and stay focused, missing opportunities to consistently serve our customers in what was—and continues to be—a challenging retail environment. As a result, we fell short of your expectations, and what we demand of ourselves.

This uncommon candor set the stage for many changes at Gap, which in turn resulted in a rebound of sales and profits. Ford is another company that is beginning to use the ability to face reality to spur its growth efforts. William Clay Ford, Ford's chairman, jolted the automobile industry by openly criticizing SUVs for polluting more than cars do, contributing to global warming, and being a menace to smaller vehicles on the roads they share.[2] He did this even though Ford had been the leading popularizer of sport utility vehicles, and even though a great deal of the company's profits came from their sale. Among William Ford's objectives was to challenge his engineers to design future SUVs that will not require customers to trade off having a fun vehicle with driving a vehicle that is clean and safe. This nudge paved the way for Ford's rapid development of the first gas-electric hybrid SUV.

Ford was probably also being mindful of a past growth initiative that was less well anchored in reality. The Ford Pinto was one of the hottest-selling subcompact cars of the 1970s. It was championed by then-Ford executive Lee Iacocca as a way to defend the small-car market from the rising tide of Japanese imports. Iacocca's goal for the Pinto was for it to be competitive by not weighing an ounce over 2,000 pounds or costing a cent over $2,000. Iacocca also required the car to be rushed into production in half the time that was usually necessary. When Ford engineers discovered a major flaw in the car's design that allowed its fuel system to rupture easily in a rear-end collision, they were discouraged from making modifications because the original goal specifications were considered beyond compromise. The car was originally a successful seller, but an increasing number of deaths and injuries from gas tank explosions eventually led to a public outcry. In 1978, 1.5 million Pintos were recalled to repair the gas tank design. Iacocca was fired a month after the recall.

When bad news is treated like it is radioactive, the future suffers. Radioactive substances can be hidden, but that does nothing to make them less dangerous. If bad news is not heard or is heard too late, face may be saved, but opportunities to turn it into good news are lost. Growth is about distortion, but what is distorted is the future, changing it from what it would have been had the grower not acted. This is very different from changing the baseline that the grower needs to calibrate progress.

This kind of truth telling is not the same as Sharon Watkin's whistleblowing at Enron or Seymour Hersh-style investigative reporting, although these can play a valuable role when normal self-correction mechanisms fail. Truth telling, as used here, is just about assembling some of the basic facts about the current situation of the business: How much of what is selling, and why? What do our activities really cost? Which activities are economically viable, and which are not? Why are customers really buying from us? Why do we have such an impressive list of noncustomers? How safe are our products? How in sync are they with emerging trends and value shifts? This is information that, on its face, does not sound like it should be all that difficult to compile. But in most organizations (especially those that have charged their accounting function with creating, not just documenting, profits), it is.

This problem is often most evident when things *just start to go bad.* What happens when sales drop after a long period of steady increases in revenue? The most common explanations offered are those that attribute the decline to temporary factors, conditions that are soon expected to change for the better. Alternative possibilities—the start of a cyclical downturn in the industry, a structural change in the market signaling a permanent drop in customer buying, the emergence of a tough new competitor, or an early warning that the current business model is not working and a new one needs to be created—are much more likely to be discounted than to be investigated. Why? What makes it so hard to investigate deviations from expectations, especially soon after they are spotted, when the maximum lead time is available to develop countermeasures and minimize damage to the business?

There are two major barriers to getting straight and useful answers to questions such as these. One is a set of beliefs and assumptions that is often deeply entrenched in many organizational cultures, even if these beliefs and assumptions contradict the values espoused by corporate leaders. The other obstacle to facing reality is even harder to deal with because it involves built-in features of the way our brains work. Let's look at each type, and then consider what options we have for ferreting out the truth of a situation in spite of them.

THE WAYS WE THINK CAN DISTORT REALITY

Many of the hurdles that keep us from seeing opportunities for growth (Chapter 5) also block our perception of current reality. To the extent that our mind is functioning as a big database, comparing each new input with what came before, we will see things in terms of what they are closest to from our past experience rather than what they actually are. These memories also evoke emotions, which can cloud our perceptions, especially if they are negative. If we are too busy reacting to all these internal experiences, we set ourselves up to miss a lot of what is really going on. This is why it is so hard to launch a growth initiative in an organization that is caught up in a struggle for its existence. The negative emotions accompanying the fixer mindset sharpen our focus, but only on the most threatening aspects of the situation. These are seldom the best ones from which to leverage growth efforts.

The best growth leaders are able to see the negative features of a situation clearly and, without denying the problems, provide others with a sense of hope and confidence. Denial, unfortunately, is practiced in the business world much more than it should be. Internal missteps are blamed on external factors. Rationalizations and justifications abound. People who once projected strength and independence begin to call themselves helpless victims. This is especially common when these people have allowed their past success to fuel excessive optimism. Circumstances may change, but the old mindset prevails. Optimism is a powerful driver of growth. It opens our eyes to new opportunities (Chapter 5), and it helps us rebound from temporary setbacks (Chapter 10). But, as with all strong medicines, the proper dosage is important lest side effects predominate.

Optimism is a useful explanatory style to cultivate. Optimists view bad events as temporary blips, limited in their impact and usually caused by external circumstances. This is a good way to approach life, but it is also important to know when to tone it down or turn it off. The "truth telling" part of the growth process is one of those times.

Mind Bugs

Just as software is prone to contain unwanted bugs, our brains have "mind bugs"[3] hardwired into their workings. Our brains are always busy, but not always in helpful ways, and often in ways that we are not consciously aware of. Here are some of the mind bugs that contribute to and are associated with excessive optimism. Many of these are recent discoveries from the new field of behavioral economics. Think of them as the occupational hazards of positive thinkers.

This is a long list.[4] It is intended to make you feel humble, because that is the best state of mind to be in when facing reality.

Misperceiving causes. We often make attribution errors, giving credit to our organization, or us, for good things that happen and attributing negative results to others or to external factors. These are obviously self-serving errors, although they will often happen automatically rather than through our intent.

Exaggerating our sense of control. We often think that we have more control over events than we actually have, and we discount the extent to which things really happen as a result of luck or chance. Risk is seen as a challenge to be managed with our skills. Few possibilities are seen as being beyond our control, so we generally underestimate the likelihood of things going wrong.

Fixating on the first thing that we hear. The first estimate we make becomes our reference point for any estimates that follow. Sellers start negotiations with as high a price as they dare, knowing that this will set the context for the offers that follow. Proposals for new projects tend to start out with assumptions that will make the best case for the endeavor, skewing further analyses toward the overoptimistic side. This irrational influence of the first information we receive is called anchoring, and it is one of the most common and powerful cognitive biases.

Defaulting to the status quo. We are drawn to reach conclusions that perpetuate current conditions. Our brain is most comfortable with what it is already comfortable with. We give more weight to information that confirms our beliefs and prejudices. We are more likely to hang on to losing shares of stock than to sell them and put the proceeds into a better investment. We are more willing to acquire new businesses than to sell off old ones (even though research shows that it is the seller who usually comes out ahead). We do not want to look stupid in the (less likely) event that the business we sold turns out to be a good buy for the purchaser.

Justifying past choices. Our current choices are often made to justify past ones. Sunk costs drive our actions (or nonactions) more than do promises of new opportunity. We are more likely to escalate our commitment to a flawed course of action than to admit that we originally made the wrong choice. We do this even when the initial decision was a good one at the time, but circumstances have since changed.

Not wanting to lose. We worry more about losing than about winning. We will be more willing to take a risky course of action to avoid losses than to take an equivalent risk to pursue the same gain.

Assuming that cause always immediately precedes effect. Sometimes this works, but when there is a time lag between stimulus and response, or when too many things are going on at once, our intuition fails us. We then assume that something made something else happen when it did not. This is how superstitions form.

Being impatient with ambiguity. Our mind wants things settled, even if we might benefit by taking more time to explore alternatives in depth. So it often imposes patterns or relationships on things that are not really connected. This is why we need to take great care when reasoning with analogies; many of the ones we develop intuitively do not stand up to close scrutiny. It takes a lot of conscious effort for us to be aware of fine distinctions.

Filtering out novelty. In addition to seeing things that are not there, we miss things that are. We put new perceptions into categories derived from our previous experiences, force-fitting the new into the old and frequently missing the details that make something different.

Making snap judgments. Reaching conclusions without resorting to conscious thought works only when the context is right. It usually isn't. Malcolm Gladwell wrote a wonderful book about this called *Blink.*

Having selective recall. We most readily remember facts and experiences that serve to support our assumptions. We often say: "I've heard only good things about . . ." when, if we think harder, we know that there is more to the story.

Making biased judgments. Evidence that is in accord with our assumptions gets quick acceptance, while contradictory facts are subjected to a much more rigorous, and usually prejudiced, evaluation. We readily question our critics' competence, and we willingly impute hostile motives to them.

Being poor judges of the future. We tend to misestimate how much better or worse things are going to be in the future. Despite our best guesses, the future tends to be more like the way things are today than we expect.

Spooking easily. We are overinfluenced by dramatic or traumatic events. We expect them to change everything. They usually don't. This happens because of our tendency to base predictions about the future on our memory of the past. Rare but catastrophic events make deeper impressions on our memories than more common occurrences.

Being overconfident estimators. On almost all subjects, we tend to be more confident about our estimates than our accuracy warrants. According to McKinsey consultant Charles Roxburgh, we would rather be precisely wrong than approximately right.

Being overcautious forecasters. When we are making very-high-stakes decisions, we compensate for our overoptimistic estimates by padding our estimates "just to be on the safe side." We use "worst-case" assumptions to protect us from things that are very unlikely to ever happen. These often add great costs to what we are doing, while providing psychological, not practical, benefits.

Deciding on what before why. We are action-oriented. We tend to subconsciously decide *what* we want to do before figuring out *why* we want to do it. We often use goals to rationalize our action preferences, rather than choose tactics based on the needs of our objectives.

Thinking that others think just like us. We tend to believe this. We are usually wrong.

Being blinded by our egos and our organizations. We make forecasts based on our capabilities and goals, but we neglect to factor in those of our adversaries, even though, upon reflection, we realize that they have capabilities and goals also. When we see a promising new opportunity, we seldom consider that others may be targeting the same one. We think of others as features of our environment or extensions of us, rather than assuming that they are autonomous entities with minds and wills of their own.

Wanting to get along. We frequently succumb to groupthink, the pressure to think the way others in our team, department, organization, or social class do.

Finding safety in numbers. We like being part of the herd. The only thing worse than making a huge mistake is being the only person to make that mistake.

Lest you feel too glum after reading all 21 of these (and wonder how civilization managed to get where it is with human brains so defectively wired), there is some good news. These mind bugs are all defaults. They tend to be employed when we think on autopilot. They can be turned off.

The first line of defense against common cognitive errors is being aware of them. When you are collecting information and interpretations about current reality, think about *how* you are thinking as well as *what* you are thinking about. Make a copy of this list of mind bugs. Put it somewhere where you will see it and review it regularly. Find an example from your own experience of each of the 21. Pass out this list to your colleagues and team members. Ask them for examples, also. Doing all this builds awareness and minimizes the likelihood that you will operate in default mode.

BELIEFS AND ASSUMPTIONS ALSO DISTORT REALITY

People who try to work around some of the distortions caused by these cognitive errors are sometimes unfairly labeled as pessimists, even though they may want the situation to advance as much as do the overly optimistic advocates. They just want to make sure that the forward movement is grounded in reality, not in misperception. In some organizations, expressions of pessimism are equated with disloyalty and are seen as career-limiting moves. Likewise, the bearers of bad news run the risk of becoming pariahs, with their statements of fact turned against them to question their motives.

Cognitive errors are not only the product of our minds. Faulty beliefs and assumptions can be pervasive throughout a business. Some organizational cultures also foster fact distortion. Places where "failure is not an option" and those that take a strong "can-do, get the job done" positive attitude, such as that held by the NASA management team responsible for the space shuttle *Columbia* disaster, ironically tend to filter out information that, if it were brought to the surface early, could help avoid failure. The NASA managers wanted the shuttle's skin not to have been damaged by the foam pelting it received at takeoff. They wanted this so much that they refused to attempt to confirm that a problem might exist. Their positiveness created an environment in which dissent not only was unwelcome, but was even thought unneeded because the organization saw itself as special and more knowledgeable than anyone else.[5] Success-based optimism replaced any collective curiosity about what the impact of the insulating foam hitting the shuttle wing might have been. When NASA engineers became concerned about possible damage to the *Columbia*, they were accused of being alarmist. One of them could not understand why his hierarchical superiors treated negative information like the plague; another feared for his job if he spoke up.

Behaviors like these can become deeply embedded in an organization and are strongly resistant to change. In 1986 the space shuttle *Challenger* also disintegrated in flight. That time it happened shortly after its launch, also killing all its crew. The presidential commission set up to investigate that accident found:

• NASA had a recurring technical problem that it did not fully understand, but it did not think the problem was important because it had never previously led to an accident.

- Concerns of junior NASA engineers were not communicated to senior managers in a timely manner.

- Engineers who did express initial concerns backed off because they did not have the kinds of proof that management wanted, and they feared retribution from their superiors if they persisted and were wrong.

Sadly, these findings are identical to those in the report of the board that investigated the loss of the *Columbia* 17 years later!

Harvard behavioral scientist Chris Argyris calls these examples of "skilled incompetence."[6] He is pessimistic about the ability of organizations in which it predominates to detect and correct errors that are threatening or embarrassing. Declaring failure "not an option" is counterproductive. Failure and mistakes are always possibilities in the real world. Organizations that pretend otherwise breed unwritten rules that tell people to hide mistakes, all the while acting as though that were not being done. Then they make the "hiding" something that is undiscussable. And, for good measure, they make the undiscussability also undiscussable. Argyris's analysis is pretty bleak, but this is the kind of territory that growers need to understand and find a way to work with.

What Truth Do You Want to Hear?

Just as NASA wanted the shuttle's skin to be undamaged, Pentagon planners wanted weapons of mass destruction to be found after the invasion of Iraq. Reality was on neither NASA's nor the Pentagon's side. Greg Thielmann, then director of the State Department office responsible for analyzing intelligence about weapons of mass destruction, called this a belief in faith-based intelligence.[7] He observed that during the buildup to the invasion of Iraq, the war planners had the attitude that they knew the answers and they wanted to see only intelligence that supported them. This quashed the integrity and spirit of honest inquiry in many of the information-gathering agencies, as their professionals felt that they had no choice but to deliver what was being asked for. In distortion-prone organizations, deciding whether to be influenced by a new piece of information is based more on how it will affect past beliefs than on whether it is actually true.

Warren Bennis, leadership expert and University of Southern California management professor, has observed that many corporations appear to fear truth more than they do competition.[8] He even found this fear prevalent when he was a consultant to the State Department. Junior foreign service officers, Bennis found, quickly decided not to tell their bosses what they learned in the field because they assumed that their bosses would not like what they had found. This was something they learned through the "hidden curriculum" that was passed on informally to new recruits from old hands. It was reinforced by the faith-based approach to intelligence that Thielmann observed. The practice escalated up the foreign service hierarchy, with the young officers' bosses feeling the same way about telling all they knew to their bosses. The net result: a system that was seemingly dedicated to maximizing its leaders' ignorance.

Fudging the Numbers

Early in his career at Burlington Northern, Bill Greenwood (whose efforts to turn truckers into railroad customers were described in Chapter 4) learned how senior executives' biases led to fact distortion, a lesson that eventually prepared him to effectively challenge his president's fear and loathing of the trucking industry. As a new recruit to the railroad in the mid-1960s, Greenwood was assigned to assist an outside consultant who had been hired to find out how much, in those pre-Amtrak days, it was costing the railroad to run its passenger trains. Actually, as Greenwood soon figured out, the real purpose of the consulting study was to make a case for requesting regulatory permission to eliminate the passenger service. Unlike many railroads of that era, Burlington Northern took pride in its passenger trains, the famed Zephyrs, and provided excellent service on them. Customers responded well to the clean stainless steel trains and their on-time service, frequently filling every seat that was offered for sale. But in 1965 a new president, Louis Menk, arrived. Previously the head of the Frisco Railroad, he had a reputation there for scuttling its passenger service, and everyone at Burlington Northern expected him to try to do the same there.[9]

Menk lived up to their expectations. When he arrived at Burlington Northern, he quickly sensed the pride that the managers felt in having a first-class passenger operation at a time when other railroads were ditching theirs. Knowing that they would be resistant to his plans, Menk did what many new CEOs do to rally support for a new way of doing things. He called in a consultant.

Young Greenwood spent the next six months working with Menk's adviser, a bald, bespectacled, heavy-set fellow with an intimidating manner and a doctorate in mathematical physics. Their bottom-up cost accounting study was originally planned to take several weeks, but the time period was continually extended because the numbers would not add up the way Menk wanted them to. Greenwood's job was to track down every conceivable cost that could be attributed to running the passenger trains. The consultant, an expert in statistical analysis, tutored him in every possible way to add in extra costs and to present the least favorable case for the passenger business. He knew that quantification was as much a matter of judgment as of measurement, and he also knew what kind of judgment his client expected. The task turned out to be a lot like trying to pick up a handful of Jell-O—one useful fact would be found at the same time another slipped away.

In the end, the analysis showed that Burlington Northern was making millions of dollars in profit by carrying passengers, and that no case could be made for applying for permission to get out of that business. Menk refused to believe the results. They contradicted everything he "knew" was true from his past experience. Seeing that he was not getting anywhere with the cost study, he transferred the manager responsible for the highly successful passenger marketing effort to a similar position on the freight side of the business. He hoped that without the manager's ardent work selling seats, revenue would decline. Feeling that he was being punished for doing his job too well, the manager resigned instead.

Menk went to great lengths to tell people that he had no sentimental attachment to passenger trains. He maintained that he was a businessman, and businesspeople see things objectively, not emotionally. They just do not like to see things lose money, he maintained. Of course, the truth was that the trains were making money. Menk was trying to relive his defining moment at his previous job, even if it made no economic sense in his current one.

Who was the consultant who taught Greenwood so much about the relativity of numbers and the irrationality of some executives? This was a person who was relatively unknown then in the United States because he had spent most of the previous decade working in Japan. There W. Edwards Deming was hailed as a master fixer and given a lot of the credit for that country's rapid economic boom, which was driven in large part by his gospel of statistical quality improvement. Deming's coaching was to serve Greenwood well later in his career as he put together an unshakable case for Burlington Northern's entering a new business that its then-president was dead set against.

Sugarcoating

Eventually the growth of jet plane travel and interstate highways demolished the economic basis for profitable passenger trains. Three decades after the Deming project, Menk declared with the benefit of hindsight: "You couldn't make money then, can't make money now, and won't make money ever on intercity passenger trains."[10] While his history may be a bit distorted, Menk had a better grasp of contemporary railroad economics than did most of the leaders of Amtrak, the government-established corporation that took over the operation of passenger trains from private railroads like Burlington Northern. For decades, Amtrak's presidents kept promising their funders in Congress that profitability was just around the corner. They kept releasing long-term projections showing that their trains could be self-supporting, all the while knowing that this was a near impossibility. These fictions continued, and Amtrak's economics and performance declined, until David Gunn, a grower with a knack for facing reality, was put in charge. Gunn's directness and candor convinced Congress to give him funds to ameliorate pressing performance problems. His reality-based proposals for creating a trust fund for passenger rail service along the lines of those used to subsidize highways and airports offered Amtrak its best hope ever for seeing a light at the end of its tunnel.

Telling people what you assume they want to hear is probably the most common way in which reality is deliberately distorted. Sometimes it is done for self-serving reasons. Jürgen Schrempp admitted that he dubbed Daimler-Benz's combination with Chrysler a "merger of equals" because he wanted the deal to go through, not because it characterized the kind of organization he planned to create.[11] Other times, telling this sort of fiction is done out of a feeling of dependency, assuming that if one is really straightforward with others, they will feel offended, will not buy in, and might even leave the team or the company. Or, even worse, if they have hierarchical power, they will ask the excessively direct person to go.

The common, but generally unwritten, rule of *getting along by going along* is a close companion of telling others what they want to hear. It substitutes harmony and loyalty for confrontation and candor. It also favors passivity over action, a behavior that is unlikely to move a situation forward. One underlying assumption of both of these rules is that talk does not have to be walked. Another is that people are fundamentally brittle, cannot take the punches, and prefer to be dealt with indirectly, and that any misgivings about them are things to be kept private.

Chris Argyris's research into the causes of learned ineffectiveness makes it clear that an overemphasis on being positive is clearly counterproductive. It overlooks the useful early warnings that negative information can provide—as long as it is faced up to, not buried. Argyris also asserts: "The emphasis on being positive condescendingly assumes that employees can only function in a cheerful world, even if the cheer is false."[12] This is a trap that Winston Churchill never fell into. He never thought that offering only "blood, toil, tears and sweat" would demotivate anyone. He knew that despair comes, not from bad news, but from the lack of a good plan to deal with it.

Subordinating Truth to Higher (and Lower) Objectives

Truth is sometimes crippled for understandable reasons. Canon never announced its intention of seizing a profitable chunk of the copier market to Xerox. Churchill never extended his candor to his enemies; instead, he authorized a massive deception campaign to keep knowledge of the Normandy invasion location away from the Germans. ("In wartime, truth is so precious that she should always be attended by a bodyguard of lies.") In both cases, reality was distorted in the service of a higher objective.

When the higher objective seems to have more to do with narrow self-preservation, distorters deserve less sympathy. Daniel Ellsberg, the whistle-blowing leaker of the Pentagon Papers during the Vietnam War, has criticized himself and many of his Department of Defense colleagues for succumbing to the get-along-by-going-along syndrome. Loyalty, not honesty, was the main measure of success for the planners of that ill-fated war. Ellsberg saw this tendency as coming from the top of the organization. In October 1966, Secretary of Defense Robert McNamara flew back to Washington after an inspection trip to Saigon. Throughout the long flight, he acknowledged in conversations with his colleagues how much worse the situation in Vietnam had really gotten. Then when the plane landed at Andrews Air Force Base in Washington, McNamara immediately went up to the microphones placed on the tarmac and spoke to the waiting reporters about the great progress the United States was making in every aspect of the war.[13]

The story of the Vietnam War is a long, sad tale of deception. In 1961, President Kennedy was pressured by many of his national security advisers to increase American involvement there. By the end of the year, he agreed to provide increased military assistance. The general he sent to lead the U.S. command in Saigon was a close friend of one of these advisers. Even though the general discovered many potential obstacles and setbacks, his loyalty to his friend kept him from reporting anything that would suggest that the U.S. role ought to be rethought.

Economic incentives, like the excessive use of stock options described in Chapter 2, can play a similar role in tempting people to distort reality, especially when reality is followed (too) closely every quarter. Pressures to meet stock analysts' quarterly projections can be immense and, if not resisted, can lead to a company's essentially outsourcing its strategic direction to Wall Street.

Mission Blinders

Some forms of truth distortion are less intentional, but just as pervasive. When an organization has a distinctive competence, it tends to interpret information in a way that implies that there is a continuing need for that competence. As the U.S. Forest Service became associated with preventing and putting out forest fires (Smokey the Bear), it became for many years resistant to the idea that controlled burning in forests could be beneficial and might actually reduce the damage caused by large, out-of-control fires. Any type of burning had become an anathema to the

Forest Service. It became so wrapped up in its fire-fighting work that it could not accept arguments or research data that suggested that fires could be a blessing in disguise. These ideas became undiscussable in the Forest Service, threats to the prevailing ideology that were never fully investigated by the service's research arm. Not until there was a public outcry, after a series of disastrous fires fed by accumulated undergrowth and debris that would have been eliminated had controlled burning been practiced, did the Forest Service change its policies.

Shooting the Messenger

Fear is one of the most persistent causes of accurate information not being brought out and thereby remaining unavailable to serve as a platform for growth. Unwritten rules of the kind described in this chapter combine to send a sharp warning to many truth tellers that bad things are likely to happen to bearers of bad news. Pleas to "not shoot the messenger" too often seem to have the opposite effect, so potential carriers of discordant information often lie low, and important facts that could guide action stay buried. Samuel Goldwyn, the famous Hollywood studio magnate, was once so frustrated with this behavior that he implored a subordinate to tell him "exactly what's wrong with me and with MGM even if it means losing your job."[14]

I would not have wanted to be the person telling Carly Fiorina that combining two bad personal computer businesses was only going to result in one big but still bad business for Hewlett-Packard. Or the one suggesting to Maurice Greenberg, patriarch of insurance giant American International Group, that something might be amiss as his company appeared to defy gravity by producing smooth and steady results for many years while operating in a highly volatile and cyclical industry. Ironically, there might have been a chance that both these, since dethroned, chief executives could have kept their jobs had they been able to face the realities of their situations. Both of these would be hard messenger assignments, but they pale in comparison to the challenges confronting some would-be growers who take on complex social problems.

In the mid-1960s, James Coleman from the University of Chicago did the largest social-science research study ever attempted up to that time. He used powerful statistical-analysis techniques to try to find the relationship between the level of funding that schools received and the educational achievement of their students. His study found that there was very little relationship: If more was spent, most kids would not do any better. What he found did matter was what kind of family the kids came from. Children from intact and better-off families did better.

This finding mirrored a report prepared a year earlier by Daniel Moynihan, an assistant secretary of labor in President Johnson's administration. Moynihan argued that removing legal barriers to equal opportunity for African Americans was not enough to enable them to fully participate in society. He said that for many blacks, poverty and the aftermath of slavery were responsible for the breakdown of the family structure, and widened the gap between the races.

When these studies were released, a firestorm of controversy ensued. Both men were accused of being tools of conservatives who were trying to cut spending on social programs. Some teachers' groups misinterpreted the findings, saying that they could not be held responsible for poorly achieving minority students if the real problems were with their families. Some civil rights leaders said that Moynihan and Coleman were putting up a smoke screen to slow down desegregation and antipoverty efforts, which was not at all their intention.

If we fast-forward 40 years, it is apparent that the problems these studies address have not gone away. But, fortunately, some solutions are beginning to emerge.

UMBC—Making Smart Cool

Freeman Hrabowski's business is selling educational opportunity. He heads the University of Maryland–Baltimore County campus. This is a school that, until he took over, was an undistinguished commuter branch of a large state educational system. That has all changed. Now UMBC is second only to Harvard College in the number of places at Harvard Medical School filled by its graduates. Hrabowski's school is also the leading producer of African Americans going on to earn Ph.D.'s in science, engineering, and math in the United States. UMBC recruits, and frequently enrolls, the same top high school students that are offered admission by MIT, Harvard, Johns Hopkins, and Yale. The school awards more chemistry and biochemistry degrees to African Americans than any other college in the United States.[15]

Hrabowski had a clear goal when he joined UMBC in 1987 as vice provost. At that time, he said, if visitors were to see a group of African American men walking across campus, they would most likely think: "There goes the basketball team." What he wanted was for them to, just as reasonably, assume that they were watching the chemistry honors society or the chess team. With the help of two Baltimore philanthropists, Robert and Jane Meyerhoff, he launched a program two years later that, within a decade, made this vision a reality.

The odds did not favor Hrabowski. Young black men were more likely to be murdered or imprisoned than to graduate from college. More were in jail than were in universities. Of those who did go on to college, math and science were the least popular majors. Although African Americans make up 12 percent of the population, they account for only 2 percent of the math, science, and engineering doctorates awarded. Half a century after the Supreme Court decision that officially ended racial separation in education, patterns of segregation continue for most black and Latino children. Many attend schools that are still, according to Hrabowski, underfunded, underachieving, and unequal. Even in wealthy school districts, he notes, the majority of black and Latino children lag dramatically behind their white classmates.

There are almost as many explanations now for what is behind this bleak situation as there were in the mid-1960s. Hrabowski did not want to get caught in the mire that limited the usefulness of the studies by Moynihan and Coleman. His goal was to do something: to create a new possibility for black males. So he zeroed in on two realities that seemed pivotal to the problem he wanted to address:

1. "It's not cool to be smart" was a prevailing attitude in the culture in which many African American young men lived.
2. Most traditionally taught college science and math curriculums seemed more oriented toward weeding out weak students than toward broadening the base of capable ones.

One of these observations was an indictment of prevailing practices in higher education, the other a criticism of popular culture. Hrabowski attacked each head-on. He turned UMBC into a place where it was very cool to be smart. This is a school without a football team. But it does have a world-class chess team, a frequent title winner at the Pan-American Chess Championships, the NCAA tournament for college chess players. Team members sport smart jackets. Cheerleaders, a marching band, and a smoke machine herald their accomplishments. Players are recruited away from Harvard and MIT with full and partial chess scholarships. For a smart chess player, life doesn't get much better.

It takes more than chess to attract math and science majors. Critical mass is important, too. So each year 50 students enter UMBC as Meyerhoff Scholars (out of 1,500 who apply). They all bond at a mandatory six-week summer boot camp before the freshman year officially starts. In addition to courses in science, math, and African American studies, they take a seminar in time management and start to study together in small groups, a practice that they will continue until graduation. From day one, the program staff emphasizes what comes next in their education: graduate school. Still fresh from their SATs, they are given detailed information about the GRE, graduate school entrance requirements, and a list of the top schools in their field. Keep in mind that this all happens before regular freshmen orientation. By the time their freshman year ends, all the Meyerhoff Scholars will have written the first draft of their graduate school application essay.

In addition to organizing people into study groups, UMBC finds other ways to create a sense of community among the students so that they all feel some responsibility for one another's progress. Sophomores are expected to help freshmen, seniors tutor juniors, and so on. Math and science, unlike many other subjects, are progressive. You have to master one week's work before you can do the next and become proficient in one subject before you can take the next. Most people who drop out do so because they fall behind and find it impossible to learn the current lesson. The UMBC support system watches everyone like a hawk, catching students before they can do any serious falling behind. The result: 95 percent graduate in their intended majors.

When Hrabowski greets each incoming freshman class, he reminds the students that when he was in their place, it was not unusual to hear the convocation speaker say, "Look to your left; look to your right; one of you will not graduate." At UMBC, he tells them, we prefer to say,

"Look to your left; look to your right; our goal is to make sure that all of you graduate." He tends to meet this goal, and in instances when it is not met, Hrabowski feels that this is an indication that he and his faculty are doing something wrong, not the students.

This blend of equally high emphasis on nurturing and academic achievement works. Unlike the situation at most American universities, at UMBC there is no academic achievement gap between minority and white students across all the disciplines taught. UMBC once compared the performance of its graduates with those of students who qualified for the program but decided to study elsewhere. It found that its Meyerhoff Scholars were twice as likely to graduate sticking with their original math, science, or engineering major and five times as likely to go to graduate school in their field. UMBC is free of the negative stereotyping and expectation of mediocrity that African American students still face elsewhere. This school has become a model for what is possible in terms of minority high academic achievement, and it is often swamped by visits from representatives of other universities, foundations, federal agencies, and companies. Hrabowski's program originally served African American males because that group had the greatest achievement gap. Now it is also open to women and students of all races.

A Bulletproof Messenger

The realities that Hrabowski chose to address were ones in which, unlike Coleman and Moynihan, his background immunized him from criticism. A math prodigy, he graduated from college with highest honors at 19 and received his Ph.D. in statistics and education at 24. He has excellent credentials to support his criticism of prevailing teaching methods.

His background also gave him the bona fides to point out dysfunctional aspects of the culture in which many young black males live. Hrabowski was the name of a Polish immigrant who became a plantation owner in Birmingham, Alabama. When he died, he left his land and his name to his slaves, one of whom was Freeman Hrabowski's ancestor. The Birmingham of the 1950s and 1960s, in which Hrabowski grew up, was ground zero for the civil rights movement. The year after he started elementary school, Rosa Parks's refusal to give up her seat on a Montgomery bus and move to the back sparked a decade of protests. Hrabowski was jailed at age 12 for protesting segregated education. A participant in the famous Children's March of 1963, he planned to go with several hundred others to the steps of city hall and pray. Just before arriving, they were stopped and arrested by the Birmingham police. Police commissioner "Bull" Conner personally singled out Hrabowski as one of the protest leaders and spit in his face as he was being hauled away. That was a hellish year in Birmingham. One of the four young girls killed then in the bombing of the Sixteenth Street Baptist Church was a classmate of Hrabowski's.

Freeman Hrabowski illustrates how growth starts with a razor-sharp focus on what needs to be different from what is now. His success shows how critical telling the truth about the current reality is if efforts to grow beyond it are to succeed. It is possible to be aware of and acknowledge all the complexities of a situation, and then select from among them the aspects that will provide the most traction to reach your growth goals. Hrabowski focused on two aspects of the situation of African American males, issues that he had great personal credibility to address, and used those as markers of what needed to be changed to reach his goal.

TECHNIQUES TO TEASE OUT AND CONVEY THE TRUTH

Telling the truth, like knowing where to look, puts a premium on the use of observational data, not judgmental interpretations. Judgments beget blame and rationalization, shaky bases from which to move forward. Growers focus on what is actually there. If they had a bad year, they say that they had a bad year, and they say what they are going to do differently in the next one. If they had a good year, they avoid becoming so caught up in self-congratulations that they fail to identify just what it is they are doing right (so that they can keep it up) and what they are doing wrong (so they can fix it). Most important, they don't minimize what's wrong just because it doesn't seem to be holding them back. Yet.

Searching for Truth

There are a wide variety of truth-seeking and truth-telling techniques that growers have found helpful. Here are some of the most useful practices for seeking the truth.

Pull the plug on PowerPoint. Not long after Louis Gerstner took over the top job at then-troubled IBM, he found himself sitting through countless meetings dominated by slide presentations about the state of the company's various businesses. It did not take him long to realize that the fancy graphics were masking more truth than they revealed. So he just stood up and unplugged a presenter's projector. He said that he had heard enough spin. Let's just talk about what's really going on in the company. Throughout IBM, this episode quickly became known as "the click that went around the world," a sound that marked the start of the company's reality-facing.[16]

Start with the last slide. Jim McCann, president of 1-800-FLOWERS, offers a variant on Gerstner's move.[17] McCann believes that the first sentence in a presentation should tell him what the last sentence does. So when people visit him to make a presentation, he asks if they have a summary slide. If they say yes, he insists that they start off with it. This also cuts out a lot of spin.

Listen to the voices of strangers. You are more likely to get the straight story from someone who is a stranger than from a person you have worked with for years, says Harvard Business School professor Michael Wheeler.[18]

Short-circuit the hierarchy. Think Shakespeare, *Henry V.* The night before the decisive battle of Agincourt, King Henry dresses in an officer's cloak and wanders among his soldiers, trying to get a fix on their morale and the likelihood of victory the next day. He got a much more accurate reading this way than if he had asked his officers.

Be wary of misguided loyalty. Some subordinates overly idealize their bosses. This tendency is intensified in time of danger and change. In trying to protect their leaders, and their images of them, they may filter out bad news that it would be useful to hear sooner rather than later. Self-deprecating leaders have less of this problem than narcissists. Humility begets more honesty than grandiosity. Treat flattery like chewing gum. Enjoy it. Just don't swallow it.[19]

Try cash. When candor completely breaks down, try cash. Offer a sizable cash bonus to the individual or team that comes up with the best argument against doing what you planned to do. Encourage competition among the contenders.

Use directly observable data. Procter & Gamble's Deborah Henretta (Chapter 3) did not need to pore over market research or focus group data. By setting up a diaper-testing center down the hall from her office at headquarters, she literally brought the consumers of her baby-care division's products into her day-to-day work life. It doesn't get more real than this.

Offer a limited amnesty. UNICEF's operations take place in difficult, and frequently dangerous, working conditions in some of the world's poorest countries. Local field offices often need to make creative adaptations to policies issued from headquarters in New York. Knowing when an adaptation is too creative is often a difficult judgment call. In the 1970s, auditors from headquarters visited each office once or twice a year to assess how well UNICEF's financial and operational rules were being implemented. The auditors, many of them with past experience working in field offices, knew that how they approached their work would determine how much effort the local staff would put into covering up deviations from official policy. So they worked hard to be seen as potential helpers, not just policemen. They told the local offices that, except in cases of outright fraud or corruption, they would not report departures from accepted practices as long as the departures were reported to (not discovered by) the auditors. The departures would then be openly discussed, and either the auditor would sanction the adaptation or both parties would agree that it would be corrected by the time of the next audit.

Assert and *be open to challenge.* Most of us are better at the first part of this. Tell people exactly what you think (so that they don't have to guess or fish around for it), and then, just as directly, let them know that this view is open for debate. Ask what others think. Make it easy for people to question what you are saying by laying out the assumptions behind each assertion. When discussing what you make of a situation, try to start from a common body of facts whose validity all those present accept. Science does not get ahead by making new discoveries; progress starts when old ones are disconfirmed. If you want to go for progress, you need to be open to challenge. After minds are made up, always ask:

"What fresh facts would cause you to revise or change your mind?"[20] Barry Diller, chief executive of the Internet company InterActiveCorp (Home Shopping Network, Ticketmaster, Expedia, LendingTree), has tried hard to foster this kind of culture of debate in his business. Diller says that he wants subordinates who will call him a fool and tell him he is wrong. One of them, Karl Peterson of Hotwire.com, thinks Diller has pulled this off, holding meetings where people are really interested in finding the right answer, not just affirming the one they came into the room with.[21]

Offer candor and respect. Bill Greenwood's business, railroading, is about as far from InterActiveCorp's as a business can be. But the behaviors he encouraged in his intermodal team (Chapter 4) run on the same tracks as Diller's. Issues that could not be easily resolved during the team's regular morning progress reviews were tabled until the next Sunday afternoon, when the whole group met at Greenwood's home to thrash things out. There was a lot of disagreement among team members; it comes with the territory when you try to do something you have never done before. But it was carried out in an atmosphere of self-respect and respect for one's teammates that Greenwood went to great lengths to encourage. The team members shared a goal: Get the new intermodal business up and running. This gave them a common reference point to use as they debated tactics. They faced a lot of hostility from many powerful people in the railroad, but they took care not to succumb to the bunker mentality and the data blinders that are usually associated with it.

Take time. Truth suffers when we feel pressured to make decisions too fast. Build some lag time into how you operate. I was a trustee of a Quaker school at the same time I served on the boards of two business corporations. Without question, the decision-making process of the school was much more effective than that of either business. Decisions in Friends' organizations are made by consensus, not by voting. It takes longer, but the decisions stick better. This school board also had a practice that after consensus had been reached, the decision would be automatically tabled for final resolution until the next meeting. General Motors, in its glory years under Alfred Sloan, operated this way at times also. At the end of one executive committee meeting, Sloan observed that all present seemed to be in complete agreement on an important matter. He then proposed postponing further discussion of the issue until their next meeting so that they would have adequate time to develop some disagreement among themselves. Sloan felt that the lack of such disagreement might be a warning that they really did not understand what the decision was all about.

Use advisers, not consultants. Advisers can provide an early warning about emerging problems, signals that are often missed by a consultant's sharp focus on eliminating the problem at hand. These are two very different roles. It's hard for one person—or firm—to act well in both capacities at the same time. Arthur Martinez, the CEO who led Sears's successful turnaround, had a reputation as one of industry's shrewdest users of outside professional help. He likes to call on consultants when Sears has a *clear-cut problem that is in need of solution.* But when he uses an outside adviser, Martinez has already thought through several possible solutions. The job of the adviser is to serve as an impartial sounding board, a sparring partner to help Martinez *test his ideas* and then *identify the pros and cons* of proposed courses of action. Consultants are problem solvers. They excel at developing and selling ideas, and they can be great simplifiers. Good advisers, though, often muddy the waters, leaving their clients with a new and often broader perspective. They are better problem definers than problem solvers. At their best, they contribute to strengthening their clients' capacity to solve their own problems.

Have a kitchen cabinet. If one adviser with a fresh perspective and new insights can help, imagine what a small group of them can do.

Have devil's advocates and court jesters. The gift of humor can make it much easier to convey some truths. So can putting someone in the role of devil's advocate, charged with arguing against the decision you are contemplating. Do not select the same person as devil's advocate all the time. Institutionalizing this role, as President Lyndon Johnson did with George Ball during the Vietnam War, undercuts its effectiveness.

Use multiple advocates. Some situations are more complicated to sort out than the back-and-forth with a single devil's advocate allows. If there are several possible interpretations or ways in which things might happen next, assign a person or a team to flesh out the logic of each. Then have the people or teams argue, courtroom style, for their position.

Try to learn from and synthesize all the viewpoints rather than pick a clear winner.

Don't give an anchor to your outsiders. If you make the answer you want to hear too obvious, you will be much more likely to hear it. We all like to give people what they want. Be careful not to ask leading questions that only invite confirmation of your beliefs.

Telling the Truth

The telling usually turns out to be a bigger problem than the finding of the truth. Here are some useful practices for telling the truth.

Fishbowl the findings. Rather than having an investigative task force present the results of a study that is likely to arouse controversy and defensiveness in the senior managers who need to hear about it, convene a fishbowl meeting. Place the task force members around a round table in the center of the room. Seat the senior executives in comfortable chairs along the walls. Let the task force discuss what it has done and found, making no final judgments or recommendations. Convey information through conversation and back-and-forth dialogue among the task force members, rather than with slides and bullet points. Allow the members to present differing points of view. The job of the executives is to sit quietly and take notes, with questions at the end for clarification only. Then, after the task force finishes, is thanked, and leaves, the senior executives debate among themselves what to make of what they have heard and what course of action should be taken. This is a helpful separation of roles: One group identifies what is, then the executives deal with what should be and how to get there.

Provide quotes, not interpretations. As a consultant I frequently had to present the results of organization studies to the senior executives who commissioned them. I would usually try to schedule an interim meeting with the clients when the project was nearing completion. Rather than start off with what I thought, I would present a series of disguised quotations from my interviews, arranged to illustrate key themes that had emerged. Then I would ask for their help in figuring out what was the meaning behind the quotations—an easy request, since they did not expect my personal recommendations at that point in the project. Since problems were identified in the words of those in the organization, I was seen less as the messenger of bad news.

If you are to be a person to whom the truth is willingly told, heed the advice just given and try some of these techniques. Know what the common cognitive errors that drive overoptimism are. Understand the facets of your corporate culture that are most likely to fuel spin and distortion. Let people know how much you value honest messengers. Actively seek out those who see the world differently from you. Figure out your most common defenses, and learn how to turn them off when they get in the way. Manage by results, not blame. And keep the classic injunction in mind: The truth will set you free—but first it is likely to make you really mad.

Realism Drives Decisions; Optimism Propels Action

This chapter has been about realism. For growers, telling (and being told) the truth about the current state of affairs in relation to where they want to go is essential. Otherwise there is no sound basis for selecting a course of action, and no way to measure progress once one has been chosen. I've purposely been hard on optimism here. Too much of it clouds judgment and good decision making. But growth involves much more than sound thinking. Growers must also use creative tension, win the support of others, generate momentum, and bounce back from adversity. These all involve knowing how to build enthusiasm for taking effective action, something that is best guided by optimism and mobilizing positive emotions.

8

CREATE TENSION TO GENERATE
FORWARD MOVEMENT

The role of a leader is to define reality and to give hope. [1]

—Kenneth Chenault

COGNITIVE DISSONANCE DRIVES CREATIVE TENSION

What happens when you hold two ideas in your mind that are inconsistent with each other? One might be an idea about how things are now, the other an idea about how you want them to be. A psychologist, Leon Festinger, invented the concept of *cognitive dissonance* to describe this situation.[2] It is one of the most influential theories in the field of social psychology. It says that our psyches don't like this dissonance and will work overtime to change one idea to make it more consistent with the other. Which is the most likely to change? The one that is most threatened is the one that is least attractive or desired. Festinger found that the existence of dissonance also encourages us to seek out others who agree that the idea we see as attractive is the one that should be established or maintained.

Growers have learned to take good advantage of this hard-wired human tendency, using it to move the world around them closer to where they want it to be. On the one hand, they articulate, at every opportunity they have, their growth goal. Then, in almost the same breath, they lay out what the current state of the business is in relation to the objective. It's the *tension in the gap* between the two, not the vision itself, that generates the energy to move forward.

Kenneth Chenault, American Express's CEO, sums up this dual thrust: "The role of a leader is to define reality and to give hope." Here's how things are today; here's how we want them to be tomorrow. Articulate this persistently enough and a *new context for activities* within the business is created. Fill the context with efforts focused on the growth goal, and eventually something has to give. Stay focused on the target by getting those around you excited about the benefits that will ensue, and ideas for ways to close the gap will emerge. If you can't get to where you want to be from where you are, change where you are, the current state of the business. Actions that influence forward movement are guided by what is wanted, but they are directed toward changing what is.

Dissonance theory lays out a way in which forward movement can happen. But it does not make it inevitable. The status quo, as most growers well know, is often very resistant to change. For some individuals, it may be very attractive, something that they feel is worth hanging on to. Growers overcome this by keeping their eye on their prize and by inventing creative approaches that destabilize the current reality.

Focus on the Gap, Not the Goal

Growers need both a goal and a sense of current reality. With only a goal, efforts are unconnected to reality and may fly around, unattached to what needs to change in order for the goal to be realized. If actions are rooted only in the current situation, however, it is easy to lose a sense of possibility and pursue only incremental changes. When all the focus is on current reality, the motivation for forward movement can dissipate when the flaws in the current situation are fixed, and growth is likely to stop. Growth occurs when people are pulled toward something new and desired, not just pushed away from what is present but unwanted.

When you want to *excite* people about what the future can be, focus them on your growth goal. When you want to *motivate* them to work to bring the future into reality, focus them on the gap between the goal and the current situation. Creative tension involves the gap, not the goal. Growers have to be willing to tolerate this discrepancy for as long as it takes to reach their goal. Not tolerating it leads to premature closure, usually in favor of what is easiest to make happen: continuing with the status quo.[3]

Much of the time and energy of growers is spent closing the gap. Its existence is more important than its magnitude. Fixating on the size of the gap may lead to despair and frenetic activities, not purposeful movement forward. Purposeful movement gets you closer to the goal; action just for the sake of action produces hit-or-miss results. It leads to diffuse, scattered activity, driven more by feelings of stress and anxiety about the discrepancy than by optimism and hope about the goal. This is the emotional terrain that the grower needs to navigate, steering toward positive emotions and away from worry, fear, and anxiety.

When you articulate the gap, you set the context for judging growth strategies. It is the nature of the gap that must drive the choice of tactics to close it. If the starting point becomes "what should we do" rather than "what's the result wanted, and what distance are we from it," means become confused with ends. Tactics and techniques take on lives of their own when they lack this breach-closing context. Instead, their application becomes the de facto objective. Execution is valued, but growth is lost.

CREATE A SENSE OF URGENCY

Urgency is one of the most effective drivers of forward movement. Articulating the gap and the goal defines a mission. If creative ideas about how to close the gap are to be generated, growers usually need to stimulate a sense of meaningful urgency about what needs to be done.

Urgency is a strong medicine, though, one whose dosage needs to be carefully calibrated. Too little, and nothing happens. Too much, and people are likely to feel overwhelmed and despair of ever reaching the goal. An excess of urgency usually means that negative emotions, especially fear, are predominant. Guilt and shame then take over as the primary motivators, and they usually provide weak support for the kinds of creative risk-taking that growth efforts require.

Time Pressure and Creativity

Recent research at Harvard Business School[4] offers some helpful advice for growers who are looking for the best way to use urgency. It finds that, in addition to being given in the right dosage, urgency needs to be accompanied by a certain set of working conditions if it is to really pay off. This research also confirms Barbara Fredrickson's idea (Chapter 4) that positive emotions have the ability to undo the harm of negative ones. The Harvard investigators, led by Teresa Amabile, looked closely at how several hundred employees in seven U.S. companies experienced time pressure as they worked on projects that demanded high levels of inventiveness. The employees' ability to think creatively when under significant time pressure was studied by sending them daily e-mail questionnaires throughout the course of their projects.

What the researchers learned explains why some people seem to do their most creative work under tight deadlines, while most people find that this kind of pressure produces only plodding productivity increases rather than real insight and creativity. Extreme time pressure leads to overwork and burnout when people feel as if they are on a treadmill and are experiencing:

- Constant distractions and workdays fragmented into many different activities
- Little control over their time and many last-minute changes in plans and schedules
- More time spent in meetings and group discussions than is available for collaborating one on one
- Little sense that what they are doing is especially important

On the other hand, it is possible to have identical intense deadline pressure and produce ingenious solutions and creative insights if some of these conditions are changed so that people see themselves being on a *mission*. These individuals feel that they:

- Are doing something important that they have bought into and that offers them a positive challenge
- Have better control of their time because they are allowed to focus on a single activity for a major portion of the day
- Have been freed from doing less-essential tasks
- Are able to set their agenda by working on issues they have identified as relevant to the mission, as well as those they have been assigned

Working conditions that allow a degree of control, autonomy, and protection from short-term distractions, according to Amabile's research, help convert urgency into creativity. Without these conditions, time pressures are likely to undermine, not spur, creative thinking.

A strong sense of being on a mission feeds the "got to make it happen" drive of the innovative grower. It also distinguishes the more discovery-oriented creativity of the less time-pressured academic and R&D lab researcher from the minimal creativity usually exhibited by individuals working on autopilot with neither a mission nor a difficult deadline. The job of a growth leader is to use goals and a sense of urgency to turn off these autopilots and treadmills. The sense of hope, optimism, and possibility conveyed by the grower can also, as Fredrickson has found, act as an antidote to the anxiety and fear that otherwise tend to accompany intense time pressure.

Speeding Up Science

Michael Milken has found that it is even possible to add urgency to the usually slow-paced, deadline-free discovery efforts of medical researchers. Milken is an experienced grower. Once one of the most powerful people on Wall Street, he invented the junk bond method of debt financing, a technique that moved traditional investment banking well beyond the limits that had once defined it. He also served 22 months in prison for breaching the limits of the securities laws related to insider trading. Milken is much more likely to be remembered, though, for his subsequent crusade to dramatically change the way in which cancer research is conducted.[5] A few days after Milken was released from prison, he had a routine physical exam and found that he had advanced prostate cancer. He was given less than 18 months to live.

Milken spent the next year beating his cancer into remission, and the next decade revolutionizing the business model for medical research. He created a foundation that is the world's largest private sponsor of prostate cancer research, and he used the strings he attached to its grants to create a completely different approach to funding and carrying out research. Before Milken, research on prostate cancer was a medical backwater, despite the disease's affecting one in six American men. With most research grants going to other diseases, studying this cancer was seen as a career-destroying move. What little money was available often took years to get into the hands of researchers and required hundreds and hundreds of pages of documentation for funding applications.

Milken's foundation took a different approach. It wanted to flood the field with fast cash, at the same time telling the medical research community that the foundation was most interested in sponsoring innovative and unconventional ideas. It asked for proposals for the things the researchers dreamed about doing, not the "safe" things that were known to be most easily fundable. It wanted ideas that could lead directly to new therapies rather than new theories. The application form was all of five pages long. Grants would be awarded within 90 days. And, most important, the researchers had to agree to work fast and present their results in a year's time—fast money in exchange for fast results.

This last requirement, going public with findings, was the most jarring to the medical establishment. It did not allow time to patent new compounds or submit articles to prestigious medical journals. Milken also controlled the presentation venue—his own annual prostate cancer scientific retreat at Lake Tahoe. Grantees would find their peers and colleagues, their scientific rivals, and drug company representatives in their audience, all waiting to grill them mercilessly about their findings, and then possibly steal their best ideas for further development. And they would have a similar opportunity to return the favor as they attended the other presentations.

Milken's insistence on rapid sharing of findings is key to his hope to accelerate the search for medical cures. He tries to pack each four-day annual gathering with just the right people, fill the agenda with back-to-back compelling presentations (often to standing-room-only audiences), and seed the sessions with Nobel Prize winners and leading nonscientific thought leaders—all in an effort to create a spirited sense of urgency. Each event becomes a marker of forward movement as Milken tries to get otherwise fiercely independent researchers to see themselves as part of a fast-paced relay race, rather than the solo long-distance scientific marathons that they are accustomed to running.

After a decade, results are coming in. Twenty-five percent fewer people have died from prostate cancer over the 10-year period. Milken's focus on results, mandated collaboration, and urgency has created a new model for medical research, one that is now being rapidly adopted by groups concerned with juvenile diabetes, cystic fibrosis, pancreatic cancer, Lou Gehrig's disease, and Parkinson's disease.[6]

When Milken began planning to attack prostate cancer, he thought about creating a "Manhattan Project" type of organization, bringing together the world's leading researchers under one roof. But upon further reflection, it was obvious to him that the bigness approach that had worked in the pressurized wartime atmosphere to create an atom bomb was the wrong model for encouraging aggressive entrepreneurial focus in a decentralized community of medical researchers. Bigger is not always better, Milken appears to have concluded.

Imposing a time frame on what was an amorphous set of minimally coordinated efforts is one way to instill urgency. Another is to encourage competition.

Competition

Toyota may have stumbled into the hybrid auto market when its efforts to develop competitive diesel cars did not succeed, but Ford's decision to develop its own gas-electric technology and China's automakers' attempts to copy Toyota technology are what will keep the Japanese car maker at the top of its game. Competition, especially in the early stages of a growth effort, begets creative tension.

Competition also can spur progress in knowledge creation. In 1990, a large-scale, multigovernment, public-private collaboration to map and sequence all the genes in the human genome began. Eight years later, with hundreds of highly qualified scientists mobilized on what they expected to be their life's work, 5 percent of the job was done. That was when J. Craig Venter set his own company, Celera Genomics, to use a faster computer-intensive technology to compete with the big ongoing effort. Venter announced completion of the human genome decoding only two years later. He used competition to spur discovery along the same lines that the double-helix structure of DNA was initially uncovered in the early 1950s in a race between a team of researchers led by James Watson and Francis Crick and another team headed by Linus Pauling. This intense rivalry undoubtedly induced each side to work harder to solve DNA's mysteries.

STARTING POINTS

How do growth efforts like these begin? Many of them start with a conversation, not a business plan. Growers discuss their goal and the distance between it and current reality widely. "Here's where we are. Here's where we ought to be. Do you have any ideas about how to close the gap?" they ask. The focus is on what is to be, leaving room for others to start thinking about how to get there. The idea here is not to lay out a detailed plan, but rather to solicit many views and get a new conversation about the business's future going. Hold off developing action steps, milestones, and assignments. Tolerate ambiguity and uncertainty for a while.

If you do this enough, and in an engaging way (focusing on the hopeful possibilities of what could be, not on negative grumbling about the present, which often monopolizes many current ongoing conversations), your presence itself may be all that is needed to trigger people's thoughts about what the business might become. This is a different way to be "in someone's face." Yale psychologist John Bargh calls this nonconscious goal pursuit; you can stimulate people's motivation without their even knowing that you have done so.[7] You make yourself into a lightning rod for ideas about the future. And by continuing to solicit their suggestions for next steps, you are likely to find that you have enlisted some supporters. Don't try to get them all to buy into some compelling vision. That is too grandiose a starting point. Settle for a willingness to toss in a few ideas and maybe take on responsibility for one or two start-up activities.

Dissatisfaction

Dissatisfaction with the status quo can be helpful at this point, depending on how intense it is. Dissatisfaction works along the same lines that urgency does. People who are content with things as they are aren't likely to propel change. Nor are those who are so deeply dissatisfied that they have become paralyzed with frustration, unable to do more than tell you all about what has not worked. It is those with more moderate anxiety about current conditions who will make the most effective early allies. They tend to have the greatest readiness to learn about new alternatives and the greatest readiness to change.[8]

Information from outside your organization that is related to the growth objective may have more credibility at this stage than anything you might do or say. External wisdom can help raise important questions about the appropriateness of maintaining the status quo. Al Bru of Frito-Lay did this when he invited two well-known health and fitness gurus, Dr. Kenneth Cooper and Dr. Dean Ornish, to participate in a cross-divisional nutritional summit that he organized. At the summit, Bru asked them what was the single biggest thing that Frito-Lay could do to improve the health of its consumers. They quickly answered: "Remove trans fats from the company's snacks." Bru announced, on the spot, that Frito-Lay would do so. And to reinforce his sense of urgency to the managers at the meeting, whom he looked to for an ongoing stream of ideas about improving the nutritional value of their products, Bru insisted that the reformulated Doritos and Tostidos be introduced without even bothering to test-market them.

Seek out ways to prod your organization, be it in the form of industry association studies, benchmarking and best-practices data, books, articles, consultant's reports, or outside speakers. Stage events likes Bru's summit. Find out which outside sources count the most with decision makers inside your company. Seed their ideas with key internal opinion leaders. Keep some distance from them also, when appropriate. Remember, you want to play the role of information connector, not carrier of bad news.

The hope here is to trigger a series of internal conversations that will ultimately establish a rationale for change and move some people from content and complacent to moderately anxious.[9] This, in turn, can create demand for some of the initial growth efforts you want to launch. Do not worry if the early conversations seem ill defined or ambiguous. The fact that they have happened can serve as a reference point for later actions. You are trying to create tension, not resolution, here.

Feedforward

You want the tension to resolve in favor of growing beyond your organization's current limits. Consultant Jon Katzenbach and executive coach Marshall Goldsmith have developed a technique that they call "feedforward" that might be helpful.[10] Their approach was developed for a different context (performance reviews and coaching), but there is no reason not to also use it for growth planning. It is a way to encourage people to spend time creating the future, rather than dwelling on the mistakes of the past or the muddle of the present. Katzenbach and Goldsmith note that many appraisal and coaching sessions dwell on reliving what someone did wrong, sometimes through a careful cataloguing of all instances when performance was not up to par. These are offered as "helpful feedback," the fixer's approach to encouraging improvement and change. This common approach, which relies on generating negative feelings of shame and guilt, leaves many growers cold.

Feedforward can actually cover much of the same ground as feedback, but its focus is more positive because it offers only ideas about what someone can do better in the future. This parallels the appreciative inquiry methodology discussed in Chapter 5. No critiquing or bringing up of the past is allowed. The dominant mood is one of hopeful optimism, not blame and regret. These same ground rules for dealing with individuals can also be used to guide a productive conversation about an organization and where it should go. When someone brings a problem to you, resist offering a quick solution. Instead, describe a way in which things could happen that would make the problem either go away or seem irrelevant.

What Will Have Been

Feedforward generates ideas about potential outcomes. The next step is to encourage people to think backward from these potential outcomes and specify what events would need to happen for that particular outcome to be created. This way of thinking, popularized by social psychologist Karl Weick, helps anchor those you are talking with in the future.[11] It implies conversing in the future perfect tense ("In three years we will have . . ."). Most planning usually begins by thinking of actions that will take from where you currently are, an approach that can crimp the imagination and is not necessarily guaranteed to lead to where you want to be going.

These are ways to avoid searching for the future by looking through a rearview mirror. This is the problem that constantly plagues commissions that are set up in the wake of major disasters—the 9/11 Commission, the panels that investigated the space shuttle disasters, and the post-Iraq invasion intelligence inquiry. These groups have dismal track records in guiding preparation for the future because they are so anchored in the traumas of the past. Many of their recommendations have a "closing the gate after the cow has already left the barnyard" quality to them, focusing on what should have been done to deal with past circumstances. Dealing with future challenges requires first an appreciation of what the future circumstances might be, rather than a projection of past ones.

Red Teaming

One way to help people break the lock of the past on their thinking about the future dwells more on the negative than most growth tactics do, but it can be a useful antidote to complacency. Called "red teaming," it attempts to simulate potential future threats that might not otherwise be apparent. This approach was developed by the U.S. government in the 1970s to test the security of computer systems and networks. Teams of experts ("ethical hackers") were asked to do their best to break into these systems, and then report how they did it and what vulnerabilities they found. More recently, red teams have been employed to probe for weak spots that terrorists might use to attack potential targets, such as nuclear power stations and government offices. Often "blue teams" are organized to defend the facilities, and the exercise becomes a simulated war game. Frequently the red teams win, although this is always a better way to learn of risks and weak spots than having them attacked in reality.

This can be a good exercise to use with people in your organization who are staunch supporters of the status quo. Designate the brightest and most creative of these people as your company's red team. Ask them to assume that it is three years hence and they are the leadership group of your business's toughest rival (or regulator). Have them figure out what steps to take to demolish your company's position in that future marketplace. Alternatively, ask them to assume that they represent an emerging trend (a demographic shift, a major about-face in consumer preferences, sky-high energy demand and prices, currency collapse, and so on) that presents a serious risk to the company over that same time frame. Let them prepare a pull-no-punches statement of the trend's impact on the business. Then later, after the air clears, return to your favored alternative for the future. Discuss how it might offer better resistance to these threats.

The objective of all these starting-point tactics is to create a state of nonequilibrium in your organization. It may not feel comfortable, but it is growth's best friend. By this point you have probably done enough to raise expectations, and are possibly personally on the hook to get something moving.

Don't Make an Elaborate Master Plan

It is surprising how little planning or analysis is needed before taking a first step toward a growth goal. Actually, according to the University of Michigan's Karl Weick, the less the better.[12] He finds most plans too specific, with their detail creating an illusion that the grower grasps everything that is going on and knows more than he or she actually does. To illustrate this, Weick delights in telling a story about a platoon of Hungarian soldiers that was lost in the Alps. The soldiers were in an area that they had never been in before, felt very disoriented, and started to panic. Then one soldier found a map in his pocket. They huddled around it, matching markings on the map to features of their terrain. Soon they were able to select a direction to travel and were able to find their way out of the mountains safely. Later, when the soldiers were back in their barracks, they reexamined the map that they had so successfully relied on. Upon close inspection, they found that it actually was a map of the Pyrenees, a mountain range between France and Spain over 400 miles from the Alps.

There are many lessons in this story. When you are confused, Weick maintains, almost any plan can help you discover what is going on and figure out what to do next. At the least, it will help you over a hurdle that is frequently worse than moving in the wrong direction—panicking and not moving at all. This is something that could have done these troops in, as they were not properly equipped to spend the night camping in the frigid Alps. When you need to initiate action in a realm of high uncertainty, sometimes the best advice is, as Weick says, to leap before looking. He turns around the traditional look-before-you-leap cautionary advice because sometimes the best way to get a sense of the reality of your surroundings is to try to change them a bit. This can get you to a point where the view is better.

Activity Cycles Drive Forward Movement

The idea here is to take a first step away from your current situation in the rough direction of your goal. Do not move too far, though. The idea at this stage is to learn what works and what does not work, not to shatter speed records for distance traveled. Act, see where it gets you, evaluate where you are, make any necessary adjustments, and then act again. With each move, if you keep the goal in mind, you will have changed the current reality a little, bending it in the direction you want it to go. Think of this as an ongoing cycle of activities, a cycle that spirals toward your target.[13] When skilled growers like Bruce Aylward of WHO's polio-eradication program (Chapter 6) look back on the route they took to achieve their objectives, they invariably find that it curves and circles around much more than it moves straight ahead. They also note that it is better to start out knowing that this is how things are likely to happen than to mistakenly feel like a failure halfway through.

Get Feedback Fast

Small steps make for rapid feedback (here we want feedback, not feed-forward). Missteps and mistakes are easy to correct if they are caught quickly. Risk is reduced. The growers who get in the most trouble are those who feel that they need to think everything through before doing anything. Weick has studied people with these tendencies. He finds that the difficulty they have in defining and refining their plans, without testing them, is that the world keeps changing on them. Their assumptions and hypotheses get further and further outdated and eventually become irrelevant. Long-range plans that do not lead to concrete changes within a few months of formulation tend to never have any effect at all.

Rapid feedback also pays another dividend. It sets the grower up to experience one of the most sought-after positive sensations: flow.[14] Flow is what happens when you are so immersed in a task that time stops. You are doing exactly what you most want to be doing. Flow comes from doing a challenging task that requires a measure of skill, one with clear goals and immediate feedback. It is not a common experience, but when it is present, it is a good sign that the grower is using creative tension just right.

Big, well-thought-out plans tend to be arguments in favor of a single course of action. They are things to be PERT-charted and implemented, not magnets to attract data that may disconfirm them. Growers, at least when starting out, will do better to have multiple plausible interpretations of what is going on. Each may suggest a different action to take; some may conflict with others. This is fine. Try some. The consequences of each action will let you know if it makes sense to move further in that direction, and this will help prune the list of possibilities.

A key to success here is to keep placing your actions in the context of the current realities of your organization, as well as in relation to the growth goal. The realities keep changing for many reasons, including the actions you are taking to modify the status quo. All of these need to be monitored and updated on a regular basis, because this is what defines the gap you will use to drive the next action. The usual tendency is to think about current reality as something rock solid, whereas a goal or vision is ephemeral and fluid. Growers know that the reverse is often more true. They see reality the way Weick does, not as something concrete and all black or white, but as a fluid entity that is half imagined and half created by the organizations that espouse it.[15]

THE SULLIVAN PRINCIPLES

Many successful business growers are masters at employing these kind of techniques—Andy Grove at Intel and Ryuzaburo Kaku of Canon are especially good examples. But the most skillful use I have seen of driving action forward through creative tension was that orchestrated by a former member of the General Motors board, Reverend Leon Sullivan.

Sullivan was pastor of Philadelphia's largest church. Like Freeman Hrabowski (Chapter 7), he had been active in civil rights activities since his youth. In the late 1950s, he led a "selective patronage" campaign to discourage consumers from doing business with Philadelphia firms that restricted or barred minority hiring. The drive was successful, but it soon became apparent that many African Americans lacked the basic job skills needed for the positions that the protests had now opened to them. Undaunted, Sullivan, with the help of local church congregations, pennies collected by school kids, and a second mortgage on his home, raised funds to open a job-training facility. Called the Opportunities Industrialization Center, its programs placed over 80 percent of their graduates in jobs. This success led to over a hundred centers being established throughout the United States and in 18 other countries.

Sullivan and South Africa

Sullivan's positive approach to change impressed General Motors' leadership, and in 1971 he became the first African American director of a major corporation. He was no quieter on the GM board about issues that concerned him than he was from his church pulpit, and soon Sullivan announced his support of an activist shareholder proposal that GM pull its operations out of South Africa to protest that country's apartheid policies. The idea of withdrawal was bitterly opposed by many in business, who felt that a company's role should be purely economic and that firms had no place advocating political or social change, especially outside their home country. The *Wall Street Journal* even editorialized against Sullivan, and some of his fellow board members went so far as to turn their backs on him each time he raised the issue of divestiture.

Sullivan obviously had different views about all this. In 1975 he flew to South Africa to inspect GM's operations there firsthand. GM, then America's largest corporation, was also South Africa's largest employer of blacks. Compared to those of many South African employers, GM's working conditions were laudable, and it was not until Sullivan tried to board his flight back to the United States that an idea crystallized. He was stopped at the gate by an armed guard, herded into a small room at the airport and strip-searched by a gun-brandishing police officer. He was the only passenger on his flight who was subjected to this uncommon (in pre-9/11 times) indignity. Sullivan felt humiliated as all his clothing and belongings were being pawed over, and his thoughts went back to the hostility he had felt decades before when he led sit-ins at segregated lunch counters in the United States. The officer doing the searching was embarrassed, and he told the GM director standing in front of him that he was only doing his job, only doing what he had to do. Sullivan smiled, looked back at him and said, "I understand." Then he told the guard that, when he got back home, he was going to do what he had to do, also.

A Code of Conduct with Teeth

What Sullivan did was to write a code of conduct for American companies. Sullivan's South Africa Statement of Principles was unlike many such codes, both then and now. It had teeth. He maintained that the only legitimate rationale for doing business in apartheid South Africa was to work hard to help bring about a peaceful end to that system. Sullivan set up a process that used creative tension to guide companies' efforts toward this end:

- Every company that signed these voluntary principles agreed to provide Sullivan with a detailed report each year on what it was doing to implement them.

- The financial and quantitative information in each report had to be certified as accurate by the company's auditor.

- Sullivan hired a large international management consulting firm, Arthur D. Little, Inc., to evaluate each company's activities and give each company an annual grade (A, C, or Fail) for its efforts.

- Some of the principles were graded on a pass/fail basis (provide a desegregated workplace, follow equal-employment practices, provide equal pay for equal work, and pay a minimum wage). A signatory failing any of these would fail for the year.

- The other principles were graded on a curve. These included training nonwhites for white-collar jobs, documenting nonwhites' advancement into supervisory and management positions, community development, and (eventually) political lobbying efforts. The ratings were adjusted based on the size of each company's operations in South Africa. Then the companies whose efforts that year, relative to those of the other signatories, placed them in the top tier of their peers were given an A (Making Good Progress). The second tier received a C (Making Progress), and the others a failing grade (Need to Become More Active).

- The ratings for each company were published annually. They received considerable publicity. They often formed the basis on which investors decided to sell shares, and activists targeted laggards for public pressure. Eventually the ratings were used as a basis for determining the eligibility of the U.S.-based parent company to compete for some public contracts.

Sullivan initially recruited a dozen companies to join the effort. These included some of America's largest and best-known companies: Citicorp, Ford, General Motors, IBM, and Mobil. By the mid-1980s, this number had grown to almost 200 signatories. The Sullivan Principles were essentially a pledge to violate many of the apartheid laws of the country in which the business operated. They required desegregated washroom and lunchroom facilities when both local custom and law did not allow that. They promoted nonwhites into jobs that these employees were not legally, at that time, allowed to hold because of a system of "job reservation" then in force. What the companies received in return was a seal of legitimacy for them to operate in South Africa at a time when many apartheid protesters were demanding that they leave. It also gave them an opportunity to do good.

Using Tension to Drive Progress

It was the grading of companies relative to the performance of the pack that caused the most discomfort for the signatories. They would have been much happier with fixed standards so that they would know how much money they would have to spend or how many people they would have to promote to receive a top grade. This is where the Sullivan-induced tension came in. The uncertainty it created caused many companies to increase their contributions annually and take more aggressive actions than they might otherwise have done. He made effective use of companies' skills in competition, although in this case they were competing for Sullivan ratings, not market share. For Sullivan, the goal was the peaceful end of apartheid, something that was hard to quantify in terms of the inputs needed to bring it about. But it was clear to Sullivan that the intensity of the effort needed to continually increase, something that the rating system was designed to accomplish. Each year's progress would change the current reality a bit and set a new baseline for the next year.

Sullivan avoided imposing a static code on a moving target. He knew that conditions in South Africa at that time were in considerable flux.

There were many possible outcomes, from an entrenchment of the white minority government and a tightening of the apartheid system to the establishment of a democratic, nonracially based South Africa. While Sullivan used broad and flexible language in his principles, the annual evaluations used very specific, often quantifiable measures that were adjusted upward each year to reflect the changing circumstances. The Sullivan requirements were phased in. One year a company might be asked to show signs of starting up or making progress in an area; in the next rating cycle or two, actual results would be required and measured. Learning was built into the system.

What Sullivan did that is still rare today in the implementation of codes of conduct was to use the mindset of the grower, not the fixer. He did not want to punish companies for being in South Africa; instead, he wanted to make use of that existing reality to promote positive change. His focus was progress, not compliance. Compliance is a rearview measure—meeting last year's standard. Progress focuses on efforts to achieve a goal in the future. Compliance is often a minimal effort aimed at avoiding punishment. Progress is forward movement toward something that is wanted.

Over the decade in which the principles were most active, Sullivan could also observe a measure of progress in many of the signatories as well. A number of the managers and executives who were most closely involved in the effort underwent a change of personal motivation. Initially they worked hard because they wanted to get a good rating; eventually they were working, often harder and more creatively, because they wanted an end to apartheid. A few of these were among the leading international bankers who helped the government of South Africa fund its economy. By the late 1980s, they became convinced that the existing political system was not viable, and they balked at further refinancing, one of the factors that helped convince President de Klerk to release Nelson Mandela from prison and begin the negotiations to dismantle apartheid and create an inclusive democracy.

* * *

Few growers find that they can do it all alone. They need partners and helpers, cheerleaders and approvers. The need these people's ideas and OKs, as well as their time and energy. The key to getting these, since real growth feeds on active commitment, not passive compliance, lies in knowing how to win their hearts and minds.

WIN HEARTS AND MINDS

An idea will not move from the fringes to the mainstream simply
because it is good; it must be skillfully marketed before it will actually
shift people's perceptions and behavior.[1]

—*David Bornstein, author of* How to Change the World

A new scientific truth does not triumph by convincing its opponents and making them
see the light, but rather because its opponents eventually die, and a new generation
grows up that is familiar with it.[2]

—*Max Planck, physicist*

ARE FORCE OR MANIPULATION THE ONLY OPTIONS?

Who is more right, Planck or Bornstein—"skillful marketing" or waiting
out the opposition? Most growers put a lot of time and energy into trying
to win supporters for their cause. Few have the patience, or the luxury
of time, that Planck counsels, although for some issues the physicist's
wisdom is the more realistic. Growers know that they do not have to win
everyone's approval, but winning the hearts and minds of a critical mass
is usually vital to their success.

Winning people over is not the same as getting their compliance.
The most common ways to get people to do what you want them to do
involve either force or manipulation (sticks or carrots). Force is not

socially acceptable in most organizations, although in today's downsizing-prone organizations, most employees do think twice before ignoring a direct request from their boss. Force can be mental as well as physical. Aggressive arguments delivered by a person with formal power are popular with some leaders. This tactic has been a key part of embattled Harvard University President Larry Summers's tool kit, although even he has begun to question its effectiveness: "Over time, I came to see that mutual interest was often a more important catalyst to agreement than compelling logic."[3]

Manipulation is subtler; carrots are usually more popular than sticks and are often sought after. There is also a large body of knowledge that builds on using psychological insights to gain control over people and trick them into doing what you want.[4] Used car salesmen and cult gurus have mastered these techniques over many years, and password-seeking computer hackers dub them "social engineering." They trade on common tendencies such as people's desires to be liked, to reciprocate other people's kind gestures, to defer to authority and follow others' leads, to follow through on public commitments, and to be reflexively trusting and willing to give others the benefit of the doubt—common qualities, but qualities that can be dangerous when thus manipulated. Kevin Mitnick, a masterful computer programmer who succumbed to the dark side, served a five-year sentence in a federal prison for his skill in this realm.

Neither manipulation nor coercion is a good option for growers seeking allies and supporters. Both are forms of control that are intended to elicit compliance. They are key parts of the fixer's arsenal. Their impact is usually temporary; they change short-term behaviors, not long-term mindsets. When the threat of punishment or the promise of reward ends, people tend to revert to their previous behaviors. This makes these tactics costly motivators. They are also mistargeted; it is usually the person responsible for their application, not those on the receiving end, who is most motivated. It is difficult to "control" people toward growth; the impulse to break through the limits that define a business is something that has to come from inside. This is more a matter of commitment than of compliance. Free will, not coercion, must drive it. Growth is about feeling personally able to influence the future, not just being a player in someone else's game.

EVERYTHING STARTS WITH THE GROWER

Start by being very clear about your own goals, values, and motivation. Don't ask others to be committed to a growth goal unless you are. The era of the self-promoting executive, the leader with a lust for aggrandizement, has left a cynical residue among many in business. Many successful growers are rewarded with career advancement. But if this is your primary objective, keep in mind that your potential supporters will grasp this fairly quickly. They may still support your endeavor, but they will most likely do so on a transactional basis: They support you, and, in turn, you are expected to support them. A lot of things get done very successfully this way, but it is seldom the way real growth happens. It is too easy for growth goals to become lost or subordinated to all the horse trading and deal making that accompany transactional leadership.

Humility and competence, a willingness to get your hands dirty and the ability to engender trust, are qualities that distinguish real growers from bubble merchants. Mindsets are contagious; the ideas, values, and beliefs of one person can be incorporated into the mindset of another if that other person wants to identify with you. It's hard, though, identifying with someone who obviously isn't walking the talk.

Fortunately, this is not a problem with most growers. Those around them see a grower as a person who has made an extraordinary commitment to bringing about a result that truly matters. This kind of commitment can have two different positive effects on people. Some will share the grower's enthusiasm and rationale. This is enough for them to willingly ally themselves with the grower's cause. Others will also join in, but for an additional reason.

Be Aware of the Effect You Are Having on Others

Followers often idealize their leaders. They see them as better than they really are. Some growth leaders are thought to be all-knowing. These leaders are readily given the benefit of the doubt when they stumble, and their followers often feel motivated to take on more risks than they might otherwise. Bonds of intense and unquestioning loyalties form. This type of "emotional glue" that binds people to a grower sounds nice, and it can be very functional as long as the idealizations are not too far removed from reality.[5] But this type of magnetism can easily get out of control, especially in the stressful times that accompany many growth initiatives. Most growers move things ahead by learning as they go. If they are also expected to walk on water, something may have to give, and it is usually the leader's credibility and the followers' morale as they face the inevitable disappointments caused by inflated expectations.

This sort of idealization is something that growers need to be aware and wary of, lest they suffer the negative consequences. Cultivating humility is a good defense against the grandiosity that can come from believing all your reviews. Resist the temptation to let your supporters create a myth about you that bears no relationship to fact. If the myth is allowed to persist, people will distort reality to protect you from unwelcome facts, and in so doing will take away just the feedback you may need to keep the growth effort on track. Michael Maccoby, a psychoanalyst who has studied this problem extensively, advocates insight and honesty as the best ways to ward off the dangers of overidealization that all growers are susceptible to. Know yourself, and find a few trusted advisers who are far removed from your growth initiative to keep you on an even keel. Be open with your teammates about your foibles; don't pretend to be something you are not. Keep people focused on the challenges ahead, not on you.

Also, select your supporters carefully. Choose them for reasons beyond their willingness to board your bandwagon. Pick people who are also able to get off if necessary. Strong growers ensure that their allies do not give up their capacities for independent judgment as the price of coming on board. The more committed you are, the more attractive you become to others. Keep your eyes open to the pros and cons of this. People align themselves with your growth goal by identifying with and attaching to you. This can put you in a situation of having considerable influence and power over others. Be careful not to abuse it. If you do, you will feel very powerful, but you will have lost the kind of mature support you really need from others.

BEGIN BY LISTENING

Walking your talk is important. Talk, though, may not be the best place to start. Few growers accomplish their aims alone, and many find that they have more success at converting skeptics to committed allies by listening, not talking. These growers know that it is possible for people to act in unison with others, even if they have significant disagreements with them, as long as they feel that their views have been heard and understood. So the grower's first step in winning support is often giving support through listening.

Hitting the Ground Running vs. Active Listening

Before Carly Fiorina's first day on the job as Hewlett-Packard's chief executive, she carefully did her homework, learning all she could about the company and its products and markets.[6] In her round of introductory meetings across HP, she took great pride in being able to field every question that was thrown at her. Fiorina thought her great store of knowledge would help reassure HP's employees that this new outsider really understood them and could be trusted to set the course for HP's future. Instead, the result was the opposite: People felt intimidated.

The back-and-forth give and take of Socratic dialogue had long been a part of HP's culture. Saying "I don't know" or "I need some time to think about that" was seen at HP as a mark of strength in a leader. Fiorina's projection of herself as someone with all the answers raised concerns that she was not interested in getting to know them and their views about the company. She did not distinguish between facts and her interpretation of them, nor did she offer the possibility that there might be some usefulness in considering different interpretations of the same data.

Henry Schacht was once Fiorina's boss at Lucent. His advice for someone in her situation is to start off by doing nothing. Schacht urges new leaders to fight the strong temptation to hit the ground running. He says that if they yield to this temptation, they are certain, regardless of the amount of research and advance prep they do, to make mistakes. Strong leaders seldom know as much as they think they do. Schacht also observes that beginning an assignment by imposing your views on others, even indirectly, almost inevitably weakens those people's commitment to support your efforts later, in times of great need.

When Carlos Ghosn arrived to lead the troubled Japanese car maker Nissan in 1999, he took a different approach from Fiorina's.[7] In his first weeks, he engaged in what he calls his "active listening" mode. He care-

fully sought advice from many people inside and outside the organization. What many of them told him was not what he wanted to hear—you
can't cut headcount in Japan, you can't close factories, you can't move
fast. Even though these opinions contradicted his own beliefs about what
needed to happen, he still listened carefully, taking steps to make sure
that each person he talked with felt that Ghosn fully understood his
views.

Then Ghosn did what he felt he had to do. Acting rapidly, he shut
down factories and reduced headcount. He told people that Nissan's
precarious financial situation left him with no choice. Feeling that they
had been listened to earlier, they understood and gave him their support.
Ghosn also made use of something he discovered during his listening
campaign: Japanese managers tend to be suspicious of big ideas and
lofty concepts. Especially in the engineering-driven culture characteristic
of automakers, they believe in numbers and results. So he avoided announcing a bold, new vision for Nissan. Instead, he expressed his plans
in terms of measurable statistics, an approach that Nissan managers felt
very comfortable with.

Ghosn's efforts were very successful. Nissan's profits returned, its
debt dropped, its market share increased, and its new car models won
rave reviews. He became a folk hero in Japan and was promoted to
head Nissan's corporate parent, Renault. Fiorina failed. She followed a
strategic course that was equally as unpopular as Ghosn's, but she failed
to build support for her plans, and her board fired her at about the time
Ghosn was packing his bags to move on to Paris.

A Great Opportunity to Ask Dumb Questions

Take good advantage of beginnings. They are, as Robert Eckert, CEO of
Mattel, likes to point out, your one great opportunity to ask stupid questions. Eckert found, when he moved from Kraft Foods to Mattel, that
acknowledging dependence on his new subordinates actually helped him
earn the right to lead them.[8] People want to be listened to. People want
to be heard. Lay out your thoughts about the challenges facing the organization. Let people know what you think and how you got to that point.
Suggest a new direction that might be taken. Then ask: "*What do you
think?*" Don't say a further word about your ideas. Don't defend any-

thing. Speak only to ask questions that will help you better understand what you are hearing. Write down what you are being told. It will help your memory as well as signify to others you value what they are saying.

Then go off and think about what you have heard. The real take-away from good listening is that you will have acquired more than just your way to interpret a situation. When people see that you have this ability, they will be more willing to join forces with you. Try to attune yourself to spot new opportunities in the comments people have made. Even negative and highly critical views can prove valuable. If nothing else, they can give you an idea of the lay of the land ahead.

GROUND RULES FOR MOVING FROM LISTENING TO DIALOGUE

After a wide-ranging round of listening, it can be useful to pull together the people who have expressed the strongest interest in helping to further the growth initiative. This is a time to focus on future possibilities and what needs to be done to bring them about—not a gripe session on the past and why things may have gone so wrong. Set some ground rules to keep the discussion most productive:

- *Rule 1:* Agree not to look for ways to discredit one another's views; maximizing the group's collective wisdom should be everyone's prime objective. This can best be done by making the most of the different perspectives that people bring to the meeting. Ask others *what leads them to the conclusions they have come to.* Let people know why you are questioning their point of view and what is making you uncomfortable with what you are hearing.

- *Rule 2:* Come together not so much to share your thoughts as with a real willingness to be influenced by others: "Here's what I think. Do you see things differently?" Ask others to help you identify the implications you may have missed by looking at things your way.

- *Rule 3:* Advocate your position by laying out the facts and logic on which it is based ("Here's what is leading me to believe this."). Encourage others to help identify your assumptions and open them up for questioning. Ask if others can see gaps in your reasoning.

- **Rule 4:** Positions are things to be understood, not just agreed with or refuted. Polarizing debate seldom leads to shared understanding. The problem with polarized argument is that everyone's negative emotions are aroused. In win-lose discussions like these, important information is often withheld, big-picture vision lost, creativity blocked, and collective insight seldom achieved.

- **Rule 5:** The object is not to end the discussion with everybody feeling "aligned" or "on the same page" (those are fixer goals), but for everyone to leave feeling that he has been heard and understood. This, rather than a rush to premature closure, will lay the strongest groundwork for future unified action.

When a discussion seems to be headed toward an impasse, ask what could be said, or found to be true, to remove the roadblock. Be sure you understand what could be done to alleviate others' concerns ("What might I say or do that would convince you otherwise?"). Look for common goals that can span disagreements. Lay out specific points of agreement, and note what issues are still in question. Ask others how the group might proceed, taking the differing views into consideration. Keep in mind that the idea is not to try to resolve all conflicts, but to mine sources of disagreement so that the collective understanding of growth possibilities is as strong as it can be.

At the end of a session like this, conduct a quick postmortem.[9] Ask everybody how satisfied she felt with the discussion on a scale of one to seven, with seven being "very pleased." Invite anyone who gives the discussion a rating of one, two, or three to say why. If something comes up that is resolvable on the spot, great; do it. Otherwise pledge to deal with these issues the next time you gather.

Without guidelines such as these, discussions tend to be less productive, doubts are unspoken, and agreements are superficial and less likely to support the mutual effort that a growth initiative requires. Meetings tend to drift from polite conversation to pointed debate, but they seldom lead to new understanding or shared commitment. Some groups bring in an outside facilitator to teach and enforce these guidelines. This may sometimes be useful, but not always. A presence of a skilled facilitator sometimes takes the onus off the group members to internalize this logic.

Discussions then become productive only when the third party is around. Try circulating these bullet points ahead of the meeting and asking if participants would be wiling to adopt them for the discussion.

Four Essential Roles

How can such discussions keep a degree of balance while moving the group's thinking forward? What is necessary for harmonious disagreement to prevail? These are issues that William Isaacs has spent several years researching at MIT's Sloan School Dialogue Project.[10] He has identified four roles that a person can play in any conversation:

Movers: Initiators of ideas and providers of direction

Supporters: Elaborators on and fleshers-out of movers' ideas

Opposers: Challengers of what is being said, devil's advocates

Observers: Active noticers of what is going on (and what is missing from the discussion) and providers of perspective, linkers of ideas, and builders of bridges among meeting participants

All four roles are necessary; they are all equally important. Although people often gravitate toward a favorite role, discussions will go better if individuals shift from one to another during the course of the meeting. In the most productive discussions, there is a sequence of interactions that touch each of these. To the extent that one of the four roles is missing or underemphasized, the quality of the group effort suffers. In less functional groups, a person may be stuck in one role, often that of mover or opposer, and the other balancing roles are deemphasized. This may work for a college debate, but it is not a good way to discuss growth options.

If the five ground rules described in the preceding section are to drive the discussion, there needs to be some rough equivalence between people who are advocating positions (movers and opposers) and those who are furthering inquiry (supporters and observers). Without this, advocacy dominates. Real listening is neglected, as habitual advocates, as Isaacs points out, are too busy reloading for their next volley. People will impute motives to others and make assumptions about what is being discussed without testing whether they are right or inquiring into what others really meant. Good, but unspoken ideas remain unsaid. Ignorance prevails, and the groundwork for the group's next blind spot is laid.

When this sort of imbalance threatens, the most skillful growth leaders tend to step in and either take on the roles that are missing or encourage others to do so. The payoff is a discussion that all present feel they have an active part in, and in which all sides of the issues are addressed. Participants are then often struck with the sense that the group seems to be speaking with one voice, especially when they start to hear their own thoughts being articulated by others. Formal decisions may not even need to be made, as the appropriate next step seems almost automatically obvious to everyone. Having a group that is able to act this way is a great asset for a grower. It is well worth the trouble it takes to get it organized.

HELP PEOPLE LOWER THEIR DEFENSIVE BIASES

In a fixer's world, defensiveness is an enemy, something to be overcome. Growers, however, think of it as another of humankind's features, not flaws. Defenses are part of the territory, something to be expected and worked with. People build up their characteristic defenses over a lifetime.[11] These are what an individual has found most useful in trying to adapt to the changes and challenges that life has put before him. Launching a direct assault on a person's defenses is seldom successful. Some defenses are actually very functional: anticipation, altruism, humor, sublimation, and suppression. Others may be less so: intellectualization, repression, and temporary denial; and some are outright dangerous: projection, passive-aggression, distortion, and delusion. Do not expect people to set all of these aside just to join in your growth effort. Effective growers take advantage of the functional defenses and compensate for or protect against those that contribute less to the growth effort. A grower is not a psychotherapist. You job is to deal with the implications of people's defenses, not to try to change them or reorganize them.

Work with Optimists *and* Pessimists

Growers often find that optimistic people are easy to win over; just focus them on all the positive benefits that will ensue from the growth initiative you are championing, and then get out of their way. They make strong allies. They are great opportunity spotters and are fun to be around because they are usually happy. Keep in mind, though, that not all of those whose support you need will share the optimist's mindset. And, as mentioned in Chapter 7, there are times in the growth process when it is important to tone down optimism lest it stand in the way of accurately perceiving the reality that you want to change. A growth team with a mix of optimists and pessimists is likely to adapt better to changing circumstance than one with only optimists. Each outlook has particular strengths and vulnerabilities. Pessimism is usually associated with anxiety, optimism with confidence. Crippling anxiety and extreme overconfidence can be equally dangerous.

Do not try to convert the pessimists you find into optimists.[12] It is hard, distracting work, and it is likely to reduce their level of performance. What may work better is to deal with them on their own terms. If pessimists are feeling anxious about being in a situation that appears out of control, reassure them. Provide a structure for their involvement. Be willing to tolerate their anxiety; it is often a useful motivator of action for them. Their expectations of success may be low; use this as a way to bracket the results you are aiming for and to generate worst-case, but tolerable, fallback scenarios.

Pessimists pay attention to details that optimists might gloss over. They anticipate problems; they are natural risk managers. Pessimists will tend to think hard about all the things that might go wrong with your plans. They are also good at coming up with ways to keep these bad things from happening—something that will make the positive outcomes you are seeking more likely. Listen to them. If you approach them as a useful resource, rather than as an emotional drag on the endeavor, you will be immunized from their negative mood. Make sure the optimists on your team understand the pessimists' contribution. Do not try to shower the pessimists with unwanted encouragement, ask them to lighten up, or tell them to think positive thoughts. This will only weaken their ability to perform.

Why People Hang On to Outmoded Beliefs

Growers know that people hang on to outmoded beliefs when doing so helps them protect their perceived worth and integrity.[13] Laying out the "facts" or presenting a sound "business-case" rationale for moving forward is seldom sufficient to win allies. We also need to help those we want to reach lower their defensive biases so that they can better hear and accept our message. The motivation to maintain self-worth is a very powerful one. It can cause people to resist, deny, or distort information that would otherwise be very beneficial to them. This happens all the time when people who are at high risk of heart disease or cancer are told to exercise, cut out smoking, and improve their diet. They may agree intellectually with the information and analysis they are given. But most of them do not change their behaviors. Even threats of death from continuing with their habits lead few to improve their lifestyle. When given the choice of change or die, 90 percent of health-threatened individuals choose to hang on to their death-promoting behaviors.[14]

The conventional wisdom that crisis is always a great motivator is just not true. This is because informational and confrontational strategies do nothing to address the self-worth issue. These strategies attempt to contradict core beliefs that many people may hold about their freedom from risk and their perception of themselves as fundamentally healthy. Regardless of whether these beliefs are being mistakenly held, they have become central to these people's identities. People do not want to believe anything that may suggest that they have been misguided. Fear is more likely to prompt denial (a stabilizing mechanism) than long-term behavior change.

Self-worth issues also arise in organizational situations. Many people identify with their employer. They see their job performance as a validator of their worth. If they are told that there is a problem with either of these, they are more likely to discredit the messenger or blame external circumstances. Losing sports teams usually blame their defeat on external factors such as luck, while winners take personal credit for all their victories. In both cases, self-worth is maintained. This may help team members keep their spirits up for tomorrow's game, but it runs the risk of ignoring potentially beneficial information. The losers risk missing opportunities to improve, as do the winners, who may be sliding by and resting on their laurels.

Provide an Alternative Source of Identity and Self-Worth

What should you do if you suspect that self-worth issues may be involved in people's fears about your growth initiative? One way to help lower these biases is to provide an alternative source of identity for the people you are trying to reach. This could provide them with another way to save face and maintain a positive self-image without having to shield themselves from otherwise threatening information and ideas.

Researchers from UCLA and Yale have found that people respond in a less defensive and more open-minded manner when this alternative source of identity is provided *before* belief-disconfirming evidence is presented. They would ask people to reflect on an important value they held that was unrelated to the threat. Other research subjects were given positive feedback about an important skill that they possessed. People who were about to face a wrenching series of changes at work were asked to think about some other settings in which they played important roles, perhaps as a parent, as a partner in a significant relationship, as a member of a professional organization, or in their community. Just having some time to mull over these alternative sources of integrity made a significant difference in how able these people were to reduce their biases, be open to new sources of information, and change their behaviors based on what they learned.

The publisher of the *New York Times* helped his reporters accept the changes necessary to rebound from a scandal involving fabricated news stories by reminding them of the paper's underlying positive characteristics. He positioned the incident as a temporary straying from the ideals they all held. He told them it was now time to come home.

When Steve Jobs returned to lead Apple Computer, he prefaced all the changes in organization, products, and strategy that he planned to make with a marketing campaign that highlighted people with the boldness to "think different." While the media blitz was aimed at customers, Jobs admitted that it was even more directed at Apple's employees. He wanted to remind them of who their heroes were and, by extension, who they were: a small elite, not a marginalized player in the PC market-share battle.

Winston Churchill faced a grave situation when he became Britain's prime minister in 1940. Through his celebrated speeches, he managed to impose his imagination and will upon his countrymen. He idealized them with such intensity that Isaiah Berlin, an Oxford philosopher, observed that they began to approach his ideal, seeing themselves as he saw them. Berlin credits Churchill with transforming cowards into brave

men.[15] Churchill actually was just borrowing an approach from (ironically) a German, Johann Wolfgang von Goethe: Treat people as if they
were what they ought to be, and you will help them become what they
are capable of being.

Make It Easier for People to Question Their Fundamental Assumptions

Affirmation can make the sting go away. It can also elevate people's
moods, which can be very useful because, when they are in such a state,
people's openness to persuasion often increases. The most difficult job
of persuasion facing many growers has to do with encouraging people to
critically examine the assumptions behind business as it is currently
being conducted. The grower's hope, of course, is that if this is done, the
logic of pursuing a growth goal will become apparent and the assumption
examiners will turn into supporters.

Unfortunately, this is usually a steep uphill climb for many growers.
What often keeps the change from happening is the way in which the
confronting of assumptions takes place. Challenging a person's deeply
held beliefs about the business and where it is going often triggers strong
negative emotions such as anger and embarrassment. A grower who does
this is more likely to be seen as a threat, someone who is trying to take
something away, than as a helpful guide to the future.

Some behavioral scientists, such as Chris Argyris, have maintained
that these emotions should be taken as indicators of a person's faulty
thinking process and that the person expressing them should be con-
fronted and then reeducated. The problem with this steamroller approach is that it is very likely to elicit even stronger negative protective
feelings. These, in turn, will further restrict the individual's ability to
think broadly and to reflect creatively on the beliefs she holds about the
business. (See Chapter 4 for more information about the consequences
of negative emotions.) Head-on, hardball confrontation in these circumstances is usually counterproductive because it marshals a person's feelings and entire nervous system against what the grower is trying to
accomplish.

Myeong-Gu Seo, a University of Maryland professor of management, has identified a way out of this dilemma.[16] He suggests making use

of the research about positive emotions described in Chapter 4 to lay the groundwork for whatever challenges a grower may need to make. Rather than starting with strident confrontation, make use of the power of positive emotions to help the person you want to reach broaden his thinking repertoire and undo the defensive effects of negative feelings. In other words, you will have an easier time bringing a trusted friend around to your way of thinking than bringing around someone with whom you do not already have a close emotional bond. That is a good starting point, but most growers find that they need a broader base of support than their circle of friends can provide. Growers can benefit by generally cultivating the ability to "disagree without becoming disagreeable." This can happen through:

- Skillful use of humor (especially the self-deprecating variety)
- Always approaching people in a friendly and respectful manner (something that seems obvious, but is often lost in the haste of trying to move an effort along)
- Being willing to explore others' feelings and subjective experiences regarding the issue at hand
- Speaking in a way that shows that you identify with them (say "we" a lot more than "I")

Many people want to connect with others. This is a powerful motive for growers to tap into. People will often take much bolder action when they are part of a group than they ever would as individuals. On Lou Gerstner's first day as CEO of IBM, he met with the company's 50-person management board. He noticed that everyone in the room was wearing a white shirt. Gerstner's was blue. A few weeks later, the board met again. Gerstner, the newcomer to the company, wanted to fit in, so he wore a white shirt. When he got up to speak, he looked around and found himself in a sea of blue shirts. His people also wanted to fit in. This was when Gerstner knew that the time was right to start this group down the path that eventually led it collectively to see IBM as a technology and consulting-service provider, not just the builder of computers it once was.

Pave the Way with a Win-Win Success

Seo's research also suggests that growers consider a multiphase approach to building support for their objectives. Start by dealing with an issue that offers a win-win victory for all concerned. Look for cooperative solutions where everyone gains. Then build on the groundwork of positive emotions that ensues to face more difficult issues. As an example of this, he cites the way Branch Rickey, general manager of the Brooklyn Dodgers, successfully integrated his baseball team in the years following World War II.

Rickey knew that racial integration was on the horizon for major league sports. He thought it was the right thing to do, and he thought it was something that could benefit the Dodgers. He also realized that not everyone shared his views. Rickey began by presenting to his board of directors a plan for recruiting African American players. The plan said nothing about social justice or ending racial discrimination. It was just a solid economic case for broadening the scope of players the Dodgers sought. He focused his directors' attention on the future and the need to build up a better stock of talent for the team rosters during a time when competition for talent was expected to be intense. (Many people assumed that Rickey's motivation was finding a source of cheap talent.) The board approved his plan, and Rickey then presented the same rationale to his fans.

One of his early black hires, Jackie Robinson, proved to be a quick success. Not only did Robinson break baseball's color barrier, but he was the catalyst for the Dodgers' winning six pennants in ten seasons. Robinson's overwhelming popularity provided Rickey with a reservoir of public goodwill and positive feeling. Rickey was then able to use this to begin a dialogue about social justice as the rationale for integrating his team, other baseball clubs, and American society in general.

Skillful growers know that the shortest distance between two points is not always a straight line. They also realize that for every action, there are likely to be multiple rationales that can be used to provide support for it. Picking the rationale that triggers the least amount of defensiveness is often the best way to move forward.

Sometimes Hearts and Minds Have to Come Along Later

Seo is a realist. He knows that not all situations that require assumption rethinking allow the time necessary to take the long way around or to build a positive and trusting relationship with those you are trying to influence. In these instances (such as the concerns NASA engineers had about safety issues on the *Challenger* and *Columbia* space shuttles, described in Chapter 7), where reevaluation needs to happen very fast, Seo suggests leveraging opposing forces instead of positive emotions. For example, if NASA's engineers had built alliances with other power centers in the organization, such as senior executives or the astronauts themselves, they might have found ways to get around the dismissals of their concerns that they received from the management hierarchy. Even if they did not short-circuit the chain of command, their managers' awareness that they *could* reach out to other parts of NASA might have been enough to earn these technical experts a fairer hearing.

Seo has even put together a template of how such a conversation between the NASA engineers and their supervisors might have gone:

> *We understand your concerns about changing the customary shuttle procedures. But if anything goes wrong, the issue will involve more than a difference of opinion between us. It concerns NASA as a whole, and the life or death of the astronauts on board.* [Broaden the perspective on the issue.]
>
> *We realize it is up to you to make this decision, but we also feel as engineering professionals we have a responsibility to ensure that information about a serious threat to the shuttle's safety is widely known.* [Acknowledge your boss' authority; also assert your own authority base.]
>
> *So we ask you to inform at least your immediate superior and the shuttle crew of what we are recommending. If you do not, we will feel responsible to do this.* [Offer a way to save face. Make clear what you feel you need to do otherwise.]
>
> *Would you like a few minutes to discuss this among yourselves?*[17] [Provide some breathing space.]

PEOPLE WANT TO CONNECT WITH SOMETHING LARGER

In some situations, political pressure is the only alternative. Most growth initiatives, however, offer more time to overcome resistance and build a base of supporters. Even Seo's scenario for NASA engineers began with an appeal to overarching concerns that they and their managers shared—NASA's reputation and the lives of the shuttle crew.

It takes skill and preparation to give weight to such an appeal. Phil Jackson, who coached the Chicago Bulls and LA Lakers basketball teams, is a grower who has mastered this approach. "The most effective way to forge a winning team," says Jackson, "is to call on the players' need to connect with something larger than themselves."[18] Mushy idealism? Perhaps. But the best growers all use the power of purpose skillfully to win allies and recruits.

Roy Vagelos led Merck in the days before the pharmaceutical industry became a captive of the blockbuster syndrome (Chapter 1). In the 1980s, he made one of his most controversial decisions: to give away a drug that had been developed in Merck's labs. It was a medicine that cured river blindness, a disease affecting tens of millions of poor Africans. People inside Merck and throughout the drug industry worried that this would set a dangerous precedent. Drug companies were expected to earn profits by selling their discoveries. Without profits, they would not be able to fuel the next round of R&D. Vagelos ignored the criticism, knowing that the good publicity the company received would be invaluable. His move also energized the Merck labs, gave everyone in the company a strong sense of mission, and for a decade made it possible for the company to recruit almost anyone it wanted. A life-size bronze sculpture of a boy using a wooden stick to lead his river-blinded father is prominently displayed in Merck's headquarters building lobby, a reminder of the 250 million doses of the medicine that have been donated to date, and the disease they cured.

Vagelos, like all growers, knew that many of us hunger for a sense of mission in our work. Pride counts. It brings coherence and focus. It breeds gratification beyond what a paycheck and a fistful of options can provide. Many people will be willing to work long hours to solve apparently unsolvable problems if they can give an affirmative answer to the question, "Am I making a difference?" Feeling this way is the best way to leave the confines of a narrow job (or the part of our ego that misleads us into thinking that the world, and those in it, revolves around us). The open-source software movement—several hundred thousand programmers generating programs and upgrades that are unpatented, unlicensed, and freely available to all takers—is a clear demonstration of this power. It's what's behind Linux, the fast-growing computer operating system;

Apache, the market leader in Web-server software; and Wikipedia, the online encyclopedia.

Tap into the Underground Economy

The open-source movement taps into the "esteem culture": people who feel compensated when they earn the esteem of their professional peers. Open-source projects include a list of credits, or a "history" file. This includes the name of everyone who has done something important to advance a particular part of the software code. It is a permanent record, and appearing on several of these lists is the same as an artist's work being accepted to be shown in juried exhibitions or at the top galleries in Basel, Cologne, or Manhattan. In addition to gratified volunteers, this system leads to pretty good quality software because every programmer knows that his work product will be carefully scrutinized by thousands of others before it is released. Peer pressure and concern for reputation lead to error-free work, as does the lack of the opportunity to shift blame that is readily available in all the large corporate software bureaucracies.

Growers who are able to engender the degree of trust that the open-software movement represents often discover that there is an underground economy in their company. Most exchanges in the business world are commoditylike transactions: hours or raw materials for money. Many growers in the early stages of their initiatives find themselves excluded from this economy—the budget cycle exists to fund what is, not what might be. So where do they find the talent and resources they need to move an idea to the stage where its worth becomes obvious?

Some beg, borrow, or steal. Greenwood's growth group (Chapter 4) did all three, as do many corporate bootleggers. Others discover, and tap into, a parallel economy that is alive, though often sub rosa, in many organizations. This is the gift economy, one whose currency is respect and trust, not dollars and options. These forms of payment, and the opportunity to do something that can make a real difference, are often the sum total of many growers' start-up budgets.

The Gift Economy

Ron Avitzur was one of many young programmers working under contract with Apple Computer in the early 1990s.[19] He was dismissed when the project he was working on was canceled. He had been creating a computer version of the powerful handheld graphical calculator that is now in common use by high school students. Avitzur thought it was important to finish the programming because the calculator would be an important addition to Apple's Macintosh lineup. So he never bothered to turn in his badge on his last day of paid work. Instead, he recruited another laid-off contractor, found some unoccupied cubicles, and kept coming to work, gratis. Eventually, during their six-month escapade, the two programmers obtained the stealth help of actual paid Apple employees, and they finished the programming. Finally, after a 2 a.m. visit to Avitzur's hideout, an Apple official looked over their labor of love, liked it, and agreed to ship it with the next Mac release. The two developers were paid by an embarrassed Apple for the rights to their software, but Avitzur and his buddy felt that their real pay was seeing their handiwork in over 20 million Macs.

In the gift economy, an emotional bond is established between the giver and the recipient, because the giver is, in a sense, giving a part of herself. Supply and demand is not the key driver here. When Robert Levering investigated the differences between those companies that earned a place on his lists of Best Companies to Work For (Chapter 6) and those that did not, he quickly found that the better employers often had an active gift economy that went beyond the tit-for-tat commodity exchange of time for money. These were the companies with the overflowing employee suggestion boxes, the ones with the most active programs to recognize worker accomplishments and the greatest willingness to delegate and decentralize. People give things away and get a sense of community in return. Levering noticed that the less-good workplaces take a narrower view of their relationship with their employees and, in effect, often refuse ideas and gifts that they are voluntarily offered.

Refusing ideas and gifts is a luxury growers do not have. They are active traders in the voluntary gift currency. They find people who can be paid with trust and recognition, using the efforts and donations that the gift economy offers to make possible pilot projects and limited-scale efforts. The early successes that these produce create a taste of new possibilities that will, in turn, change how some people in the business perceive what's possible. Growers then build on these new perceptions. After a while, more members of the organization start thinking hopefully, and these thoughts provide positive emotions whose energy can be channeled to move a project along.

GIFTS GENERATE NEW STORIES TO TELL

Giving people a new story to tell about the business and where it is going is a very effective way to jump-start growth. It certainly works when the objective is to get people thinking and behaving differently. When I joined the Arthur D. Little consulting firm after graduate school, my boss did not tell me that the place was nonhierarchical and customer-driven, or that he expected a lot of initiative from all employees. Instead, he told me a story featuring fear, courage, and noblesse oblige. It had to do with the time a junior consultant in charge of a small client assignment needed the specialized expertise of retired General James Gavin, Arthur D. Little's then-chairman of the board, on his project team. With more than a little trepidation, the young staff member bravely knocked on Gavin's door on the top floor of the headquarters building. Gavin said come in, gave him a warm welcome, and said of course he would be glad to be the consultant's subordinate on that assignment if that was what would most benefit the client. From that day on, no ADL executive or manager refused a request to roll up his sleeves and serve on any client project.

Or, at least, that is how the story ended. It sounded nice when I first heard it. I am not sure I completely believed it, at least not until a few months later, when I read a newspaper article about a new White House initiative to completely rethink how international aid programs would be managed. I thought that could be an interesting challenge for a management consultant, and I wondered how I might get to help out. I mentioned the situation to a few colleagues, and one of them suggested that I see Gavin. Before coming to ADL, Gavin had been President Kennedy's ambassador to France, in part because he had commanded the paratroopers who liberated the first French village on D-Day. Gavin still had many connections in Washington, and I, remembering the folklore I had heard when I was hired, went off to see him. He was as gracious as the story made him out to be, and he turned out to be a personal friend of the head of the new presidential commission. One quick phone call later, I found myself on a plane to Washington, ready to start work. Stories, I realized, are not just ways to convey history. They are ways to get people to do things.

Change the Old Story

Word of mouth tends to build support better than PowerPoint. Growers communicate through stories instead of bullet points. Slides and graphics can describe something that has happened, but when events are recounted through stories, they come alive. An experience being recounted makes a sharper impression than a concept being taught.

It is hard for bullet points to evoke emotions. Telling, retelling, and listening to stories about early small victories have great strength because the act of doing so reshapes people's experiences. Stories provide a painless way to see reality a little differently—sometimes in new categories, often with a new understanding. Telling a story that highlights *the way things might turn out* gives listeners an opportunity to actually experience these new realities—something like a taste test or a rehearsal of the future. A story packages facts along with a framework for explaining those facts—the story line. It also can depict complex cause-and-effect patterns that are too hard to reduce to understandable flowcharts and diagrams.

Stories are a lot easier to remember than flowcharts, too. James Zull, a researcher of brain function at Case Western Reserve University, says that stories work because the sensation of movement toward a goal that they evoke stimulates the brain's pleasure centers, which are also activated by physical activities such as dancing or running. When our pleasure centers are activated, we tend to remember the cause. Stories are sticky.

Spread the Word

How does word of a grower's accomplishments spread? How does the flywheel get started? This happens through networks of social connections that cut across an organization's departments and hierarchy. Some people are better connected to others in the organization than most. They are the ones with ample social capital, often living at the intersection of social worlds within the organization. They are the people whom everyone seems to go to for an explanation when something puzzling is happening. Find them. Connect them with your ideas and with other similar "connector people." Feed them information about your early successes and the implications of these successes for a "new story" about the business.

Only a few strategic connections are needed to turn a large organization into a small world. But they won't happen if all you do is talk to people you know well and feel very comfortable with. Spending most of your time preaching to the converted wins few new converts. Instead, put your efforts into getting out word through your weak ties: people you vaguely know, people whose social networks have minimal overlap with yours. This is where the real action is. Close friends, as Jeff Howe, an editor at *Wired* magazine, has observed, are great for road trips, intimate dinners, and the odd interest-free loan.[20] But these folks tend to know the same people you already know. It is the people you just barely know who are the best sources for blind dates and job leads—and the best way to get your growth idea talked about in distant parts of your organization.

Do not spend a lot of time at this stage trying to make proposals to, or curry favor with, what it is becoming popular to call the "core group." These are what business author Art Kleiner calls the people in the organization with the ability to get others to confer legitimacy upon them.[21] They are the inner circle, the people who seem to be calling all the shots in the business. (Kleiner also feels that, in some instances, the company seems to be run more for these people's benefit than for that of its customers or shareholders.) It is important to know who these people are, and to keep in mind that some of them may have more at stake in the status quo than in the direction you are trying to move the organization toward. As a growth effort builds momentum, its leaders are likely to find themselves grafted into this group. But before that happens, it is often wise to minimize the need for members of the core group to take a stand on a growth project. Do not put these people in a position to say no to something before its early viability has been demonstrated and word of its success has gotten around.

As information spreads, be sure its flow is a two-way street. Use your new connections to keep abreast of developments inside and outside the organization. Listen closely to these people as well as tell them your stories. They might well be sources of new and helpful ideas, perhaps ones that they have not yet realized how to make use of, but that you can use. It is often hard to stay open to outside influences in the early stages of a growth effort, but it is essential if you want to keep yourself and your supporters from turning into a self-sealing cult.

CHANGING WHAT THE FIELD OF PSYCHOLOGY IS ALL ABOUT

An idea is really sold when its purchasers feel better about *themselves* for having bought it. That is what is happening in spades in the positive psychology movement created and led by Martin Seligman (noted in chapters 3 and 5). The job of a psychologist has traditionally been to find out what is wrong with you. Positive psychologists are different. They want to find out what is really right with you, and then figure out how to get you to use it more often.

When Seligman received his Ph.D. in 1967, psychology was close to being a faith-based discipline. Freud's never-rigorously-tested ideas dominated the therapy side of the field. What passed for its popular image as a science was often limited to experimenters giving electric shocks to rats in basement laboratories. Determinism dominated most discourse, and virtually all funding in the field was earmarked for the negative aspect of psychology: helping sick people get better. Psychology had little to offer to those who wanted to do more than just correct weaknesses. In his career as a University of Pennsylvania professor, American Psychological Association president, and leader of the positive psychology movement, Seligman has done a great deal to change all that.

One of his graduate students, Susan Johnson, describes him as one of those people who never grew up, who still thinks he can change the world and has never shirked from taking on outlandish goals. I just call him a quintessential grower.

Seligman characterizes the first 30 years of his career as having been focused on misery. His research made him the world's leading expert on "learned helplessness." This is his name for a groundbreaking theory that helped redefine the way psychology views and treats the mental illness of depression. Seligman's theory said that a major component of depression is a "learned" pessimistic way of thinking. How we think about our problems has a lot to do with either relieving or aggravating depression. Since these thought processes are learned, as Seligman discovered through his research, they can also be unlearned. Seligman and his colleagues then developed ways to help people change their explanatory style to one that is more optimistically oriented. These now well-proven techniques are commonly used by therapists to treat people with depression, and by educators to successfully immunize children against it.

When Seligman decided to write a mass-market book about his work, he had a life-changing discussion with his literary agent.[22] The agent warned that while "learned helplessness" might be a fine label for his work among professional psychologists, it could be a real turn-off for lay readers. Why not emphasize the positive and call it "learned *optimism*" instead, he suggested. Seligman, who had been laboring under the impression that he had been studying pessimism all those years, quickly saw the agent's point, and in so doing transformed himself from a leading expert on pessimism and depression to the world's top scientific authority on optimism. He learned how much better it is to sell the solution, not the problem, and went on to write a bestseller.[23] This shift of mindset may have also helped start him thinking about a bigger issue—the nature of his profession, psychology, and how it had come to define itself.

Professions, like industries, chase after their markets. After World War II, billions of dollars of funding for psychology came from the Veterans Administration and the National Institute of Mental Health. And most of this money went to study and treat mental illness. The medical mindset dominated the profession; 90 percent of scientific psychological research was based on the disease model. Victory happened when a distressed person moved from a -7 to a -3.

Seligman's rise through the ranks of his profession, based on the fame earned by his disease-model-based research, led to his election as president of the 155,000-member American Psychological Association (APA). When he assumed this office in 1998, he made the observation that his field had gotten sidetracked over the past 50 years. Psychology, he told the APA members, is not just the study of weakness and damage. It is also concerned with strength and virtue. Treatment, he felt, should not be limited to fixing what is broken in people; it should also nurture what is best in us. Psychology could offer the preventive medicines of strength and resilience, as well as the remedial therapies that currently defined its product line. Seligman urged his colleagues to grow their profession so that it could also offer individuals a way to move from + 2 to + 6.

Seligman's efforts over the years since his APA presidency have all been focused on identifying and designing the elements of what he labeled "positive psychology." This is a discipline that is as oriented toward increasing the net tonnage of happiness in the world as traditional psychology has been toward decreasing the tonnage of suffering. He is a grower extraordinaire. The steps he has taken to move his field beyond the limits that had come to define it offer ideas for leaders of growth in other professions, as well as in business settings, where the key to success is winning the support of others. Here are some of Seligman's key initiatives. Think about how they reinforce each other, and how they might translate to your situation.

Build Bridges to Unite Warring Factions. For a decade or more before Seligman headed the APA, this organization had been the site of a near civil war between its research-oriented members and its therapist-practitioners. The scientists wanted APA to lobby for bigger government-funded research programs; the clinicians were more concerned with ensuring that their services were covered by health insurance plans.

Seligman demonstrated how these opposing camps could make common cause by showing how psychological science could be used to validate which therapies worked and identify those that didn't. This gave the researchers a key role in resolving many controversies that had plagued psychology since Freud, and it gave the practitioners the evidence they needed to establish the validity of their "talking cures" with the keepers of managed health care's purse strings. Everyone was happy, and Seligman had a victory upon which to build his further initiatives.

Don't Dismiss the Past, Declare Victory. Seligman began his APA presidency by praising all that "negative" psychology had accomplished since World War II. In 1950, no major mental illness was really treatable. What passed for care was all smoke and mirrors. Now, fourteen mental illnesses are treatable and two (panic disorder and some phobias) can be completely cured. These results occurred, according to Seligman, as psychology moved from a practice to a science, with an emphasis on classification and measurement, and the use of tools like longitudinal and placebo/control studies.

Start with Your Peers. Many academics, when they want to create a new field, set themselves up as the guru and start by building a small army of dependent followers—junior faculty members and graduate students. This often results in the creation of academic silos and splintered disciplines. Seligman began horizontally, not vertically, by initially reaching out to his like-minded peers. These were among the most well-established and renowned figures in psychology, including Mihaly Csikszentmihalyi, Edward Diener, and George Vaillant. He did not ask his peers to submit to a new authority or doctrine, but he helped them see the benefits of positioning their work as key pillars of something bigger.

Seek Out Rising Stars. When Seligman began his term as APA president, he wrote to the top 50 people in psychology. He asked them for the names of the field's up-and-comers, the people most likely to become department heads while their careers are relatively young. From these lists, Seligman invited groups of 25 at a time to spend the first week in January with him in Akumal, a resort town in Yucatan (see Chapter 5 for more details). These sessions, held for four consecutive years, helped flesh out the elements of positive psychology and enlisted some of the profession's most promising talent to work on it.

Broaden the Resource Base. Seligman reached beyond the traditional government funding sources to find the seed capital needed to fund positive psychology's networks, gatherings, and early research. He enlisted the Gallup Organization as a private-sector partner, and he tapped into the resources of places like Atlantic Philanthropies and the Annenberg, Mayerson, Pew, and Templeton Foundations.

Use Incentives to Shape Agendas. The Templeton Positive Psychology Prize is now psychology's most lucrative award. It is given for the best work done by a scientist under 40 years of age. Barbara Fredrickson was the first winner of this $100,000 prize for her work on positive emotions (see Chapter 4).

Organize Forums to Structure Efforts and Take Stock. Out of the Akumal meetings, Seligman created the Positive Psychology Network to coordinate the ongoing efforts that were born under the bright Mexican sun. Positive psychology summits are also held annually in Washington, D.C., to bring together leading scholars and their graduate students. Seligman's most recent effort, dubbed "Medici II," is intended to bring many of the world's leading researchers (including the Akumal alumni) in positive psychology to the Penn campus in the spring and summer of 2005, 2006, and 2007. This multiyear gathering will include major research presentations, seminars, lectures, and planning sessions, and— according to Seligman—a lot of sitting around, drinking beer, and exchanging ideas. He is modeling this event after the sessions in Copenhagen before World War II hosted by Niels Bohr that brought the world's leading atomic scientists together for work and play. Out of those annual Danish conferences emerged a consensus about what the structure of the atom actually involved.

Create New Metrics of Progress. Seligman realized that a key reason that traditional psychology was able to make so much progress in dealing with mental illness was that it, with the encouragement and funding of the National Institute of Mental Health, developed a common set of diagnostic criteria for mental afflictions. Called the DSM (the *Diagnostic and Statistical Manual of Mental Disorders*), it has served for decades as the plumb line around which reliable diagnoses and treatments could be built. Seligman realized that positive psychology needed the same thing. He recruited a leading University of Michigan professor, Christopher Peterson, to direct its preparation.

Funded by the Mayerson Foundation, this three-year effort examined all the world's major religious and philosophical traditions to come up with a catalog of six virtues that almost every single tradition endorsed (wisdom and knowledge, courage, love and humanity, justice, temperance, and spirituality and transcendence). Taken together, these provide a working definition of "good character." For each of these virtues, Peterson identified several measurable and acquirable strengths whose exercise would enact the virtue. This catalog of human strengths, 24 in all, gave positive psychology researchers something to assess and study, and provided positive psychology therapists with a curriculum to coach from.

Stimulate Demand by Going to Your Customers' Customers. Seligman has never been a publicity-shy academic. Both *Newsweek* and *Time* have done cover stories about his work, and he is frequently quoted in newspapers such as the *New York Times* and *USA Today*. He has written a book for the general public about the emergence of positive psychology, *Authentic Happiness*, and has set up a web site to allow people to use the questionnaires and instruments the field has developed to identify their own signature strengths and try out the interventions that are being developed.[24] These mass-market awareness efforts, in turn, stimulate demand for psychologists who are able to use positive psychology as part of their tool kit.

Retrain Practitioners. Seligman has helped psychologists meet the demand he has stimulated through a new master's-level degree program in applied positive psychology at the University of Pennsylvania and a multimonth teleconference coaching program for coaches, counselors, therapists, and educators who want to get up to speed on positive psychology.

Infuse, Don't Fragment. Positive psychology is intended as a change of focus for the entire field. Its goal is to complete and extend what has gone before, not to replace traditional mental illness–focused psychology. Seligman and his colleagues have resisted efforts to create a new journal or specialized departments for positive psychology. (Journals are the traditional calling cards that announce a new academic specialty.) Instead, they encourage positive psychologists to publish in the media that are already available, as a way to infuse this perspective throughout the broad field, rather than create a new subspecialty in competition with the dozens already established.

Seligman's approach to growing psychology illustrates how growers' efforts can lead to more balance. He moved the field in the direction of great complexity (see Chapter 3) by adding positive psychology to supplement its mental illness focus. He also maintained and augmented the linkages between the field's researchers and therapists, providing win-wins for all concerned.

Seligman's efforts suggest that disciplines as well as companies can grow beyond their established boundaries, and they offer some clues about what it takes to reorient an academic field and a profession. He is a skilled grower, able to find openings and opportunities, a user of facts to drive forward movement, and a master at rallying support for a new direction in a domain of fiercely independent thinkers. Few growers are as good as Seligman at getting other people to drop whatever they are doing and come along to support another's vision.

* * *

Building support for a growth initiative requires doing the kinds of things that Seligman has done: paying attention to heads, hearts, and hands. New ideas provide an intellectual rationale for changing people's logic system. They help people perceive reality differently and better appreciate the new possibility that the grower is trying to bring about. Doing things that stimulate positive emotions increases receptivity to the rationale and makes the trip a lot more fun and gratifying than it would be otherwise. Giving people an opportunity to develop the skills and techniques they need to master in order to function in this new reality is also vital. Winning people's hearts and minds is the biggest hurdle a grower needs to overcome. It is what will move a growth effort to its tipping point. Chapter 10 addresses what comes next, two of the most important capabilities that growers must acquire if they are to continue to prevail: the ability to generate momentum and the ability to bounce back from setbacks.

MASTER MOMENTUM AND BOUNCE

Success begets failure because the more that you know a thing works, the less likely you are to think that it won't work. When you have had a long string of victories, it's harder to foresee your own vulnerabilities.[1]

—Leslie Wexner

MOMENTUM IS DRIVEN BY A SERIES OF SMALL WINS

Wexner is CEO of Limited Brands. The good news buried between the lines of his comment is that, initially at least, success begets more success. This is good, especially if you have the foresight to remain aware of your potential vulnerabilities while you are enjoying the long string of victories. This awareness can provide at least a partial immunization against the failure he prophesies. Momentum and resilience are actually two sides of the same coin.

Momentum comes from creating a series of small successes. Where does the first early win come from? By focusing their time and resources, growers find a way to accomplish something, however small, in the direction in which they want to move. Directional focus is important; dogged and indiscriminate application of effort alone does not guarantee actions that will reinforce one another. *Growers know that motivation does not precede action, but rather comes from it.* So the basic idea behind generating momentum is simple: Do something—something easy if possible—that is likely to advance your cause. This primes the pump and motivates more action, which further ratchets additional motivation.

The Bronze-Medal Effect

The idea of initial *small* successes is important. Ironically, limited early success may be more useful for motivational purposes than an initial bigger win. Call it the "bronze-medal effect." Studies of Olympic Games winners find that bronze medalists tend to be happier about their victory than those winning the silver.[2] Olympians, and the rest of us, tend to compare what occurred with what might have been. For bronze-medal winners, the most likely alternative was getting no medal, whereas most silver medalists focus more on having lost the gold than on their victory over the bronze winners. It is possible to be objectively better off than others, but feel worse about it—our minds work in strange ways. Expectation management is an important part of momentum creation.

Small wins are also safer. They are visible enough to establish an idea's viability, but not so large as to arouse jealousy or threaten already well-established activities. A string of small victories at the outset of an initiative can be more useful than one lucky big win.

Fail Early and Often

Start by doing. Work with the resources you can get; don't wait for what you think you need. David Kelley, leader of the product-development-for-hire company IDEO, has made a religion of "enlightened trial and error." He feels that failing early and often always trumps failing late and big. Failing often lets a company succeed sooner. An IDEO product designer, Peter Skillman, advocates small-scale, rapid prototyping: When he gets an idea, he makes the product right away so that it can be seen, tried, and learned from. Most progress is the result of trial and error, so start off by getting some good errors on the table. Upstream problems are always easier and cheaper to fix than those that are discovered later.

Growers make good errors and bad errors. The bad ones are those that are unnoticed, or that are discovered but then quickly swept under the carpet. These will eventually pop up and block your best efforts at rebounding. Good failures, on the other hand, are what drive sustained growth. Growers who rarely fail are growers who are not pushing the envelope hard enough. Google is a company that has taken this to heart more than most, perhaps because its primary product—Internet search results—is always imperfect and riddled with errors. Perhaps this has

rubbed off on the Google culture. Productive failures have two key characteristics, says Google project manager Urs Holzle: "You know why
you failed, and you have something you can apply to the next project."[3]
If you publicly note both of these, along with a log of the missteps that
led to the failures, you will be well on your way to creating a culture that
knows how to rebound.

Google is more willing than most companies to put its new ideas out
for public display through an ongoing stream of high-visibility beta tests.
Is there a better way to recruit several hundred thousand unpaid quality
checkers? This habit accelerates failure finding (and bouncing back).
When an idea checks out, it also builds momentum quickly. It allows
early successes to get visibility (and more resources) within Google more
quickly than any invariably politically charged annual budgeting or strategic planning process might allow. It also permits faster visibility in the
marketplace. Beta testers are the kind of people who will go to great
lengths to spread the word about a new product. They create market
momentum because each of them feels that a little piece of her is now a
part of the product. Beta testers are those that *The Tipping Point*'s author, Malcolm Gladwell, calls "mavens." These are the people others go
to for advice on what to buy. They are good folks to have on your side.

Google's hiring policies also include an aim to drive rapid failures.
This company seeks two types of technical talent. One group of new
recruits fits the young and brash mold. Google expects that these people's inexperience will lead them to have no fear about trying hard projects that are far outside the bounds of what they know. They are the
high-energy mistake generators. Type 2 hires are the Ph.D. superstars
from the best computer science schools. Their job is to quickly find and
fix the errors that the first group creates.

The alternative to Google's willingness to search quickly for facts is
"faith-based product development." How many companies do you know
of that have stuck with the wrong features on the wrong product for far
too long? Without fast facts and feedback, cheerleaders and true believ-
ers take over, executive supporters find themselves in positions they
can't back away from, and failure is seldom far behind.

Getting Things Moving with Gut Feel

In the military, the price of failure is measured in lost lives, not points
of market share. The U.S. Marine Corps tries to operate in a fast and

bold manner, believing that its troops have a better chance of prevailing in combat if they set the pace and course of the battle. They try to do this by having a decision-making loop that is more streamlined than the process used by their opponents. This means making many small, frequent, and rapid decisions when the information upon which these decisions have to be based is sketchy and unanalyzed. At each point in time, a Marine combat leader has to be able to boil down a complex, confusing, and ambiguous situation and discern its "actionable essence." Then the leader acts fast, updates his reading of the situation, and repeats the process, all with the objective of keeping momentum on his troops' side, not their opponents'. Growers may or may not have to outshoot their competition, but in the early stages of an initiative, it is vital to keep constant track of the project's actionable essence, its "what needs to happen next."

Gary Klein is a cognitive scientist whom the Marines like to invite along on their combat training missions as an outside observer. Klein has made a career of studying how people make good do-or-die decisions.[4] He has examined firefighters, Black Hawk helicopter pilots, and hospital emergency-room teams. None of these seem to follow the classic decision-making strategy taught in business schools: Identify alternative actions, evaluate each, rate the options against one another, and then implement the one rated most highly. These people all use intuition, not analysis, to figure out what they need to do. Klein uses his skills at analysis to figure out just what intuition involves.

Intuition starts with a recognition of cues or patterns in the situation at hand. This is where past experience comes in. The more of it there is filed away in a person's memory, the easier it is to make a match between current and past situations. Then instinct takes over; a gut feeling about what to do almost invariably arises, based on what worked before when similar clues were present. Few fast decision makers spend time developing other action alternatives. If some come to mind, they may be compared with the instinctive favorite, although this is mainly to justify the experienced expert's first impression. These experts then "qualify" their favored course of action by imagining how it might unfold and ultimately play out. This is like running a fast mental simulation. If everything checks out, they do what their first instinct told them. If the mental preview suggests problems, they quickly abandon that solution and come up with another option. They do not compare the alternatives; they just keep coming up with others until one passes their imaginary trial. According to Klein: "They don't need the best solution. They just need the one that works."[5]

This is not a good way to do strategic planning. Nor is it the way presented in Chapter 5 to uncover new growth opportunities. But it is the right technique to use to get things moving once an opportunity has been identified.

Postmortems and Premortems

Not all gut instincts work out. When Klein studied professional forest firefighters, he found that after every major blaze, the leaders run a feedback session. They review exactly what happened, what worked, what did not work, and why, and then they collectively agree on lessons to carry away for dealing with the next fire. The U.S. Army uses a similar practice, called the After Action Review. It has the same purpose: to identify what needs to be improved in order to achieve the results that are desired. These reviews are about learning, not about assigning blame or identifying heroes (those are the responsibilities of the Army hierarchy). During the invasion of Iraq and its aftermath, this process migrated to an intranet, making use of e-mail message lists and web pages to help newly deployed troops get up to speed quickly by tapping into the accumulated wisdom of the soldiers who were already in place.

Learning from war stories and postmortems is very useful, but Klein has found that it is even better to fix problems before they occur. To do this, he has invented the "premortem." This is a form of mental simulation intended to discover a growth initiative's hidden flaws. At the end of a project's kickoff meeting, team members are asked to pretend to stare into a crystal ball, looking six months ahead. They are told that the glimpse they received of the future was not a good one and the initiative has failed. They are given three minutes to run a simulation in their heads to uncover why the project collapsed. They then write down and share their reasons.

A candid discussion usually ensues. Pushing the failure date six months into the future makes it easier for team members to say what they really think. Minutes of the discussion are taken and distributed.

The idea here is not to reopen the planning process, but to lay out all the foreseeable speed bumps before action begins. People are fore-warned about what to be on the lookout for as events unfold, and there-fore are in a smarter position to take quick remedial action. The tendency to start out with gung-ho overconfidence is minimized, and eyes-open positive realism is enhanced.

Some activities move too fast to lend themselves to useful premor-tems. The University of Connecticut women's basketball team has found a way to obtain some of the benefits of premortems, though. Before games, they simulate the most difficult circumstances imaginable by hav-ing their starting players practice against eight opponents, rather than the five they will face in the real game. Doing this invariably makes the actual game seem easier.

Organizing for Momentum

Organizations that generate momentum have little resemblance to those that have traditionally been used to create new products. When Ford committed itself to building a gas-electric hybrid SUV, it faced the chal-lenge of creating the most technically advanced product it had ever mass-produced.[6] Even though the company has been making cars for over 100 years, these have all run with one motor. Hybrids have two, and they require a host of new-to-Ford technologies to make the two motors work together. To develop this car, Ford pulled researchers out of its lab and sat them next to the design engineers who were building the car proto-type. These and other members of the hybrid team stayed in close physi-cal proximity throughout the project, and the entire team stayed together until the project was completed.

Just like the SUV they were creating, this group had two engines. One member of the team, Prabhaker Patil, was a Ph.D. scientist. His job was to inspire creativity and invention. Another group leader, Mary Ann Wright, a veteran of many successful Ford car launches, was is the feet-on-the-ground person. Her job was to keep things on schedule. She was the disciplinarian who forced the scientists, who naturally like to keep refining (and refining) their work, to wrap things up. Ford's head of product development also ran interference for the group with the com-pany's top management. He freed the team from the normal time-consuming management reviews and progress report requirements, allowing it to focus on the must-win technical battles of the project, not the needs of the bureaucracy.

Contrast the hothouse process Ford used to play a critical game of catch-up with its rival hybrid maker, Toyota, with the product creation system that Bill Gates designed for Microsoft. There, responsibility for each new product passes from the "incubator" of an idea, usually a re-searcher in one of Microsoft's divisions, to the product "definer" (some-one in marketing or a division manager), and then finally to the "owner," which is a development team, which supervises the programmers who do the real work. Notice that the originator of the idea is not considered its owner and is not kept with the project through its completion. A host of other Microsoft managers play varying roles throughout the develop-ment cycle. Some are participants; others have reviewer or approver/ coach roles. Microsoft calls this integrated innovation, although its em-phasis seems to be more on fostering the integration than on fostering the innovation. Complex matrix systems like this are almost guaranteed to destroy momentum and result in long-delayed product introductions— which, when you think about it, might make sense for a company like Microsoft, whose new products primarily compete with its established products.

Extreme Programming and Other Tricks of the Trade

Growers cast a wide net when they are looking for ideas about how to keep progress accelerating. They borrow from successful college endow-ment fundraisers their practice of conducting a "quiet phase" of their campaigns, in which 30 to 40 percent of their total goal for donations is raised before the drive is formally announced publicly. Likewise, skillful growers line up a critical mass of resources and supporters before they officially announce their initiatives.

Some growers avoid Microsoft-style bureaucracy by following the lead of Seattle's other technology company, Amazon. Its CEO, Jeff Bezos, makes use of small, highly autonomous task forces to innovate and test new features for the Amazon web site. His rule about team size is, no more mouths than can be fed by two pizzas. Keeping the size of the group to seven or fewer also keeps it at the point where every participant can feel real ownership in what is produced. When groups get too large or too permanent, they are susceptible to the trap of wanting to *be* something, rather than to *accomplish* something.

Momentum can be thought of as an organizational equivalent of the state that Mihaly Csikszentmihalyi calls flow: the ability of an individual to be completely absorbed in whatever is being undertaken. Both flow and momentum require clear goals, rapid feedback, a balance of tough challenges and ample skills to meet them, and enough autonomy to provide flexible control over time.

A lesson for growers can also come from the new breed of computer programmer that is promising to revolutionize segments of the software industry. These are the practitioners of something called extreme programming (XP).[7] Most large software projects devote a great deal of time to up-front planning. They then make microscopic divisions of labor to an army of individual programmers who work by themselves. After all these people produce their contributions, another significant amount of time is spent putting the pieces together and correcting mistakes and wrong assumptions. This process invariably results in late projects and cost overruns.

XP works differently. Relatively little time is spent on planning. Programmers dive in and write the software, making course corrections wherever needed. Simple, but complete, versions of complex projects are designed quickly, then tested before elaborations are made. The idea is to produce a one-step-better working version of something with each cycle of work, rather than a piece-of-a-piece of something bigger that cannot be checked out until even more elements are finished.

XP's most striking feature, and one that is worth migrating outside the software world, is that a pair of software writers does all the programming—two people sharing one monitor and one keyboard. XP has completely thrown out the assumption that computer coding is a solitary activity that must be done by socially inept nerds. It is an incredibly productive approach. When one programmer reaches an impasse, he does not spend hours feeling lost and frustrated. His alter ego is inches away to immediately lend a different perspective. Paired programmers catch each other's mistakes, resulting in fewer bugs to find and destroy later. One partner types while the other scans the screen to check for logic (and typos). The traditional solo approach to software design is a bit like trying to drive a car on a strange, dark, hilly road with many surprise turns, all the while trying to read directions or consult a map. Not much fun. XP adds a navigator sitting next to you, and a relief driver for the long trips. Many tasks that growth teams need to accomplish can also be designed so that they can be assigned to a pair, rather than to individuals. Try it!

Sustaining Your Lead

Successful growers do not assume that they know why they are successful just because they have had a successful launch. When Fred Smith successfully modeled his overnight air delivery system on the hub-and-spoke model used by banks to clear checks and phone companies to route calls, he did not declare victory and just settle down into operating mode. After a few years of listening carefully to customers about why they used Federal Express, Smith realized that the company was not in the business he thought it was in. Smith had assumed that the business was all about the overnight transportation of goods. But his customers told him that what they were really buying was peace of mind. In other words, his computerized package tracking system was delivering more value than his fleet of airplanes. This was hard news for Smith to accept—he was a pilot who had worked his way through college flying charter flights—but he accepted it. And he quickly invested in handheld computers and transmitting devices for every one of his drivers to strengthen FedEx's lead in what he found really counted most with his customers.

A Columbia University sociologist, Duncan Watts, has studied how momentum feeds on itself by creating social chain reactions.[8] These occur when people start to buy a product just because other people are buying that product (the bestseller phenomenon). The key to taking advantage of this bandwagon effect lies in how you think about your market. Do not think about it as a preexisting entity, calm and quiet, just waiting for your efforts to penetrate it. Market demand is something that is created more dynamically, driven, as Watts has found, in large part by the growing success of the product itself. This is how FedEx grew, with its customers, not the FedEx marketing department or Fred Smith, really creating the product's rationale. Smith, fortunately, had the grower's ability to listen for what the market was telling him. Then he amplified its message, instead of getting caught up in his original plans for ongoing rollout and penetration.

OPTIMISM DRIVES RESILIENCE

Just as momentum is fueled by early action, so is rebounding. Many of the lessons about creating tension to generate forward movement that were covered in Chapter 8 are also relevant to staying resilient. Frequently the people who get in the most trouble during unexpected crises are those who attempt to think everything through before taking any corrective action. In situations where everything around you is changing quickly, attempts at exhaustive analysis can only prepare you for yesterday's reality. Instead, you need to develop multiple quick-and-dirty, conflicting interpretations of what's going on. Then do something, and, based on what you've tried, confirm some of the interpretations and throw the others out. Then repeat the process, each time getting a better fix on reality, as well as avoiding crisis paralysis by staying in motion. Karl Weick, the academic who has thought these steps through better than anyone else, likes to suggest that leaders "leap before they look" when everything around them is fogged in. It's often the best way to move to a point where the visibility is better.

Moving Beyond Yourself

Where does the courage to take such improvisational leaps come from? What does a grower need in order to be able to snap back (not snap) when faced with an unexpected setback? It is not hard to collapse into despair mode when you realize that all you have to fall back on is yourself, and you have just found that self to be a bit lacking. Growers, fortunately, have cultivated an ability to move beyond themselves, to look at situations from the outside in, not just outward from where they sit. This is how they have acquired the ability to see opportunities where others find only problems. This is how they measure progress by seeing the world as it is, not as they wish it to be. And this is how they are able to step back and learn from their errors.

Growers do not make their sense of self-esteem contingent on every-

thing always going according to plan. Growers feel good about themselves because they have made a commitment to move something
forward, to bring something new into being. They cultivate humility because it is a good antidote to thinking of themselves as infallible. They
know that acknowledging mistakes is essential to moving forward, and
that this acknowledgment calls a person's infallibility into question.

Don't Dig Deeper; Don't Demonize

Growers have a number of tactics for dealing with setbacks. They start
by *not* doing two things. First, they resist what is often a strong temptation to save face by redoubling their efforts along the same lines that got
them into trouble in the first place. They follow Warren Buffett's wise
counsel that the best thing to do when you find yourself in a hole is to
stop digging. Growers also resist demonizing their adversaries or blaming other people for their difficulties. Demonizing makes others seem
larger than life—not the best perception to have of an obstacle that needs
to be dealt with. Exacting revenge seldom breaks losing streaks, either.
In Apple Computer's early years, a lot of energy was spent portraying
first IBM and then Microsoft in this way. It is unclear that Apple really
benefited from this, and it is likely that focusing on IBM and Microsoft
distracted Apple from listening to its customers and better aligning its
products with those customers. Demonization and blame stimulate negative emotions and all the growth-destroying side effects that accompany
them.

New Course, Same Destination

Instead, growers are better served by refocusing on the goal they are
trying to reach. When you are sailing on choppy seas, you will quickly
get in trouble if you are totally focused on your course rather than your
destination. There is no point in trying to return to the route you were
originally on if your boat has been thrown off course. Focus instead on
your destination and plot a new path to get there from where you are
now. Stay attached to your goal, not to your assumptions about how to
reach it.

  If you are not in a sailing boat where you have to react instantly to changing circumstances, take a time-out. Disengage from what you are doing. Find something to distract you, something that will elevate your spirits and put you in a positive mood. Mentally relive some good experiences from your past. Recall the feelings that these evoked. This is the best way to prepare yourself, through marshaling positive emotions, to become clearheaded before figuring out what to differently. Then you are ready to:

- Look broadly, and ask what you should do based on the evidence you now see before you.
- Make sure your new efforts are in sync with your goal; do not hope for one thing to happen while you are rewarding others for something else.
- Ask if all the parts of your effort are serving the purpose of the whole, rather than having come to exist for their own sake.
- Be sure you have not missed any of the broader (social, political, technical, or economic) implications affecting what you have set out to accomplish. Keep in mind that these are often moving targets.
- Don't try too hard (competing aggressively when strategically co-operating would be more appropriate) and don't run too fast (out-running your supply lines and finding your effort capacity-constrained).
- Don't cross lines you don't mean to cross. People who fall just short of their goal are often the most tempted to behave unethically and to set themselves up for later failure.[9]

Resilience in Polio Eradication

The effort to eliminate polio from the world (described in Chapter 6) has not been without major setbacks. As I write this, it appears uncertain that the target date of 2008 will be met. Regardless, the ultimate goal has not changed. It can't. A handful of cases of polio remaining would eventually lead to thousands and then hundreds of thousands of cases. But the strategies and the timetable have evolved as circumstances required. When the Global Polio Eradication Initiative began in 1988, its target for declaring the world free of the disease was 2000. The deadline has slipped several times, although progress has been steady, with the number of polio cases having declined from over 350,000 to only 124 reported as this is being written in 2005. In addition to the immense logistical challenges inherent in ensuring that every person on the planet has been vaccinated, the effort—several times, in the midst of bloody civil wars—has been a victim of misinformation and fear.

Two years ago, just as the initiative, coordinated by the World Health Organization's Bruce Aylward, was closing in on its target, a group of radical Islamic preachers in northern Nigeria told parents not to allow their children to be vaccinated. They maintained that the immunization program was part of a plot by the U.S. government to infect Muslims with AIDS or render them infertile. The polio eradication program there came to a standstill until an intense international lobbying effort directed toward the Nigerian government, and a creative decision to provide vaccine that was manufactured in another Muslim country, Indonesia, convinced officials to resume. By then, though, the damage had been done. Migrant workers from Nigeria had spread the virus across a number of African countries, and some African Muslims brought it with them to Mecca during the 2005 annual pilgrimage, which drew over two million visitors. Since then, cases have been reported as far away as Indonesia that have been traced back to the strain of polio virus common in Nigeria.

The recent spread of the disease has forced Aylward to ramp up massive and costly reimmunization programs in countries that had been declared polio-free years before. If you ask him about the setback in Nigeria, though, all you will hear is praise for the extraordinary effort made by officials and clerics in the north to resume the vaccinations after the program ground to a halt for 12 months. Since most of the remaining polio-plagued countries are Muslim, he sees this as an opportunity to redouble his fundraising efforts in the capitals of the oil-rich Gulf states. Missed target dates have also provided an excuse to summon the health ministers of the affected countries to Geneva to sign a public declaration of their strong and ongoing commitment to free the world of polio. For Aylward, there is no such thing as bad news. He is a firm believer in taking good advantage of whatever goes wrong.

Aylward is an optimist. This characteristic, more than his energy and brains (both of which he has in ample supply), fuels his resilience and that of the global effort he coordinates. According to psychologist Martin Seligman, what matters most is what you think when you encounter adversity. Optimists are people who interpret setbacks as surmountable, specific to a single problem or instance, and caused by temporary circumstances or other people. Seligman says that optimists are brisk bouncers-back from troubles, and they also get on a roll easily after an initial success. He has demonstrated that optimism is a strength that can be cultivated, and he has developed a number of techniques that growers can use to acquire this habit of thought.[10] If Aylward had been a pessimist, he would have viewed the situation in Nigeria as his personal fault, something that would undermine the entire polio eradication effort, and an event whose consequences would be permanent. If he thought this way, he probably would have quit his WHO position years ago, and would be back in his native Newfoundland quietly working as a physician and treating only his nearby patients.

USE "OPEN SPACE" TO TAKE STOCK

Both momentum maintenance and bouncing back can benefit from taking time out to take stock of the situation that a grower initiative is in. This is especially useful when an effort is well underway, involves an increasing number of participants, and is at a turning point in its direction or is facing serious obstacles and challenges. Toyota has an approach for doing this that it calls "oobeya." This is the Japanese word for "big, open office," and the auto maker uses this mechanism to bring people from all parts of the company together to share information about a particular product or issue. Not to be outdone, Honda uses something similar, as the company has realized that even seemingly straightforward problems can have far-flung causes that are seldom really sorted out until a broad range of institutional knowledge is collected in one room. My favorite way to do this, though, involves a meeting technology invented by an American, Harrison Owen.

Owen discovered what he calls "Open Space" when he was hired to spend a year organizing an international conference for 250 participants. Although the meeting came off very well, Owen and all the participants agreed at its close that the most useful element was the coffee breaks. This led Owen to wonder if a meeting format could be designed that had all the energy, synergy, and excitement present in a good coffee break and dispensed with all the formal presentation, papers, and panel discussions that filled the time between the breaks.

What he came up with was a way in which complex business issues could be addressed by a group of a dozen to several hundred people (sufficient to include all the diverse views that were relevant) in a relatively short period of time. This is done with no advance agenda preparation and minimal meeting facilitation. By the end of the gathering:

- All issues of concern to everyone will have been identified.
- Each issue will have been discussed to the extent anyone cared to, and next steps will have been proposed.

Open Space meetings work best when they address an issue that no one (including the grower in charge who convenes the meeting) knows the answer to, but for which people are willing to collectively try to find an answer. Everyone who comes should care about the issue and feel that she has something to contribute to its resolution. No one should have an unchangeable attachment to a particular outcome.

These sessions can take place in one very crowded day, but taking two or three days is usually better. This allows ideas to be recorded and participants to have time to reflect on (and possibly rethink) what has been said. An outside speaker or preplanned presentation may be appropriate at the start of a session, but never afterward, lest it interrupt whatever energy has been generated to go out and take action on what has been discussed.

Space requirements are simple: one room large enough to allow everyone to sit in a circle, or several concentric circles, without crowding. The room should have a large wall on which notices can be taped up. Ample space for breakout sessions is also necessary. Aside from arranging for a venue and timing, the only advance planning involves specifying the theme or issue to address and inviting the participants.

The meeting opens with a statement of its theme. All participants are sitting in a large circle—no classroom or bowling alley–style seating arrangements are allowed. They get in the way of free discussion, and they signify that the person in the front is the main authority on the subject at hand. In the next two hours or so, the entire agenda for the rest of the meeting is planned. Each participant is asked if he has an issue or opportunity related to the meeting theme that he would like to bring up and take responsibility for seeing that it is discussed. One by one, each of these people comes to the center of the circle and writes a short title for his breakout session and his name on a piece of paper. He then introduces himself to the group, says a few words about his specific issue, and finishes by taping his paper to the large wall. Each proposer is also responsible for designating a time and place for the discussion, and then convening it. A matrix chart can be made with all the scheduling and location information. Then, after all those who wish to propose a topic for discussion have done so, all the participants are invited to go to the wall and sign up for whatever groups they are interested in.

It may take a little time for the participants to realize that nothing is going to get discussed unless they suggest something, and that if something they are especially concerned about is not discussed, it is their own fault, but they usually catch on quickly.

The only other structure to the meeting is the entire group assembling briefly each morning for announcements and at the end of the day for a quick recap of what was discussed during that day's sessions. The session at the end of the last day is likely to be longer.

Owen has found it useful to announce at the outset what he calls the "law of two feet." It states: "If at any time you find yourself in any situation where you are neither learning nor contributing—use your two feet and move to some place more to your liking. Such a place might be another group, or even outside into the sunshine. No matter what, don't sit there feeling miserable—unhappy people are unlikely to be productive people."[11] This law reinforces the logic behind the agenda-setting process and the entire Open Space concept: Individual initiative is important; nothing will happen unless you make it happen.

Doing something like this periodically helps deal with a common problem that project teams have when they work together over a long time period. In most instances, the patterns of interaction—who talks to whom about what—do not change significantly through the different stages of the project. This happens even though the information needs of conceptualization and design work are often very different from those of rollout and rapid expansion. Once particular lines of communication have been established, they become the group's habit, and people seem loath to change them. Open Space's built-in approach to self-organization remedies all that.

Growers believe that the future is fundamentally open. Open Space meetings are a perfect microcosm of that idea.

KNOW WHEN TO LET GO—AND HOW TO SHARE THE WEALTH

Most people see their lives as stories, and the story has to move forward.[1]

—Dan McAdams

QUIT WHILE YOU ARE AHEAD

McAdams, a Northwestern University expert in adult development, has also observed that if a specific goal looms large enough and dazzling enough in a person's life, its aftermath is not just another chapter in the story. "It's time to start a whole new book," he says. The last challenge many growers face is for some the hardest: declaring victory and celebrating it, then letting go and moving on.

Quitting while you are ahead is probably management's most underrated practice. It's what Jerry Seinfeld knew that his boss, Jack Welch, forgot. Welch extended his retirement date in a frantic, but futile effort to prolong General Electric's record of double-digit earning increases by acquiring Honeywell. Welch's attempt to do this tarnished his reputation, as he was unable to convince the European Union regulators to approve the deal. On the other hand, Seinfeld's reputation soared as he turned down the biggest financial deal ever offered a television star when he decided to close down the most popular American television sitcom of the 1990s. Some observers thought Seinfeld was just abandoning his audience before it abandoned him, but the reality was that he had other things he wanted to do with his life.

Business Needs Change; People Don't

Sources of competitive advantage are never constant for very long. Thriving over time means shifting from one source of advantage to the next. This kind of adaptation is much easier if the growers who took the business to where it is today have the wisdom to pull back and strategically let go, rather than redoubling their efforts to entrench what should be surpassed. The best guarantee of renewal and rebirth is a growth leader with the maturity to move on, clearing the way for other growers to take a fresh look at what has now come to be, and plot a way to move beyond it.

Growth slows because of distraction and irrelevance. Growers tend to adopt the fixer mentality when they become responsible for maintaining what they've built. They easily become too distracted by the care and feeding of the ongoing business to send out feelers to find something new. Some also cling to the assumptions that they felt were responsible for their past triumphs—premises that were once true, but since may have lost their relevance. Lee Iacocca of Chrysler and Michael Eisner of Disney both heroically rescued their companies from decline, and both stayed in place too long afterward, steering their businesses back toward the troubled states in which they found them. Contrast them with Michael Dell (Dell Computer), Pierre Omidyar (eBay), Howard Schultz (Starbucks), and even Bill Gates (Microsoft)—all growers who stepped aside long before the growth trajectories they launched had run their course.

Dell, Omidyar, and others like them would be less the exception and more the rule if the virtues of letting go were better appreciated. "Quit while you are ahead" was the last lesson Thomas Gerrity taught when he voluntarily stepped aside as dean of the University of Pennsylvania's Wharton School. He left after the school was ranked in first place in *BusinessWeek*'s ranking of the best business schools for three years running. Gerrity explained when he left that he had seen too many executives stay on too long. "There's something about turnover," he suggested, "which involves renewal and rebirth."[2]

Realized Goals Are Not Unmitigated Blessings

Letting go is not a natural response to success. An unrealized growth goal provides structure, focus, and energy. Where are these necessities to come from when the objective is reached? If all of a person's time and priorities are organized around a hunt, then the moment right after the kill is going to produce disorientation and distress, not joy and celebration.[3]

Avoiding such a letdown requires growers to avoid thinking of themselves as people who are totally identified with their efforts. It is possible to be completely committed to achieving a result without the result also coming to define you. A grower whose work has been done well sees the proof in the achievement's taking on a life of its own—outgrowing, outpacing, and possibly even outliving its instigator. The model here is that of the successful parent, not the bigger-is-better-oriented empire builder. Empire builders frequently run the risk of becoming prisoners of their empire.

The best reason to move on is having some other pressing work ahead—McAdams's idea of starting a whole new book. Does your growth goal contain within it some logical encore? Have you been able to maintain other goals as you pursued your growth objective? Coexisting goals allow for an easier transition. Shifting focus is always a lot simpler than starting over. Alternatively, your growth goal may be part of a larger objective that you have, one that you can now find other ways to work toward. There are lots of alternatives; just don't be a grower who does not know what to do next.

Broaden Your Realm

Harvard Business School professor Michael Porter's career has involved a sequence of contributions in progressively broadening realms. He first won fame for his work on competitive strategy in companies. He expanded these ideas to consider the dynamics of competition within and between industries, and that led him to research and write about how nations themselves can hone their particular competitive advantages. His international work gave him a new perspective on the U.S. marketplace, as he realized that many pockets of urban poverty had characteristics similar to those of developing countries. This led him to found the Initiative for a Competitive Inner City to seek private investment to revitalize underserved urban markets. And his exposure to nonprofit groups working on urban redevelopment led him to his latest project—figuring out how to apply lessons from strategy to help charities and philanthropies become more effective.

This kind of broadening of a grower's horizon can happen in many directions. Jeff Hawkins, designer of the first Palm Pilot, has, as described in Chapter 5, shifted his attention to neuroscience, an interest he has had since college that was set aside as he pursued a career in electrical engineering. Gordon Moore, another Silicon Valley icon and cofounder of Intel, has cultivated an interest in preserving biodiversity and has set up an organization to find pragmatic ways of saving South American rain forests. What led him in that direction? Moore had a lifetime passion for sports fishing in obscure parts of the world. Martin Seligman (Chapter 9) is still immersed in the work of creating the domain of positive psychology, but he has managed to take time out to organize a center at the University of Pennsylvania aimed at finding ways to use psychology to reduce conflict among ethnic groups worldwide.

Be a Serial Grower

Some people are serial growers and find themselves happiest and most productive when they are starting over again on a different issue in the same realm. Publisher Jane Friedman's plans (Chapter 3) to make the name of HarperCollins into a brand that is as well known as some of the top authors it publishes have a good chance of coming to fruition, considering her track record of championing innovation. She is credited with having invented the author tour when she was a young publicist, and she was later responsible for bringing the idea of recorded books into mainstream publishing when she pioneered Random House's audio book business.

Ask Bruce Aylward (chapters 6 and 10) what he wants to do after polio is finally eradicated, and he will think for a minute about spending some long-put-off time with his family. Then he will tell you that this would be almost irresponsible considering how much he and his team have learned about how to take a good idea (ridding the world of a disease) and a proven technology (immunization) and scale it up. Aylward and his World Health Organization group intend to be first in line when an initiative is announced to take on malaria, measles, smoking, or even AIDS globally. He will have no shortage of second acts to keep him busy.

IBM has realized that growth initiatives make great second acts for the leaders of its established businesses to take on. A number of IBM's "best and brightest" managers have been (voluntarily) taken from running their multibillion-dollar divisions with thousands of employees working for them, and told to go out and start a new business from scratch.[4] In the past five years, 25 of these moves have been made; 3 of them failed, but the other 22 are generating $15 billion in new revenue and are expanding at 40 percent a year.

Some growers morph into the organizational equivalent of a statesman's role, balancing and reconciling the needs and demands of fixers and growers. Bill Greenwood's career (Chapter 4) took this turn. Others find it more rewarding to completely shift gears, and become a grower of growers.

SEEDING THE FUTURE

The greatest contribution that the leader of a successful growth initiative can make is to give something back. You prime the pump for the next generation of growers by giving away the mindset for growth.

Catherine Muther used her marketing talents to help build Cisco Systems into a global computer-networking powerhouse. Then she quit and used the wealth from her hard-earned stock options to create the Three Guineas Fund. This foundation's purpose is to make it easier for women to do what she did—have an impact on and play a powerful role in Silicon Valley. To keep her fund growing after the Cisco windfall is given away, she asks each woman-owned start-up she aids to pledge a portion of its future stock to the foundation.

Muther did not leave her grower instincts behind when she became a philanthropist. She does not focus on giving away money, she focuses on solving problems. The first problem she identified was figuring out why women were so underrepresented in high-tech start-ups that received venture capital funding. Muther's solution was to start up an organization herself, the Women's Technology Cluster. It serves as a business incubator for new technology companies in which women have a major equity stake. The cluster provides offices and equipment, and connects these businesses with the established Silicon Valley venture capital network.

Narayana Murthy also works in high technology, but half a world away from Muther. Based in Bangalore, India, he has been called "India's Bill Gates." He founded one of that country's leading software makers, Infosys, and through stock options made dozens of his colleagues millionaires, something that was unheard of in a nation in which most large businesses are privately held and are passed on to family members. Believing that what had brought Infosys to the billion-dollar point in sales (himself) might not be appropriate for the next stage of its development, Murthy yielded the chief executive slot, became the nonexecutive chairman, and took on the title of "chief mentor."

Murthy knows how important it is to allow one-on-one relationships to form between senior executives and the younger, high-potential Infosys employees who will lead the company's future growth. So when he decided to build a leadership development institute, he insisted that the company's senior executives teach all the major courses. To ensure that the program involved more that just a retelling of old war stories, Murthy hired an Indian-born, UCLA-trained behavioral scientist, G. K. Jayaram, from the United States to head the institute and to teach him and his top team how to teach.

In personally leading the sessions that train Infosys's next cadre of growers, Murthy followed the example of Roger Enrico (Chapter 3), a battle-scarred veteran of the American cola wars. In the 18 months before he became chief executive of PepsiCo, Enrico spent almost half his time running a private war college for small groups of promising mid-level Pepsi managers. He taught them how he had done what he did to become designated the next CEO (Enrico, a maverick marketer, invented the Pepsi Challenge, and as head of Frito-Lay he drove Anheuser-Busch out of the snack food business). Then he helped them craft their own growth philosophies and projects to implement then. Afterward, Enrico provided ongoing coaching, putting his personal imprint on more than 100 future Pepsi growers.

Enrico did such a good job of building PepsiCo's bench of potential leaders that he identified a well-qualified successor, Steven Reinemund, and voluntarily retired a year earlier than scheduled. Why the rush to let go? Enrico wanted to spend all his time teaching future growers how it was done.

● ● ● ● ● ● ● ● ● ● ● ●

EPILOGUE

● ● ● ● ● ● ● ● ● ● ● ●

This book was written in an attic office at my home. In front of the house stand several tall, old oak trees. They tower high over the attic and roof, providing welcome shade from Washington, D.C.'s strong summer sun. They were also a source of worry when my family first moved into the house—what if one of these giants were to fall on us? Concerned about tree disease, insect damage, and the potential dangers to our home that they could cause, I consulted an arborist, expecting to hear him recommend regular applications of pesticides and other disease-fighting treatments. But he declined to prescribe any.

The tree expert said that chemical treatments would provide short-term relief, at best. When the pesticides wore off, any insect infestation would return, necessitating further treatments. Bugs, he said, make their homes in diseased trees and find healthy ones inhospitable. Instead, he recommended a program for ongoing care of the trees—regular pruning, mulching, and fertilization. This would be sufficient to keep the oaks healthy, strong enough to fight disease and fend off insect takeover attempts.

That advice was offered many years ago. I've followed it, and I have been rewarded with an intact roof, a cool attic, and thriving foliage, but I hadn't given much thought to the reasoning behind what I was doing until September 11, 2001, as I was driving through the streets of a stunned and fearful Washington on my way to pick up my young son, William, from his school.

He and his classmates had already been told of the attacks on the

World Trade Center in New York and on the nearby Pentagon. They were all very frightened and puzzled. Why was their country the target of this horror? What must be done to keep it from happening again? I was probably in as much of a state of shock and confusion as was my son. I knew little about Al Qaeda and terrorism, and I wondered what I should say to him as I drove down the hill near his school, with the smoke from the burning Pentagon still clearly visible just across the Potomac. By the time we reached home and parked under the tall oaks, I recalled the arborist's wisdom, and I shared that advice with William.

*   *   *

Fixers and growers are found in the business world and beyond. Some people have the special talent needed to create a new future. Others' efforts are better directed toward reacting and responding to events as they unfold. The wide range of actions that have taken place since September 11 in both fighting terrorism and eliminating its preconditions provide a rich laboratory for watching these two orientations in action. At times they seem to be in conflict with each other; at other times they are mutually supportive. This is understandable. Creating the world that we most want to have necessitates a mindset very different from that required to react to the world we do have. The logic behind avoiding unpleasant and feared consequences is not the same as that which guides a builder of something better.

Both organizations and societies are at risk when both mentalities are not present, and in some rough balance with each other. As Picasso once noted: "Every act of creation is first of all an act of destruction."[1] The trick is to plan the movement from old to new in a way that does not lead to mindless destruction and chaos. This means starting out with the grower's clear idea of somewhere better to end up, and knowing what is wanted with as much clarity as what is not wanted. That's how real growth happens. This kind of growth, of course, has little to do with getting bigger or prevailing over others.

NOTES

INTRODUCTION

1. Quoted in Duane Elgin, *Voluntary Simplicity* (New York: William Morrow, 1993), p. 36. Original quotation is from Simone de Beauvoir, *The Ethics of Ambiguity* (Secaucus, N.J.: Citadel Press, 1948).
2. W. Timothy Gallwey, *The Inner Game of Tennis* (New York: Random House, 1997) and *The Inner Game of Work* (New York: Random House, 1999).
3. Jennifer Reingold, "How to Read a Business Book," *Fast Company*, November 2004, p. 106.

CHAPTER 1: IS BIGGER BETTER?

1. Peter Drucker, *Management* (New York: Harper & Row, 1974), p. 772.
2. Anne Kreamer and Kurt Andersen, "Culture," *Fast Company*, October 2002, p. 78.
3. Ibid.
4. Margaret Boitano, "Is Dynegy the Next Enron?" *Fortune*, Dec. 18, 2000, p. 168.
5. Ibid.
6. Lowell Bryan and John Kay, "Can a Company Ever Be Too Big?" *McKinsey Quarterly*, 1999, no. 4, p. 106.
7. Danny Hakim, "Ford's Ex-Chief Hired to Rebuild Polaroid," *The New York Times*, Nov. 12, 2002, p. BU 1.

8. Daniel Fisher, "What's the Hurry?" *Forbes*, Apr. 14, 2003, pp. 232–233.
9. Jim Collins, "Bigger, Better, Faster," *Fast Company*, June 2003, p. 78.
10. Reed Abelson, "States Are Battling Against Wal-Mart Over Health Care," *The New York Times*, Nov. 1, 2004, p. BU 1.
11. Anthony Bianco and Wendy Zeller, "Is Wal-Mart Too Powerful?" *BusinessWeek*, Oct. 6, 2003, p. 102.
12. Drucker, *Management*, pp. 638–639.
13. Ibid., p. 638.
14. Jerry Useem, "Introduction: Wal-Mart Forever," *Fortune*, Apr. 14, 2003, p. 90.
15. Mara Der Hovanesian, "Can Chuck Prince Clean Up Citi?" *BusinessWeek*, Oct. 4, 2004, p. 34.
16. Useem, "Introduction: Wal-Mart Forever," p. 90.
17. Drucker, *Management*, p. 771.
18. "The Fallen Managers," *BusinessWeek*, Jan. 10, 2005, p. 80.
19. John Simmons, "A World of Hurt," *Fortune*, Jan. 10, 2005, p. 20.
20. "Now You See It, Now You Don't," *The Economist*, Oct. 30, 2004, "Survey of Information Technology," p. 8.
21. "Big Mac's Makeover," *The Economist*, Oct. 16, 2004, p. 63.
22. Grainger David, "Can McDonald's Cook Again?" *Fortune*, Apr. 14, 2003, p. 120.
23. Drucker, *Management*, p. 775.
24. For more background on shareholder-value theory, its assumptions and advocates, see John Cassidy, "The Greed Cycle," *The New Yorker*, Sept. 23, 2002, pp. 64–77; Robert Simons, Henry Mintzberg, and Kunal Basu, "Memo to CEOs," *Fast Company*, June 2002, pp. 117–119; and Michael Jensen and William Meckling, "The Nature of Man," *Journal of Applied Corporate Finance*, vol. 7, no. 2, Summer 1994, pp. 4–19.

CHAPTER 2: A BIGGER STOCK PRICE IS NOT ALWAYS A GOOD THING

1. John Cassidy, "The Greed Cycle," *The New Yorker*, Sept. 23, 2002, p. 75.

2. Lowell Bryan and John Kay, "Can a Company Ever Be Too Big?" *McKinsey Quarterly*, 1999, no. 4, p. 102.

3. Margaret Blair, "Shareholder Value, Corporate Governance and Corporate Performance," in Peter Cornelius and Bruce Kogut (eds.), *Corporate Governance and Capital Flows in a Global Economy* (Oxford University Press, 2003), pp. 53–82. Quotation from abstract at http://ssrn.com/abstract = 334240.

4. Ibid.

5. Robert Shiller, *Irrational Exuberance* (Princeton, N.J.: Princeton University Press, 2000).

6. Carol Loomis, "The Whistleblower and the CEO," *Fortune*, July 7, 2003, p. 91.

7. Gretchen Morgenson, "Pennies That Aren't From Heaven," *The New York Times*, Nov. 7, 2004, p. BU 1.

8. David Stires, "Krispy Kreme Is in the Hole–Again," *Fortune*, Nov. 1, 2004, p. 42.

9. "The New Earnings Game," *BusinessWeek*, Oct. 4, 2004, p. 128.

10. Joseph Fuller and Michael Jensen, "Just Say No to Wall Street: Putting a Stop to the Earnings Game," *Journal of Applied Corporate Finance*, Winter 2002, p. 45.

11. "Fat Cats Turn to Low Fat," *The Economist*, Mar. 5, 2005, p. 14.

12. Geoffrey Colvin, "Will CEOs Find Their Inner Choirboy?" *Fortune*, Apr. 28, 2003, p. 45.

13. Mark Hulbert, "In a Twist, High Dividends Are Now a Predictor of Growth," *The New York Times*, Nov. 17, 2002, p. BU 6.

14. Jason Zweig, "Peter's Uncertainty Principle," *Money*, November 2004, p. 149.

15. John Christy, "The Dividend Elite," *Forbes*, Nov. 15, 2004, p. 102.

16. Dan Lovallo and Daniel Kahneman, "Delusions of Success," *Harvard Business Review*, July 2003, p. 58.

17. David Henry, "M&A Deals: Show Me," *BusinessWeek*, Nov. 10, 2003, p. 40.

18. Lovallo and Kahneman, "Delusions of Success," p. 59.

19. Keith Hammonds, "Size Is Not a Strategy," *Fast Company*, September 2002, p. 83.

20. Gregory Crouch, "At Ahold, Past Errors Shadow the Future," *The New York Times*, Nov. 25, 2003, p. BU 1.

21. Matthias Bekier, Anna Bogardus, and Tim Oldham, "Why Mergers Fail," *McKinsey Quarterly*, 2001, no. 4, pp. 6–8.
22. R. J. Sternberg (ed.), *Why Smart People Can Be So Stupid* (New Haven, Conn.: Yale University Press, 2002).
23. R. J. Sternberg, "WICS: A Model of Leadership in Organizations," *Academy of Management Learning and Education*, vol. 2, no. 4, p. 395.
24. Henry Beam, "Why Smart Managers Fail," *Academy of Management Executive*, May 2004, p. 158.
25. Roy Lubit, "The Long-Term Organizational Impact of Destructively Narcissistic Managers," *Academy of Management Executive*, February 2002, pp. 127–138.
26. Ibid., p. 133.
27. Hammonds, "Size Is Not a Strategy," p. 80.
28. Peter Drucker, *Management* (New York: Harper & Row, 1974), p. 772.
29. Ibid.

CHAPTER 3: GROWTH IS ABOUT MOVING FORWARD

1. Thomas Kuhn, *The Structure of Scientific Revolutions* (Chicago: University of Chicago Press, 1970), p. 111.
2. This perspective on growth was influenced by Sidney Jourard, "Growing Awareness and the Awareness of Growth," in Herbert Otto and John Mann (eds.), *Ways of Growth* (New York: Viking Press, 1969), pp. 1–14.
3. John Ellis, "Yahoo Kisses It All Good-bye," *Fast Company*, July 2002, p. 116.
4. Thich Nhat Hanh, *Living Buddha, Living Christ* (New York: Riverhead Books, 1995), p. 117.
5. For more details, see John Quelch and Nathalie Laider, *ACCION International*, Harvard Business School case 9-503-106 (Boston: Harvard Business School, 2003).
6. See Malcolm Gladwell, *The Tipping Point* (Boston: Little, Brown and Co., 2000) for a description of the skills required to induce a marketplace epidemic.
7. Joseph Fuller and Michael Jensen, "Just Say No to Wall Street:

Putting a Stop to the Earnings Game," *Journal of Applied Corporate Finance*, Winter 2002, p. 43.

8. Robert Bruner, "Why the Big Mo Is Bad Business," *The Washington Post*, Aug. 20, 2002, p. 8.

9. Fuller and Jensen, "Just Say No," p. 41.

10. Donald Graham speaking at the 2004 MBA Media and Entertainment Conference in New York, Feb. 20, 2004.

11. Herbert Otto and John Mann, eds., *Ways of Growth*, (New York: Grossman, 1968) p. 3.

12. Ibid., p. 5.

13. Richard Normann, *Management and Statesmanship* (Stockholm: Scandinavian Institutes for Administrative Research, 1978), pp. 31–32.

14. George Salk and Rob Lachenauer, "Hardball," *Harvard Business Review*, April 2004, pp. 62–71.

15. Peter Senge, *The Fifth Discipline* (New York: Doubleday/Currency, 1990), pp. 95–104.

16. As quoted by John Balzar, "Deregulation Follies Stain Capitalism," *Los Angeles Times World Report in Yomiuri Shimbun*, Mar. 17, 2003, p. 13.

17. Devan, Millan, and Shirke, "Balancing Short- and Long-Term Performance," *McKinsey Quarterly*, 2005, no. 1, pp. 31–33.

18. Julian Birkinshaw, "The Paradox of Corporate Entrepreneurship," *Strategy + Business*, issue 30, pp. 46–57.

19. Jeanne Liedtka, "If Managers Thought Like Designers," *Batten Briefings*, Winter 2005, p. 4.

20. Ibid., p. 5.

21. John Tierney, "A Tale of Two Fisheries," *The New York Times Magazine*, Aug. 27, 2000.

22. Ibid.

23. Sydney Finkelstein, "7 Habits of Spectacularly Unsuccessful Executives," *Fast Company*, July 2003, p. 89.

CHAPTER 4: ARE YOU A FIXER OR A GROWER?

1. For more information, see John Katzenbach and Douglas Smith, *The Wisdom of Teams* (New York: HarperCollins, 1994), pp. 28–40,

and Robert Tomasko, *Go for Growth* (New York: John Wiley & Sons, 1996), pp. 15–17.

2. See Joseph Jaworski, *Synchronicity* (San Francisco: Berrett-Koehler, 1996), pp. 160–182 for more detail on this perspective.

3. Robert Fritz, *The Path of Least Resistance* (New York: Fawcett Columbine, 1989), p. 31 elaborates on this distinction.

4. Ibid., p. 40.

5. Specifically, the left middle-frontal gyrus of the left prefrontal cortex is associated with positive emotions and a parallel part of the right prefrontal cortex with some negative emotions. The amygdala, a walnut-sized part of the brain, is also active when fear is experienced. For additional details, see Daniel Goleman, *Destructive Emotions* (New York: Bantam Books, 2004), pp. 179–204.

6. Martin Seligman, *Authentic Happiness* (New York: Free Press, 2002), pp. 30–44.

7. Barbara Fredrickson, "The Value of Positive Emotions," *American Scientist*, July–August 2003, pp. 330–335.

8. Seligman, *Authentic Happiness,* pp. 30–44.

9. Kathleen Sutcliffe and Klaus Weber, "The High Cost of Accurate Knowledge," *Harvard Business Review*, May 2003, pp. 74–82.

10. Reported by Barbara Fredrickson in her presentation at the Third International Positive Psychology Summit in Washington, D.C., on Oct. 1, 2004.

11. Roberts, Spreitzer, Dutton, Quinn, Heaphy, and Barker, "How to Play to Your Strengths," *Harvard Business Review*, January 2005, p. 80.

12. Reported by Barbara Fredrickson in her presentation at the Third International Positive Psychology Summit in Washington, D.C., on Oct. 1, 2004, and in Marcial Losada, "The Complex Dynamics of High Performance Teams," *Mathematical and Computer Modeling*, vol. 30, no. 9–10, 1999, pp. 179–192.

13. Simone de Beauvoir, *The Ethics of Ambiguity* (Secaucus, N.J.: Citadel Press, 1948), pp. 75–155.

CHAPTER 5: KNOW WHERE TO LOOK

1. Steven Levy, "Out of Left Field," *Newsweek*, Apr. 21, 2003, p. E10.

2. Alex Markels, "The Wisdom of Chairman Ko," *Fast Company*, November 1999, pp. 270–272.

3. Matthew Karnitschnig, "That Van You're Driving May Be Part Porsche," *BusinessWeek*, Dec. 27, 1999, p. 72.

4. Keith Hammonds, "How to Play Beane Ball," *Fast Company*, May 2003, pp. 84-88. For more details, see Michael Lewis, *Moneyball: The Art of Winning an Unfair Game* (New York: Norton, 2003).

5. Rob Walker, "The Marketing of No Marketing," *The New York Times Magazine*, June 22, 2003, pp. 42-45.

6. President Ronald Liebowitz's inaugural address, Middlebury College, Oct. 10, 2004.

7. Michael Maccoby, *The Productive Narcissist* (New York: Broadway Books, 2003), pp. 162-165.

8. For more details, see Jeff Hawkins with Sandra Blakeslee, *On Intelligence* (New York: Times Books, 2004).

9. Diane Coutu, "Psychologist Karl E. Weick: Sense and Reliability," *Harvard Business Review*, April 2003, p. 87.

10. Eric Jaffe, "Mind in a Bind," *American Psychological Society Observer*, November 2003, p. 7.

11. Lassiter, Geers, Munhall, Ploutz-Snyder, and Breitenbecher, "Illusory Causation," *Psychological Science*, July 2003, pp. 299-305.

12. Moshe Bar and Irving Biederman, "Subliminal Visual Priming," *Psychological Science*, November 1998, p. 464.

13. Egon Zehnder, "A Simpler Way to Pay," *Harvard Business Review*, April 2001, pp. 53-61.

14. Vivek Paul, "Don't Limit Yourself by Past Expectations," *Fortune*, Mar. 21, 2005, p. 100.

15. Ford, Duncan, Bedeian, Ginter, Rousclup, and Adams, "Mitigating Risks, Invisible Hands, Inevitable Disasters, and Soft Variables: Management Research That Matters to Managers," *Academy of Management Executive*, February 2003, pp. 50-51.

16. Fara Warner, "Nike's Women's Movement," *Fast Company*, August 2002, pp. 72-75.

17. Mark Maletz and Nitin Nohria, "Managing in the Whitespace," *Harvard Business Review*, February 2001, p. 103.

18. Martin Seligman, *Authentic Happiness* (New York: Free Press, 2002), p. 38.

19. Karen Gasper and Gerald Clore, "Attending to the Big Picture," *Psychological Science*, January 2002, pp. 34-39.

20. Kristin Ohlson, "Brainstorm," *CWRU Magazine*, Summer 2003, p. 32.
21. Paul Hemp, "A Time for Growth," *Harvard Business Review*, July–August 2004, p. 73.
22. Christopher Johnson, "The Best Possible World," *CWRU Magazine*, Spring 2002, pp. 14-19.
23. Roger Lowenstein, "The Quality Cure?" *The New York Times Magazine*, Mar. 13, 2005.
24. Kenichi Ohmae, "Companyism and Do More Better," *Harvard Business Review*, January–February 1989, p. 132.
25. Seligman, *Authentic Happiness*, p. 279.
26. Jack Welch with Suzy Welch, *Winning* (New York: HarperBusiness, 2005), pp. 172-180.

CHAPTER 6: KNOW WHAT THEY WANT

1. Churchill's response when asked if his government would support Russia when it was invaded by Germany in 1941, as quoted in Saul Alinsky, *Rules for Radicals* (New York: Random House, 1971), p. 29.
2. Aylward, Hull, Cochi, Sutter, Olive, and Melgaard, "Disease Eradication as a Public Health Strategy," *Bulletin of the World Health Organization*, vol. 78, no. 3, 2000, pp. 285-297.
3. William Murray, *The Scottish Himalayan Expedition* (London: J. M. Dent & Sons, 1951). This quotation is often misattributed to J. W. von Goethe.
4. Peter Senge, Roberts, Ross, Smith and Kleiner, *The Fifth Discipline Fieldbook* (New York: Doubleday Currency, 1994), p. 219.
5. Robert Levering, *A Great Place to Work* (New York: Random House, 1988).
6. Carol Loomis, "Why Carly's Big Bet Is Failing," *Fortune*, Feb. 7, 2005, p. 64.
7. Oliver Morton, "After Columbia? Go to Mars," *Wired*, April 2003, p. 33.
8. James Brian Quinn, *Strategies for Change* (Homewood, Ill.: Richard D. Irwin, 1980), pp. 79-80.

9. Sumantra Ghoshal and Heike Bruch, "Reclaim Your Job," *Harvard Business Review*, March 2004, pp. 43–44.
10. Gary Hamel and C. K. Prahalad, "Strategic Intent," *Harvard Business Review*, May–June 1989, pp. 67–71.
11. Quinn, *Strategies for Change*, pp. 67–68.
12. Ibid., p. 71.

CHAPTER 7: TELL THE TRUTH

1. Larry Bossidy and Ram Charan, *Execution* (New York: Crown Business, 2002), p. 22.
2. Keith Naughton, "Why Ford Came Clean," *Newsweek*, May 22, 2000, p. 50.
3. The phrase "mind bugs" was used by Harvard University psychologist Mahzarin Banaji in a presentation at the American Psychological Society 2001 convention.
4. This catalog of cognitive errors is derived from the research of a number of behavioral scientists and consultants. For more details, see Dan Lovallo and Daniel Kahneman, "Delusions of Success," *Harvard Business Review*, July 2003, pp. 56–63; Hammond, Keeney, and Raiffa, "The Hidden Traps in Decision Making," *Harvard Business Review*, September–October 1998, pp. 47–58; Charles Roxburgh, "Hidden Flaws in Strategy," *McKinsey Quarterly*, 2003, no. 2; and Eric Bonabeau, "Don't Trust Your Gut," *Harvard Business Review*, May 2003, pp. 116–120.
5. R. Jeffery Smith, "Mistakes of NASA Toted Up," *The Washington Post*, July 13, 2003, p. A17.
6. Chris Argyris, *Overcoming Organizational Defenses* (Boston: Allyn & Bacon, 1990), pp. 37–43.
7. David Sanger and James Risen, "CIA Chief Takes Blame in Assertion on Iraq Uranium," *The New York Times*, July 12, 2003, p. A5.
8. Warren Bennis, "A Corporate Fear of Too Much Truth," *The New York Times*, Feb. 17, 2002, p. WK 11.
9. Fred Frailey, "The Grinch Who Almost Stole the Zephyrs," *Trains*, April 1998, pp. 42–45.
10. Ibid., p. 36.

11. "In a Merger Architect's Own Words," *The New York Times*, Nov. 26, 2000, p. BU 11.

12. Chris Argyris, "Good Communication That Blocks Learning," *Harvard Business Review*, July–August 1994, p. 84.

13. "The Value of Dissent," *The Economist*, Oct. 5, 2002, p. 78.

14. Quoted in Lynn Offermann, "When Followers Become Toxic," *Harvard Business Review*, January 2004, p. 58.

15. For more information about Hrabowski's approaches, see Hrabowski, Maton, and Greif, *Beating the Odds* (New York: Oxford University Press, 1998). For more about Hrabowski and UMBC, see Chuck Salter, "It's Cool to Be Smart," *Fast Company*, April 2002, p. 34; Michael Hill, "Living and Learning in Black and White," *Baltimore Sun*, April 18, 2004; and Diana Schemo, "U. of Maryland Branch Is Beacon for Minorities in Math and Science," *The New York Times*, Oct. 14, 2000.

16. Michael Beer and Russell Eisenstat, "How to Have an Honest Conversation," *Harvard Business Review*, February 2004, p. 85.

17. Anna Muoio, "The Truth Is, the Truth Hurts," *Fast Company*, April–May 1998, p. 93.

18. Ibid., p. 94.

19. Offermann, "When Followers Become Toxic," pp. 57–59.

20. Richard Neustadt and Ernest May, *Thinking in Time* (New York: Free Press, 1986), p. 274.

21. Bethany McLean, "Diller.com," *Fortune*, May 3, 2004, pp. 88–90.

CHAPTER 8: CREATE TENSION TO GENERATE FORWARD MOVEMENT

1. John Byrne and Heather Thomas, "Tough Times for a New CEO," *BusinessWeek*, Oct. 29, 2001, p. 70.

2. Leon Festinger, *A Theory of Cognitive Dissonance* (Stanford, Calif.: Stanford University Press, 1957).

3. Robert Fritz, *The Path of Least Resistance* (New York: Fawcett Columbine, 1989), p. 117.

4. Amabile, Hadley, and Kramer, "Creativity Under the Gun," *Harvard Business Review*, August 2002, pp. 52–61.

5. Cora Daniels, "The Man Who Changed Medicine," *Fortune*, Nov. 29, 2004, pp. 91–112.

6. Ibid., p. 94.

7. Christopher Chase, "Motivational Seeker," *American Psychological Society Observer*, June 2004, pp. 27–28.

8. Allan Cohen, "Transformational Change at Babson College," *Academy of Management Learning and Education*, vol. 2, no. 2, 2003, p. 157.

9. Joseph Zolner, "Transformational Change at Babson College: A View From the Outside," *Academy of Management Learning and Education*, vol. 2, no. 2, 2003, pp. 177–179.

10. Marshall Goldsmith, "Leave It at the Stream," *Fast Company*, May 2004, p. 103.

11. Jena McGregor, "Gospels of Failure," *Fast Company*, February 2005, pp. 64–65.

12. Diane Coutu, "Psychologist Karl E. Weick: Sense and Reliability," *Harvard Business Review*, April 2003, pp. 86–89.

13. For a complementary, but slightly different, perspective on this process, look at the ideas of Robert Fritz. He is an artist who has developed an approach to creating that he calls "structural tension." He has been a significant influence on Peter Senge and his group of learning organization enthusiasts as they have developed their discipline of personal mastery. See Robert Fritz, *Corporate Tides* (San Francisco: Berrett-Koehler, 1996).

14. Mihaly Csikszentmihalyi, *Flow* (New York: Harper & Row, 1990).

15. Coutu, "Psychologist Karl E. Weick," p. 86.

CHAPTER 9: WIN HEARTS AND MINDS

1. From David Bornstein, *How to Change the World* (New York: Oxford University Press, 2004).

2. From Max Planck's *Scientific Autobiography* as quoted in Thomas Kuhn, *The Structure of Scientific Revolutions* (Chicago: University of Chicago Press, 1970), p. 151.

3. James Traub, "Harvard Radical," *The New York Times Magazine*, Aug. 24, 2003, p. 33.

4. Robert Cialdini, *Influence: Science and Practice* (New York: Harper-Collins, 1993).

5. For more detail on this process, called by psychologists "transference," see Michael Maccoby, "Why People Follow the Leader," *Harvard Business Review*, September 2004, pp. 77–85.

6. Thomas Neff and James Citrin, "You're in Charge, Now What?" *Fortune*, Jan. 24, 2005, p. 110.

7. Linda Tischler, "The Road to Recovery," *Fast Company*, July 2002, pp. 80–82.

8. Neff and Citrin, "You're in Charge," p. 112.

9. Rick Ross, "Popular Postmortems," in Peter Senge, Roberts, Ross, Smith and Kleiner, *The Fifth Discipline Fieldbook* (New York: Currency Doubleday, 1994), p. 400.

10. William Isaacs, "Dialogic Leadership," *Systems Thinker*, February 1999, pp. 1–4. I have changed some of the names Isaac uses for the roles, but the idea is the same.

11. George Vaillant, *Adaptation to Life* (Boston: Little, Brown and Co., 1977), pp. 383–386.

12. For more about defensive pessimism, see Julie Norem, *The Positive Power of Negative Thinking* (New York: Basic Books, 2002).

13. David Sherman and Geoffrey Cohen, "Accepting Threatening Information," *Current Directions in Psychological Science*, August 2002, pp. 119–122.

14. Alan Deutschman, "Making Change," *Fast Company*, May 2005, pp. 52–62.

15. William Manchester, *The Last Lion: Winston Spencer Churchill: Alone* (New York: Dell, 1989), p. 682.

16. Myeong-Gu Seo, "Overcoming Emotional Barriers, Political Obstacles, and Control Imperatives in the Action Science Approach to Individual and Organizational Learning," *Academy of Management Learning and Education*, March 2003, pp. 7–21.

17. Ibid., p. 16.

18. David Shields, "The Good Father," *The New York Times Magazine*, Apr. 23, 2000, p. 61.

19. Steven Levy, "They Hacked Real Good, for Free," *Newsweek*, Jan. 10, 2005, p. 13.

20. Jeff Howe, "The Connectors," *Wired*, November 2003, p. 174.

21. Art Kleiner, "Are You In With the In Crowd?" *Harvard Business Review*, July 2003, pp. 86-92.

22. Rob Hirtz, "Martin Seligman's Journey," *Pennsylvania Gazette*, January-February 1999.

23. Martin Seligman, *Learned Optimism* (New York: Pocket Books, 1998).

24. Martin Seligman, *Authentic Happiness* (New York: Free Press, 2002) and http://www.authentichappiness.org.

CHAPTER 10: MASTER MOMENTUM AND BOUNCE

1. Quoted in Gregory Dess and Joseph Picken, "Creating Competitive (Dis)advantage," *Academy of Management Executive*, August 1999, p. 97.

2. James Shepperd and James McNulty, "The Affective Consequences of Expected and Unexpected Outcomes," *Psychological Science*, January 2002, p. 85.

3. Keith Hammonds, "Growth Search," *Fast Company*, April 2003, p. 79.

4. Bill Breen, "What's Your Intuition," *Fast Company*, September 2000, pp. 290-300.

5. Ibid., p. 298.

6. Chuck Salter, "Ford's Escape Route," *Fast Company*, October 2004, pp. 106-110.

7. Martha Baer, "The New X-Men," *Wired*, September 2003, pp. 125-129.

8. Gardiner Morse, "The Science Behind Six Degrees," *Harvard Business Review*, February 2003, p. 17.

9. Schweitzer, Ordonez, and Douma, "Goal Setting as a Motivator of Unethical Behavior," *Academy of Management Journal*, June 2004, pp. 422-432.

10. Martin Seligman, *Authentic Happiness* (New York: Free Press, 2002), pp. 24 and 92-101, and *Learned Optimism* (New York: Pocket Books, 1998).

11. Harrison Owen, *Open Space Technology* (Potomac, Md.: Abbott Publishing, 1992), p. 72.

CHAPTER 11: KNOW WHEN TO LET GO—AND HOW TO SHARE THE WEALTH

1. As quoted in Frank Bruni, "Caveat Victor at the End of the Rainbow," *The New York Times*, Mar. 1, 1998.
2. "Special Report: The Best B-Schools," *BusinessWeek*, Oct. 19, 1998, p. 87.
3. Bruni, "Caveat Victor."
4. Alan Deutschman, "Building a Better Skunk Works," *Fast Company*, March 2005, pp. 68–73.

CHAPTER 12: EPILOGUE

1. Quoted in Stan Davis and Bill Davidson, *2020 Vision* (New York: Simon & Schuster, 1991), p. 111.

INDEX

ABC, 41
accelerators, 64–66
ACCION International, 53–55
accounting rules, 33–34, 38
action
  failing early and often and, 215–216
  master plans versus, 177–178
  mindset and, 95–96
actionable essence, 217
active listening, 188–189
activity cycles, 178
advisers, consultants versus, 163
African Americans
  civil rights movement and, 158–159, 179, 180
  education of, 155–159
  in professional baseball, 199
  social research on, 154–155, 156, 158
  Sullivan Principles for South Africa and, 179–183
aggression-driven expansion, 21
Alcoholics Anonymous, 107
Amabile, Teresa, 169–170
Amazon.com, 32, 49, 50, 60, 220–221
ambiguity, impatience with, 144
American Express, 49, 52–53, 167
American International Group (AIG), 154
American Psychological Association (APA), 207, 208–213
America Online, 12–13, 41
Amgen, 113–114, 127
Amtrak, 151
Andreessen, Marc, 99, 103

Anheuser-Busch, 236
AOL Time Warner, 12–13, 41
Aon, 22
A&P, 20
Apache, 201–202
apartheid, Sullivan Principles and, 179–183
Apple Computer, 18, 40, 50, 62, 99, 196, 202–203, 224
appreciative inquiry (AI), 114–117, 175
Argyris, Chris, 147–148, 152, 197
Arthur D. Little, Inc., 181, 204–205
assumptions
  in distorting reality, 146–159
  questioning, 197–198
attribution errors, 143
Avitzur, Ron, 202–203
Aylward, Bruce, 4, 124–125, 126, 136, 137, 178, 226–227, 234

balance, and growth, 62–63
Ball, George, 163
Ballmer, Steve, 20–21
BancoSol, 54–55
Bargh, John, 173
Bayer, 23–24
Beane, Billy, 100–101
Beauvoir, Simone de, 1, 2, 5, 95
beliefs
  in distorting reality, 146–159
  outmoded, 194–195
Bell, Charlie, 25–26
Bennis, Warren, 149
Berlin, Isaiah, 196–197

Bernstein, Peter, 38
beta testers, 216
Bezos, Jeff, 32, 49, 50, 60, 220-221
B.F. Goodrich, 94
bigness
    as counterproductive, 22-27
    progress versus, 2-3, 11-16
    self-esteem and, 3
Birkinshaw, Julian, 68
Blair, Margaret, 31-33
Blatchford, Joseph, 54
blinders, removing, 103-107
blockbuster syndrome, 23-24, 201
BMW, 16-17
Boeing, 136
Bohr, Niels, 211
Bonabeau, Eric, 117
Bornstein, David, 184
Bossidy, Larry, 139
Boston Consulting Group, 36, 38-39, 63-64
bouncing back, see resilience
Brabeck, Peter, 41
brain
    limits on size of, 19-20
    perception and, 105
    research on functions of, 104, 106-107,
        205, 234
    see also psychology
Bread Loaf Writers' Conference, 102-103
bronze medal effect, 215
Brooklyn Dodgers, 199
Bru, Al, 4, 48, 57, 60, 62, 174
Bryan, Lowell, 29-30
bubble companies, 12
Buffett, Warren, 224
bully companies, 12-13
bureaucracy busting, 21-22
Burger King, 25
Burlington Northern Railroad, 48, 75-81, 87,
    89, 94, 134, 149-151
Bush, George W., 26, 61
business environment
    inhospitable, 17-19
    organizational limitations and, 19-21
    resource constraints in, 19, 70-73
business models
    defined, 81
    for medical research, 170-172
Business Roundtable, 29-30
BusinessWeek
    ranking of business schools, 232
    on Wal-Mart, 18-19

candor, 162
Canon, 135-136, 152, 179
Case Western Reserve University, 114-117,
    205
cash
    bonuses, 160-161
    hoarding, 37-38
category-killers, 23-24
CBS, 41
Celera, 172
Central Park, New York City, 70
Chait, Jay, 12
Challenger space shuttle disaster, 147-148,
    199-200
change
    growth versus, 61-73
    in real time, 58-59
charisma, 12, 126
Charles Schwab, 40
Chenault, Kenneth, 49, 52-53, 166, 167
Chicago Bulls, 201
chief executive officers (CEOs)
    Business Roundtable and, 29-30
    growth and, 7
    stock options and, 31, 36-37
Child, John, 111
China, 19, 42, 172
choices, justifying past, 144
Chouinard, Yvon, 49
Chrysler, 16, 151, 232
Churchill, Winston, 66-67, 68, 124, 152,
    196-197
Cisco Systems, 4, 235
Citicorp, 182
Citigroup, 21, 23
civil rights movement, 158-159, 179, 180
Coase, Ronald, 39
Coca-Cola, 48, 57, 74, 121, 127
coercion, manipulation versus, 184-185
coexisting opposites, 66-68
cognitive dissonance, 166-168
cognitive errors, 43-45, 143-146, 147, 165
Coleman, James, 154-155, 156, 158
Columbia space shuttle disaster, 147, 148,
    199-200
Columbia University, 222-223
commitment
    goals and, 126
    of growers versus fixers, 84-85, 186
common ground, searching for, 129-130, 209
Compaq, 40

competence, 186
competition, 172, 225
competitive advantage, 232
complexity, 52-53
Conner, "Bull," 159
Conner, Roger, 49-50, 129-130
conscious conversations, 109-110
consensus, managing by, 162-163
constraints
  creativity and, 69-73
  in guiding growth, 68-69
  on lobstermen, 70-73
  resource, 19, 70-73
consultants
  advisers versus, 163
  appreciative inquiry versus, 114-115
  business ideas and, 27
convergence, 12-13
convergent thinking, 67
Cooper, Kenneth, 174
Cooperrider, David, 114-117
Costco, 73-74, 121
creative tension, 166-183
  activity cycles and, 178
  cognitive dissonance in, 166-168
  dissatisfaction and, 2, 173-174
  feedforward and, 174-175
  master plans, avoiding, 177-178
  rapid feedback and, 178-179
  red teaming and, 176-177
  Sullivan Principles and, 179-183
  thinking backward and, 175-176
  urgency and, 168-172
creativity, 62, 67, 69-73, 107
Crick, Francis, 172
cross-functional organizations, 78
cross-selling, 40, 41
Csikszentmihalyi, Mihaly, 67, 210, 221
customers
  customer-centric information and, 121-123
  going to, 212
Cutler, David, 115-117

Daimler-Benz, 16, 134-135, 151
DaimlerChrysler, 16, 100
decision-making
  gut feel and, 216-218
  reality in, 165
defensiveness, 193-200
  assumptions, questioning, 197-198
  optimists and pessimists and, 193-194

outmoded beliefs and, 194-195
self-worth issues and, 195-197
defining moments, 74
Dell, Michael, 232
Dell Computer, 232
Deming, W. Edwards, 151
demonization, 224
depression, 207-208
determinism, 207
Deutsche Bank, 134
devil's advocates, 160-161, 163-164
dialogue
  active listening and, 188-189
  ground rules of, 192-193
  moving from listening to, 190-193
  in Open Space meeting, 227-230
  questions, asking, 189-190
Diener, Edward, 210
Diller, Barry, 162
direct observations, spin versus, 109-110
Disney, 41, 232
divergent thinking, 67
dividend policy, 37-38
DNA, 105, 172
Dodge & Cox, 15
dominating ideas, challenging, 59-60
Drucker, Peter, 11, 22, 26, 46-47

eBay, 232
Eckert, Robert, 189
Economic Man, 30, 35
economies of scale, 39-40
efficient-market hypothesis, 30, 32-33
egocentrism, 44
Eisner, Michael, 232
Ellsberg, Daniel, 152-153
emotions, 86-95
  impact of, 86
  mindsets and, 86, 91-95
  negative, see negative emotions
  positive, see positive emotions
  pros and cons of, 89-91
Enrico, Roger, 4, 48, 236
Enron, 6, 13, 21, 31, 33, 35, 141
extreme programming (XP), 221-222

faith-based intelligence, 148-149
faith-based product development, 216
Fast Company, 8, 46, 55
faulty thinking, 43-45
fear
  confidence versus, 41

fear (*continued*)
  impact of, 121, 154–155, 195
  as negative emotion, 87
"featuritis," 24
Federal Express, 41–42, 222–223
feedback
  negative, 65
  positive, 64–65, 196
  rapid, 178–179
feedforward, 84, 174–175
Festinger, Leon, 166
Finkelstein, Sydney, 43, 45, 74
Fiorina, Carly, 131, 154, 188, 189
fishbowl meetings, 164
fixers
  described, 82–83
  goals and, 127–131
  growers versus, 83–85, 92–95, 186
flow, 221
Flying Tigers, 42
focus, blurred, 24–26
force, manipulation versus, 184–185
Ford, William Clay "Bill," 49, 52–53, 60, 140
Ford Motor Company, 2, 15–16, 39, 49, 52–
    53, 60, 118–119, 140–141, 182,
    219–220
forecasting, overcautious, 145
forgetting curve, 74
Fortune, 13, 34
  list of 100 Best Companies to Work For,
    130–131, 203
Fredrickson, Barbara, 88–89, 169–170,
    210–211
Freud, Sigmund, 207, 209
Friedman, Jane, 49, 234
Frisco Railroad, 149–150
Frito-Lay, 48, 60, 62, 174, 236
Frost, Robert, 102
future, 235–236

Gallup Organization, 210
Gallwey, Tim, 5
Gap Inc., 140
Gates, Bill, 21, 126, 137, 220, 232, 236
Gatorade, 41
Gavin, James, 204–205
General Electric (GE), 6, 117, 121, 122–123,
    134
General Mills, 26
General Motors (GM), 15–16, 162–163,
    179–183

Gerrity, Thomas, 232
Gerstner, Louis, 160, 198
Ghosn, Carlos, 94–95, 188–189
Gibson, William, 117–118
gift economy, 202–205
Gillette, 57
Gladwell, Malcolm, 145, 216
Glass, David, 18
goals, 124–138
  finding, 138
  of fixers versus growers, 127–131
  grower uses of, 127–131, 133–138,
    173–179
  impact of, 125–128
  realized, 232–233
  refocusing on, 224–225
  sense of reality and, 167–168
  in traditional business planning, 59–60
  unintended consequences of, 137–138
  wrong kind of, 131–133
Goethe, Johann Wolfgang von, 197
Goizueta, Roberto, 121
Goldsmith, Marshall, 84, 174–175
Goldwyn, Samuel, 154
Goodrich (B.F.), 94
Google, 18, 50, 215–216
Gore (W.L.), 2
government regulation, impact of, 71–73
Graham, Donald, 57
grandiosity, 45–46, 60, 186–187, 224
Great Atlantic and Pacific Tea Co. (A&P), 20
Green Bay Packers, 133–134
Greenberg, Jeffrey, 23
Greenberg, Maurice, 154
Greenwood, Bill, 4, 48, 57, 77–81, 89, 94,
    134, 149–151, 162, 202, 235
Grossman, Mindy, 111–112
groupthink, 146
Grove, Andy, 179
growers
  action and, 95–96
  appreciative inquiry (AI) and, 114–117,
    175
  blinders, removal of, 103–107
  changers versus, 61
  chief executive officers (CEOs) as, 7
  connecting with something larger and,
    200–207
  described, 83
  examples of, 4, 48–49
  fixers versus, 83–85, 92–95, 186

goals and, 127-131, 133-138, 173-179
idealization of, avoiding, 186-187
letting go and, 73-74, 231-236
listening by, 187-193
lowering of defensive biases and, 193-200
mindset of, 1-2, 5-7
nature of, 1-2, 61
new perceptions and, 117-123
opportunities, seeing, 107-114
role of, 3-5
spotting trends and, 117-118
thinking differently and, 99-103
growth
beyond limits defining business, 48-50
bureaucracy busting and, 21-22
change versus, 61-73
direction of, 52-55
growth cycle and, 55-56
innovation versus, 61-73
letting go and, 73-74, 231-236
as managerial heroin, 57
measuring the wrong things, 26-27
mindset for, 1-2, 5-7
nature of, 1
opportunities for, 57-60
people versus strategies and, 6-8
Peter Pan companies and, 56-57
progress versus bigness in, 2-3, 11-16
smart versus dumb, 47
speed of, 17-19
sustainable, 6-7, 12, 13-15, 47, 50, 62-63
thinking about, 50-57
Gunn, David, 151
gut feel, 216-218
Gutierrez, Carlos, 26, 42

Hammonds, Keith, 46
Hanh, Thich Nhat, 52
hardball approach, 63-64, 66, 68
Harley-Davidson, 100
HarperCollins, 49, 234
Hartford, John, 20
Harvard Business School, 29-30, 35-36, 56,
    160, 168-170, 233-234
Harvard University, 185
Hawkins, Jeff, 104, 106, 107, 234
Henretta, Deborah, 49, 51, 161
herd mentality, 146
Hersh, Seymour, 141
Hewlett-Packard, 40, 131, 154, 188
hidden curriculum, 149

Holzle, Urs, 216
Honda, 227
honesty, see truth
Honeywell, 139, 231
Howe, Jeff, 206
Hrabowski, Freeman, 155-159, 179
Huggies, 51
humility, 186, 187, 224
humor, 163, 198
hypotheses, 110
Hy-Vee, 73-74

Iacocca, Lee, 140-141, 232
IBM, 135-136, 160, 182, 198, 224, 235
Icahn, Carl, 29
idealization, avoiding, 186-187
IDEO, 215
IKEA, 69
illusory causation, 106
incentives, 210-211
informal economy, 53
Infosys, 236
ING Direct, 49, 53
Initiative for a Competitive Inner City,
    233-234
innovation
    examples of, 62
    growth versus, 61-73
    integrated, 220
Innovation Associates, 128
insider trading, 33
integrated innovation, 220
Intel, 179, 234
InterActiveCorp, 162
Inter-American Development Bank, 54
Internal Revenue Service (IRS), 25
Internet
    growth and, 20-21
    Internet bubble, 32
intuition, 216-218
invulnerability, 45
iPod, 62
Iraq, invasion of, 148, 218
Isaacs, William, 192-193
iTunes, 62

Jackson, Phil, 201
Jayaram, G. K., 236
Jensen, Michael, 28-30, 35-36, 38, 56, 57
Jesuit management, 80
Jobs, Steve, 62, 99, 196
Johnson, Lyndon B., 155, 163

Johnson, Susan, 207
Johnson & Johnson, 2, 127
Jong-Wook, Lee, 137
Jourard, Sidney, 58
judgments, biased, 145
Jung, Carl, 85

Kahneman, Daniel, 38–39, 43
Kaku, Ryuzaburo, 179
Kandel, Eric, 105
Katzenbach, Jon, 174–175
Kay, John, 13
Keebler, 42
Kelleher, Herb, 6
Kelley, David, 215
Kellogg, 26–27, 42
Kennedy, John F., 153, 204
Klein, Gary, 217–219
Kleiner, Art, 206
Kmart, 69
Knight, Phil, 112
"know-it-all" mentality, 60
Kodak, 135–136
Kraft Foods, 189
Krispy Kreme, 34, 35
Kuhlmann, Arkadi, 49, 53
Kuhn, Thomas, 48
Kun-Hee, Lee, 118

Lachenauer, Rob, 63–64
Lafley, A. G., 118
LA Lakers, 201
Lamphier, Thomas, 75–77, 94
Lay, Kenneth, 6, 13
learned helplessness, 207–208
learning curve, 74
letting go, 73–74, 231–236
    broadening through, 233–234
    business needs and, 232
    future and, 235–236
    importance of, 231
    realized goals and, 232–233
    serial growers and, 234–235
Levering, Robert, 130–131, 203
Levi Strauss, 44
Linux, 201
listening, 187–193
    active, role of, 188–189
    asking questions and, 189–190
    moving to dialogue from, 190–193
Livengood, Scott, 34
lobstermen, constraints on, 70–73

Lombardi, Vince, 133–134
Losada, Marcial, 91–92
Lotti, Martin, 111–112
Louchheim, Frank, 107–108
Lubit, Roy, 45–46
Lucent, 33–34, 35, 188
Lufthansa, 41, 134–135

Maccoby, Michael, 103, 187
Mandela, Nelson, 183
manipulation, force versus, 184–185
Marsh & McLennan, 22, 23
Martinez, Arthur, 163
Massachusetts Institute of Technology (MIT),
    44, 64–66, 192–193
Matsushita, Konosuke, 119–120
Mattel, 57, 189
Mayerson Foundation, 211–212
McAdams, Don, 231, 233
McCann, Jim, 160
McDonald's, 24, 25–27
McGarvey, Rick, 72
McKinsey & Co., 29–30, 38–40, 67
McNamara, Robert, 153
Meckling, William, 28
Menk, Louis, 149–151
Mercedes, 16
Merck, 23–24, 201
mergers, 38–43
    fear and, 41
    successful, 41–42
    wrong psychology for, 42–43
Meyerhoff, Jane, 156
Meyerhoff, Robert, 156
MGM, 154
Microsoft, 18, 20–21, 24, 120, 220, 224, 232
Middlebury College, 102–103
Milken, Michael, 4, 170–172
Miller Brewing Company, 101–102
mindsets
    action and, 95–96
    as contagious, 186–187
    defined, 81
    emotions and, 86, 91–95
    of fixers, see fixers
    of growers, see growers
    of growers versus fixers, 83–85
    shifts in, 207–208
mission, importance of, 169–170
Mitnick, Kevin, 185
Mitsubishi, 16

MIT Systems Dynamics Group, 64–66
Moberg, Anders, 39
Mobil, 182
momentum, 214–223
 bronze medal effect and, 215
 extreme programming (XP) and, 221–222
 failing early and often for, 215–216
 gut feel and, 216–218
 nature of, 214, 221
 Open Space meetings and, 227–230
 organizing for, 219–220
 postmortems and, 218
 premortems and, 218–219
 sustaining lead and, 222–223
momentum thinking, 74
Moore, Gordon, 234
Motorola, 45
movers, roles in dialogue, 192–193
moving forward, 48–74
Moynihan, Daniel, 155, 156, 158
multitasking, 58
Murdoch, Rupert, 12
Murray, William Hutchinson, 126
Murthy, Narayana, 4, 236
Muther, Catherine, 4, 235
mutual funds, sustainable growth of, 13–15

narcissism, 12
NASA, 132, 147–148, 199–200
Nasser, Jacques, 15–16, 49
National Institute of Mental Health (NIMH),
 208, 211
National Science Foundation, 113
natural selection, 52
NCR, 99–100
negative emotions
 demonization and, 224
 fear, 41, 87, 121, 154–155, 195
 nature of, 86–87
 pessimism, 193–194
 role of, 209–210
 triggering, 197
negative feedback, 65
Nestlé, 41, 42
News Corp., 12
Newton, Isaac, 64
New York Times, 196
New York Yankees, 101
Nidetch, Jean, 107
Nike, 4, 48, 111–112, 113, 127
Nike Goddess, 111–112, 113

Nishimura, Ko, 4, 99–100
Nissan, 94–95, 188–189
Nokia, 45
novelty, filtering out, 144

Oakland Athletics, 100–101
observers, roles in dialogue, 192–193
Olmsted, Frederick Law, 70
Omidyar, Pierre, 232
omnipotence, 45
omniscience, 44
1-800-FLOWERS, 160
Opel, 100
open-source movement, 202
Open Space meetings, 227–230
Opportunities Industrialization Center,
 179–180
opposers, roles in dialogue, 192–193
optimism, 43–44, 142–143, 193–194,
 226–227
organizational learning, 5
Ornish, Dean, 174
Otero, Maria, 4, 53–55
overconfidence, 145, 218–219
overoptimism, 90
Owen, Harrison, 227–230

Pabst Blue Ribbon Beer, 101–102
Palm Pilot, 104, 234
Pampers, 51
Pan-American Chess Championships, 157
Parks, Rosa, 158–159
Patagonia, 49
Patil, Prabhaker, 219–220
Paul, Vivek, 110–111
Pauling, Linus, 172
Peace Corps, 54
Pentagon Papers, 152–153
PepsiCo, 4, 48, 57, 74, 236
perceptions
 blinders, removing, 103–107
 brain and, 105
 changing perspective and, 117–123
 goals in changing, 126
 mindsets and, 92
 opportunities, seeing, 107–114
 of reality, 110–112
 pessimism, 193–194
Peter Pan companies, 56–57
Peterson, Christopher, 211–212
Peterson, Karl, 162
Picasso, Pablo, 107, 238

Pickens, T. Boone, 29
Planck, Max, 184
polio, eradication of, 4, 124–125, 136, 137,
    178, 225–227, 234
Porsche, 100
Porter, Michael, 233–234
positive emotions
    appreciative inquiry (AI) and, 114–117,
        175
    building on groundwork of, 199
    business case for, 113–114, 169
    educational techniques and, 129–130
    nature of, 88–89
    optimism, 43–44, 142–143, 193–194,
        226–227
    positive psychology movement and, 5, 49,
        52, 120, 207–213, 234
    refocusing on goals, 224–225
positive feedback, 64–65, 196
Positive Psychology Network, 211
Post, 26
post-industrial organizations, 22
postmortems, 218
power, problems of, 45–46
Prahalad, C. K., 74
preconceptions, 119–120
premortems, 218–219
priming, 106–107
Procter & Gamble, 49, 51, 118, 161
progress, bigness versus, 2–3, 11–16
psychology
    appreciative inquiry (AI) in, 114–117, 175
    cognitive dissonance and, 166–168
    cognitive errors and, 43–45, 143–146, 147,
        165
    defensive biases and, 193–200
    economists and, 30
    of stock prices, 42–46
    see also brain; negative emotions; percep-
        tions; positive emotions
purpose, goals and, 127

Quaker, 41
questions
    asking, 189–190
    about assumptions, 197–198
Quinn, James Brian, 137–138
quotations, 164

Ramezani, Cyrus, 17
Random House, 234

reality
    in decision-making, 165
    distorting, 141, 142–159
    goals and, 167–168
    optimists and pessimists and, 193–194
    perceptions of, 110–112
    problems in facing, 139–140
    see also truth
recall, selective, 145
red teaming, 176–177
Redwood Neuroscience Institute, 104
Reinemund, Steven, 236
Reingold, Jennifer, 8
Renault, 94–95
rent-an-engineer business, 100
resilience, 223–227
    demonization, avoiding, 224
    moving beyond yourself, 223–224
    Open Space meetings and, 227–230
    in polio eradication, 225–227
    refocusing on goals, 224–225
resources
    broadening resource base, 210
    constraints on, 19, 70–73
respect, 162, 198
restrainers, 64–66
Rickey, Branch, 199
Right Management Consultants, 107–108
risky behaviors, 36–42
    earnings smoothing, 38
    hoarding cash, 37–38
    mergers, 38–43
    stock options, 31, 36–37
Robinson, Jackie, 199
Roosevelt, Franklin, 124–125
Rotary International, 125, 126
Roxburgh, Charles, 145
Royal Ahold, 39
Royal Dutch Shell, 21–22
Rubbermaid, 44
Ryanair, 17

Sabin, Albert, 125
sales, mergers and, 40, 41
Salk, George, 63–64
Salk, Jonas, 124–125
Samsung, 43–44, 118
S&P 500, 67
Sao, Myeong-Gu, 197–200
Sattelberger, Thomas, 134–135
scale
    economies of, 39–40
    limitations of size and, 19–21

Schacht, Henry, 188
Schmitt, Wolfgang, 44
Schrempp, Jurgen, 151
Schultz, Howard, 48, 52, 57, 232
Scott, Lee, 21
Search for Common Ground, 129-130
Sears, 69, 163
Seinfeld, Jerry, 231
selective exposure, 106-107
self-worth issues, 3, 195-197, 223-224
Seligman, Martin, 2, 49, 52, 113, 120, 207-213, 226-227, 234
September 11, 2001 terrorist attacks, 41, 58, 61, 237-238
Shakespeare, William, 160
shareholder value theory, 3, 27, 28-36
    critics of, 31-36
    greed and, 30
    impact of, 28-30
    managing earnings versus business and, 33-34
    overvalued stocks and, 34-36, 38
Sharer, Kevin, 113-114
Shiller, Robert, 32
size
    bureaucracy busting and, 21-22
    economies of scale and, 39-40
    limitations of, 19-21
    as means versus end, 46-47
skilled incompetence, 147-148, 152
Skillman, Peter, 215
Sloan, Alfred, 162-163
smartball approach, 66
Smith, Bryan, 128
Smith, Fred, 222-223
social activism, 4, 49-50, 179-183, 199
Socratic dialogue, 188
Solectron, 4, 100
Sony, 2, 40, 118
Soriana, 73-74
South Africa, Sullivan Principles and, 179-183
Southern Methodist University, 40
Southwest Airlines, 6, 17, 68, 69
spin, direct observations versus, 109-110
Spitzer, Eliot, 22-23
stabilizers, 65, 66
Starbucks, 2, 48, 52, 57, 127, 232
status quo, dissatisfaction with, 2, 173-174
Sternberg, Robert, 43, 45
stock options, shareholder value theory and, 31, 36-37

stock prices, 28-47
    Economic Man and, 30, 35
    efficient-market hypothesis and, 30, 32-33
    false comfort from, 34-35
    as managerial heroin, 35-36
    managing earnings versus business, 33-34
    mergers and, 38-43
    mutual funds and, 13-15
    psychology of, 42-46
    real worth of company versus, 32-33
    risky behaviors and, 36-42
    shareholder value theory and, 3, 27, 28-36
    size as means versus end and, 46-47
    stock options and, 36-37
Stroebe, Lillian, 102-103
submarine mode, 113-114
Sullivan, Leon, 4, 179-183
Sullivan Principles, 179-183
Summers, Larry, 185
supporters, roles in dialogue, 192-193
sustainable growth, 6-7, 12, 13-15, 47, 50, 62-63
Sutcliffe, Kathleen, 90
Swissair, 41
synergy, mergers and, 40
systems thinking, 64-66

Target, 73-74
Templeton Positive Psychology Prize, 210-211
tennis, 5
Thaler, Richard, 43
theories, 110
Thielmann, Greg, 148-149
Thomas, Jackie, 111-112
Three Guineas Fund, 235
time issues
    time pressure and creativity, 168-170
    timing, importance of, 136
Time Warner, 41
Tinstman, Carl, 126
Toyota, 16, 69, 172, 220, 227
Trames, Cindy, 111-112
truth, 139-165
    cognitive errors and, 43-45, 143-146, 147, 165
    reality distortion versus, 141, 142-159
    searching for, 160-164
    telling, 164-165
    traction provided by, 139-142
turnaround situations, 139-140

Turner, Ted, 137
Tyco, 13, 31

underground economy, 53, 202
UNICEF, 126, 137, 161
United Parcel Service (UPS), 42
U.S. Army, 218
U.S. Department of Defense, 152-153
U.S. Department of State, 148, 149
U.S. Forest Service, 153-154
U.S. Marines, 216-217
U.S. Veterans Administration, 208
University of California at Los Angeles
    (UCLA), 196
University of Chicago, 28, 154-155
University of Connecticut, 219
University of Maryland, 197-200
University of Maryland-Baltimore County
    campus (UMBC), 155-159
University of Michigan, 25, 35, 74, 88-89, 90,
    177-178, 211-212
University of Pennsylvania, 35, 113, 207, 211,
    212, 232, 234
University of Southern California, 149
urgency, 168-172
    competition and, 172
    in medical research, 170-172
    time pressure and, 168-170
USA Interactive, 57
US Airways, 68

Vagelos, Roy, 201
Vaillant, George, 210
Vanguard, 15
Venter, J. Craig, 172
Viacom, 41
Vietnam War, 152-153
Vivendi, 12-13
Volkswagen, 16

Wall Street Journal, 180
Wal-Mart, 2, 18-21, 44, 68-69, 73, 121
Walton, Sam, 68-69
Washington Post, 57
Watkins, Sharon, 141
Watson, James, 105, 172
Watts, Duncan, 222-223
Wegmans, 73-74
Weick, Karl, 105, 175-176, 177-179, 223
Weight Watchers, 107
Welch, Jack, 6, 121, 122-123, 231
Wendy's, 25
Wexner, Leslie, 214
Wharton School, 35
Wheeler, Michael, 160
Whole Foods, 121
Wikipedia, 201-202
Wilde, Oscar, 42-43
Willner, Alan, 101-102
win-lose discussions, 191
Winslow, Darcy, 4, 48, 111-112
win-win success, 198-199
Wipro, 110-111
Wired magazine, 206
W.L. Gore, 2
Women's Technology Cluster, 235
word of mouth, 205-207
WorldCom, 13, 31
World Health Organization (WHO), 124-
    125, 137, 178, 226-227, 234
Wright, Mary Ann, 219
Wyeth, 23-24

Xerox, 135-136, 152

Yahoo, 50-51
Yale University, 196

Zehnder, Egon, 108-109
Zull, James, 205